Measuring Environmental Degradation

Measuring Environmental Degradation

Developing Pressure Indicators for Europe

Edited by

Anil Markandya and Nick Dale

University of Bath and Metroeconomica, UK

IN ASSOCIATION WITH EUROSTAT, THE STATISTICAL OFFICE OF
THE EUROPEAN COMMUNITIES

Edward Elgar
Cheltenham, UK • Northampton, MA, USA

Published by
Edward Elgar Publishing Limited
Glensanda House
Montpellier Parade
Cheltenham
Glos GL50 1UA
UK

Edward Elgar Publishing, Inc.
136 West Street
Suite 202
Northampton
Massachusetts 01060
USA

A catalogue record for this book
is available from the British Library

Library of Congress Cataloguing in Publication Data
Measuring environmental degradation : developing pressure indicators for Europe / edited by Anil Markandya and Nick Dale.
     p. cm.
"In association with the European Community".
Includes index.
     1. Environmental degradation—Europe—Measurement.   2. Environmental indicators—Europe.   I. Markandya, Anil, 1945–   II. Dale, Nick, 1960–

GE160.E75 M43   2001
363.7064'094—dc21

00–055115

ISBN 1 84064 380 3

Typeset by Manton Typesetters, Louth, Lincolnshire, UK.
Printed and bound in Great Britain by MPG Books Ltd, Bodmin, Cornwall.

Contents

List of figures

List of tables

Foreword by Eurostat

This collection of contributions is one in a series of publications commissioned for the European Commission's Environment Directorate General and Eurostat, the Statistical Office of the European Communities, under the reference title *Towards Environmental Pressure Indicators for the EU* (TEPI). It should be seen as a first background document to the 'Environmental Pressure Indicators Project', providing a general overview of the main issues covered by the project.

The TEPI series consists of a set of four closely related volumes, aimed at raising awareness of the pressures put on the environment as a result of human activity. This is done through the creation of a framework for the regular production of environmental pressure indicators. These indicators are intended as tools for environmental policy-making at European Union level as well as providing information to the general public. Each volume is split into ten parts, representing each of the policy fields covered by the project, that is, Air Pollution, Climate Change, Loss of Biodiversity, Marine Environment and Coastal Zones, Ozone Layer Depletion, Resource Depletion, Dispersion of Toxic Substances, Urban Environmental Problems, Waste, Water Pollution and Water Resources, based on the themes of the 5EAP.[1] The starting-points of each volume have been the results of two surveys of environmental experts, carried out by Eurostat (see Editors' introduction).

The other volumes in the series are:

1. *Towards Environmental Pressure Indicators for the EU*, first edition 1999[2]
   This is Eurostat's reference publication on pressure indicators. It contains data for the set of 60 core pressure indicators selected by expert survey (see list on page xii and Editors' introduction).

2. *Towards Environmental Pressure Indicators for the EU – Indicator Definition*[3]
   This second background document provides a description of the policy fields and their respective indicators (mainly those identified as core indicators, see (1) above), and proposes recommendations for further research activities.

3. *Towards Environmental Pressure Indicators for the EU – An Examination of the Sectors*[4]

This third background document contains six reports drafted by national statistical offices, describing the links between the indicators and the economic sectors agriculture, energy, industry, tourism, transport and waste management.

The Working Documents, together with Methodology Sheets providing methodological background to the indicators, are available (or are intended to be made available) on the TEPI Web site (http://e-m-a-i-l.nu/tepi/), which provides a comprehensive description of the work done by Eurostat on pressure indicators and gives full contact details of the project team. Another related Web site (http://esl.jrc.it//envind), situated at the European Commission's Joint Research Centre in Ispra (Italy), provides a discussion forum on research aspects of the project.

   Recent political priorities have focused on developing indicators on sectoral integration, that is, integrating the environmental dimension into sectors (mainly transport, energy, agriculture and industry). This sectoral aspect was already foreseen in the work on pressure indicators (see (3) above); however, the reallocation of priorities means that some of the future work referred to in these publications, for example the condensation of the indicators into a set of indices, has now moved further down the political agenda, although such a development is not excluded at a later stage.

The reader should be aware that the opinions expressed in these documents do not necessarily reflect the official viewpoint of the European Commission.

NOTES

1. Fifth Environmental Action Programme: Resolution of the Council and the Representatives of the Governments of the Member States meeting within the Council of 1 February 1993 on a Community programme of policy and action in relation to the Environment and Sustainable Development – Towards Sustainability (OJ 93/C 138 of 17.5.93).
2. ISBN 92-828-4978-3, EUR 36 (excl. VAT) from Office for Official Publications of the European Communities, L-2985 Luxembourg (first edition June 1999; second edition to appear in 2000).
3. Availabe as a Working Document (publicity to be provided on the TEPI Web site (http://e-m-a-i-l.nu/tepi/)
4. See note 3.

List of environmental pressure indicators developed by Eurostat in the TEPI publication[a]

Air Pollution	Emissions of nitrogen oxides (NO_x)	Emissions of volatile organic compounds (VOCs)	Emissions of sulphur dioxide (SO_2)	Emissions of particles	Consumption of gasoline & diesel oil by road vehicles	Primary energy consumption
Climate Change	Emissions of carbon dioxide (CO_2)	Emissions of methane (CH_4)	Emissions of nitrous oxide (N_2O)	Emissions of hydrofluoro-carbons (HFCs) (replacing Emissions of CFCs)	Emissions of perfluorocarbons (PFCs) (replacing Emissions of NO_x)	Emissions of sulphurhexa-fluoride (SF_6) (replacing Emissions of SO_x)
Loss of Biodiversity	Protected area loss, damage and fragmentation	Wetland loss (changed from Wetland loss through drainage)	Agriculture intensity: area used for intensive arable agriculture	Fragmentation of forests & landscapes by roads/ intersections	Forest damage (changed from Clearance of nat./semi-nat. forested areas)	Change in traditional land-use practice
Marine Environment & Coastal Zones	Eutrophication	Fishing pressure	Development along shore	Discharges of heavy metals	Oil pollution at coast & at sea	Tourism intensity (replacing Discharges of halogenated organic compounds)
Ozone Layer Depletion	Emissions of bromofluoro-carbons (halons)	Emissions of chlorofluoro-carbons (CFCs)	Emissions of hydrochloro-fluorocarbons (HCFCs)	Emissions of nitrogen oxides (NO_x) by aircraft	Emissions of chlorinated carbons	Emissions of industrially produced methyl bromide (CH_3Br) (changed from Emissions of CH_3Br)

Resource Depletion	Water consumption per capita (incl. ground water abstraction)	Use of energy per capita	Increase in territory permanently occupied by urbanization; infrastructure…	Nutrient balance of the soil (nutrient input/ nutrient output)	Electricity production from fossil fuels (mineral oil, natural gas & coal)	Timber balance (new growth/ harvest)
Dispersion of Toxic Substances	Consumption of pesticides by agriculture	Emissions of persistent organic pollutants (POPs)	Consumption of toxic chemicals	Index of heavy metal emissions to water	Index of heavy metal emissions to air	Emissions of radioactive material
Urban Environmental Problems	Urban energy consumption (changed from Energy cons.)	Non-recycled municipal waste	Non-treated urban wastewater (changed from Non-treated wastewater)	Car share of urban passenger transport (changed from Share of private car transport)	People endangered by noise emissions from urban traffic (changed from People endangered by noise emissions)	Urban land use (changed from Land use)
Waste	Waste landfilled	Waste incinerated	Hazardous waste	Municipal waste	Industrial waste (replacing Waste per product during a n° of products entire lifetime)	Waste recycled/ material recovered
Water Pollution & Water Resources	Emissions of nutrients (changed from Nutrient (N + P) use (eutrophication equivalents))	Ground water abstraction	Pesticides used per hectare of utilized agriculture area	Nitrogen used per hectare of utilized agriculture area	Waste water treatment (changed from Water treated/ water collected)	Emissions of organic matter as biochemical oxygen demand (BOD)

Note: ᵃ Indicators in parentheses are those developed in the second version to appear in 2000 which have been renamed or are new.

Acknowledgements

Within Eurostat (Environment Statistics unit), this project was initiated by Jochen Jesinghaus (now at the Commission's Joint Research Centre in Ispra, Italy).

Eurostat wishes to thank the various contributors to this publication, namely:

- the authors who drafted the essays (see Introduction to the contributors and Annex III);
- the specialized institutes which provided assistance to the authors and drafted most of the introductory chapters (see Annex II); and
- the editors, Professor Anil Markandya and Nick Dale (Metroeconomica Ltd, Bath, UK), who edited the whole publication and drafted some parts of it, including some introductory chapters.

Final editing matters have been handled and coordinated by Catherine Kesy (consultant, 2SDA Luxembourg) and Metroeconomica Ltd.

Editors' introduction

This collection of essays on the theme of developing pressure indicators for Europe has been compiled as part of the Pressure Indicators Project (PIP), undertaken by Eurostat, the Statistical Office of the European Communities. The PIP aims to produce a set of indicators describing pressures resulting from human activities, which are intended to communicate environmental information to decision-makers and a wider public without losing the scientific soundness of the original indicators. Thus each indicator should describe the pressure in a comprehensive and analytically sound way, while at the same time being easy to interpret and capable of revealing trends on an appropriate time-scale.

The PIP project is divided into ten 'policy fields' (based on the seven themes of the Fifth Environmental Action Programme[1]) chosen to reflect the decision-making structure of the central institutions within the European Union, such as national and regional governments and the European Commission, which will be the focus for policy changes to improve environmental sustainability. These policy fields are: Air Pollution, Climate Change, Loss of Biodiversity, Marine Environment and Coastal Zones, Ozone Layer Depletion, Resource Depletion, Dispersion of Toxic Substances, Urban Environmental Problems, Waste and Water Pollution and Water Resources.

Ten specialized institutes (SIs) corresponding to each of the ten policy fields were selected to coordinate much of the project's work. A list of the SIs is given in Annex II. The SIs established Scientific Advisory Groups (SAGs), selected from senior natural scientists and experts in the ten policy fields from across the EU, in order to help with the process of developing pressure indicators, mainly by responding to questionnaires. The first-round questionnaire asked SAGs for proposals for environmental pressure indicators in their respective policy fields. This was conducted in December 1995 and received a total of 2744 suggested indicators. These were used as the basis for a preliminary list of indicators for each policy field. In the second-round questionnaire, conducted in October 1996, the SAGs were requested to rank the indicators on the preliminary list for their policy field in terms of policy relevance (the importance of the indicator for policy-makers), analytical soundness (the correlation between changes in the indicator and changes in environmental pressure), and responsiveness (the response of the indicator to policy actions, in other words: the ease or difficulty in taking action substantially to reduce the pressure indicator). They were also asked to opt for a short-list of five essential indicators (a core set) based on the above criteria. This has resulted in the production of a set of 100 'core indicators' for which a full set of methodology sheets will be made available on the main project Web site.[2] The ongoing stage of the project involves data collection, methodological development and calculation of the first 60 core indicators using data from across the EU Member States (see Foreword).

As part of the PIP a number of experts from across the spectrum of policy fields and from across the EU (and in a few cases beyond) were asked to write a short essay to reflect upon and aid the process of selecting an imaginative list of pressure indicators from the perspective of their policy field. These essays are collected together here with one part of the volume dedicated to each of the policy fields. The handbook is intended for decision-makers who are not environmental experts, but will also be of interest to the wider public.

It was initially suggested that authors could structure their essays to cover the following questions:

- What are the main problems within the policy field?
- Why is central political intervention necessary?
- What physical actions are needed to reduce the problem pressures?
- What are the expected benefits of communicating trends in problem pressures to policy-makers and the wider public via a pressure index for each policy field?[3]

A wide range of approaches, both within and between policy fields, has been taken by the various authors. Many chose to stay strictly within the boundaries of the guideline questions set out above. Some have addressed broader questions of the development of pressure indices, for example, Huisingh (Chapter 29), while others have outlined areas of specialist research in environmental pressures, for example, Fiedler and Hutzinger (Chapter 25). Some of the essays that differed from the suggested format are included in this published collection to illustrate the diversity of perspectives held by the experts and in the interests of variety within the collection. It should be noted that the original essays were drafted in the period 1996–98. Where possible updates have been made to take account of developments although not all more recent developments are included.

Following the production of the second-round questionnaire results some authors chose to comment on these in comparison with their own views on indicator rankings. The introduction to each part of the book gives a summary of the questionnaire results in graphical form. Full details of the results can be found in the volume *Towards Environmental Pressure Indicators for the EU – Indicator Definition* (see Foreword). The highest core-ranked indicators for each policy field are given in Annex I of the present publication.

The introductions to each part also include a discussion of the links with other policy fields and delimitation between policy fields, an evaluation of the essays and an outline of the international policy framework for the policy field. Where indicated, these have been written by the SIs for their policy fields, otherwise they have been written by us.

It is hoped that this publication will give a valuable insight into the process of developing pressure indicators undertaken by the PIP. The essays bring out a number of questions regarding the use of this approach. What should be the rationale for defining a clearly delineated set of policy fields? How can we accommodate into this framework both environmental media-based definitions (such as air and water pollution) and issues-based definitions (such as climate change), and what are the linkages and overlaps between these different types of policy field? How do we arrive at a comprehensive, analytically sound and widely accepted set of indicators for each policy field? How should we take account of the complex interconnections between environmental pressures, for example, when a reduction in one pressure indicator is linked to an increase in another pressure indicator, perhaps in another policy field? By what process should we make changes in the ranking of indicators over time (or introduce new indicators) in order to take account of a changing world?

It is also hoped that this volume will be a useful resource for all those with an interest in the broad range of environmental issues of current relevance to Europe. It presents concise explanations and background information on the present understanding of the main environmental pressures, as well as discussion on the practical actions necessary to reduce these pressures.

Metroeconomica have been involved with the Pressure Indicators Project since its inception, providing methodological support in the development of the pressure indices through use of expert questionnaires. We would like to thank all the essayists, and our colleagues from the specialized institutes (listed in Annex II) and Eurostat, in particular Catherine Kesy, for their various valuable contributions to this publication.

A. Markandya

N. Dale

NOTES

1. 5EAP; see Project terminology in Annex IV.
2. http://e-m-a-i-l.nu/tepi/
3. Possible future work foreseen for the project is the production of a set of ten indices, one for each policy field, which condense the indicators for each policy field into a highly aggregated format.

Introduction to the contributors

I AIR POLLUTION

Professor Panos Papagiannakopoulos is the head of the Photochemistry and Kinetics Laboratory at the Department of Chemistry of the University of Crete in Greece. He has 20 years' experience in the field of atmospheric chemistry. His field of expertise covers indoor and ambient air quality monitoring techniques, quality assurance in monitoring, development of new spectroscopic measurements and detection techniques, kinetics of fast reactions in the gas phase and photochemical processes in the atmosphere. He is the author of six books and of more than 30 publications in internationally refereed journals with over 100 citations.

Bjarne Sivertsen graduated from the University of Oslo in 1969. He has more than 30 years' experience as an air pollution meteorologist, specializing in boundary layer meteorology, turbulence and dispersion modelling and power plant and industrial siting. Mr Sivertsen has been responsible for several air quality investigations worldwide. He has carried out a number of environmental impact assessment studies and has been responsible for Nordic research on power production and air pollution impact. He has participated in the development of air quality surveillance and optimal abatement strategies in several countries and has performed regional emission inventories. He has given lectures on air pollution problems, air quality modelling and impact assessment in several countries. As an Associate Research Director at the Norwegian Institute for Air Research (NILU), he has been involved in air quality planning, optimal abatement strategies, impact assessment analyses and air pollution screening. He has long experience in work within and with developing countries, and is an expert in coordinating and handling interdisciplinary projects. Finally, he has also developed training programmes on air quality in Europe and in Asia.

Dr David Guinnup received his B.Sc. and M.Sc. degrees in Chemical Engineering from Purdue University and subsequently earned a Ph.D. in Chemical Engineering from the University of Michigan in 1981. After teaching Chemical Engineering at North Carolina State University for six years, he started working for the United States Environmental Protection Agency as an environmental engineer in the Office of Air Quality Planning and Standards (OAQPS). His initial area of expertise at OAQPS was in the modelling of the impacts of sources of toxic air pollution, including accidental releases to the atmosphere. He has since worked as a manager in the air toxics programme area, specializing in risk assessment and technical support. Since 1994, he has been a group leader for the Air Quality Trends and Analysis Group, a technical support group specializing primarily in statistical analysis and interpretation of air quality data. Most recently, the group has begun working on several projects aimed at better quantifying air toxics problems and tracking efforts to solve them through the analysis of air quality and emissions data.

Christine Sansevero is a policy analysis and communication specialist with the United States Environmental Protection Agency's Office of Air and Radiation. Ms Sansevero serves as a primary communications contact in the Office of Air Quality Planning and Standards, where she is responsible for preparing communication materials for all regulatory actions (including national air quality standards and emissions standards for toxic air pollutants). She is a magna cum laude graduate of the University of Connecticut in Civil Engineering, where she concentrated on environmental engineering and public policy. Since joining EPA in August 1995, she has been involved in developing environmental indicators, preparing air quality trends analyses, communicating regulatory activities, as well as organizing a variety of public outreach efforts.

II CLIMATE CHANGE

John Sweeney (Department of Geography, National University of Ireland, Maynooth) is the secretary of the Irish National Committee for the International Geosphere–Biosphere Programme.

Sir John Houghton CBE FRS is co-chair of the Intergovernmental Panel on Climate Change (IPCC) Working Group 1. This IPCC Working Group has been established to assess the available information on the science of climate change, in particular on the effects of human activities on climate.

Hartmut Grassl is currently managing the Max-Planck-Institute for Meteorology, in Hamburg. From 1994 to 1999 he was Director of the World Climate Research Programme based at WMO in Geneva. He is the chair of the Global Advisory Board to the German government, and a member of the IPCC, and the Inquiry Commission of the German Parliament 'Protection of Earth's Atmosphere'.

III LOSS OF BIODIVERSITY

Pierre Devillers is currently head of the Conservation Biology Department of the Belgian Royal Institute of Natural Sciences, where he has worked since 1972. He gained a Ph.D. (Sciences) in 1971 at the University of California, San Diego, and a further Ph.D. (Applied Science) in 1975 at the Université Libre de Bruxelles, Belgium. His areas of specialization are conservation biology, ecology, habitats systematics and typology, eco-ethology and systematics, database conception and use, and protected area planning and management. He has extensive international experience in projects across Europe, South America and North Africa.

Marianne Lefort was the Director of the Board of Genetic Resources (BRG) from 1994 to 1999. BRG is a French national organization for coordinating activities relating to animal, plant and micro-organism genetic resources. She has also recently been involved in the National Programme for Biological Diversity (PNDB) in France. She is a quantitative geneticist who has worked for 13 years at the Plant Breeding Department of INRA (National Institute for Agronomical Research), particularly with rapeseed and maize. Dr Lefort is presently the head of this department.

IV MARINE ENVIRONMENT AND COASTAL ZONES

Professor Harry Coccossis teaches environmental planning at the Department of Environmental Studies of the University of the Aegean in Greece. He has extensive research and professional experience in coastal management, sustainable development for islands, environmental planning, sustainable tourist development planning and regional planning as consultant for various national and international agencies and organizations (EU, UNEP, FAO, OECD, the World Bank, UNESCO and so on) in the Mediterranean and East Africa regions.

Margarida Cardoso da Silva is an expert on coastal zone management currently at the Estuaries Division of the National Laboratory for Civil Engineering in Lisbon, Portugal. Her publications include papers on sustainable management and integrated environmental assessment of coastal zones.

V OZONE LAYER DEPLETION

Professor Guido Visconti is Professor of Geophysics at the Department of Physics, University of L'Aquila (Italy). His main subjects of research are numerical modelling of the stratosphere and climate, lidar measurements of aerosol and ozone, and meteorology. He has worked extensively on models to simulate stratospheric ozone transport and participated in the Scientific Assessments of Ozone Depletion of the World Meteorological Organization. He is a member of the International Ozone Commission.

Professor Ivar S.A. Isaksen is Professor at the Department of Geophysics, University of Oslo (Norway), and Science Director at the Center for International Climate and Environmental Research (CICERO), Oslo. He is the vice-chair of the Committee for the European Programme on Stratospheric Research. Further, he is a member of the NATO Science Committee on Global Environmental Change, the International Ozone Commission, and the Scientific Steering Group of the project Stratospheric Processes and their Role in Climate (SPARC) of the World Climate Research Programme (WCRP).

Dr Marie-Lise Chanin has carried out extensive studies on the influence of solar radiation, and on anthropogenic effects on the atmosphere. She has served in several international committees dealing with global change issues and is currently chairing the project Stratospheric Processes and their Role in Climate (SPARC) of the World Climate Research Programme (WCRP). She is a corresponding member of the French Académie des Sciences, Chevalier de la Légion d'Honneur and Commandeur de l'Ordre du Mérite.

VI RESOURCE DEPLETION

Øyvind Lone, M.A. (Geography), University of Oslo, 1977, has worked in the Norwegian Institute for Urban and Regional Research, Statistics Norway, the OECD Environment Directorate, and is now Deputy General Director in the Norwegian Ministry of Environment.

Professor David Pearce, OBE, MA (Oxon) is Professor of Environmental Economics at UCL (University College London) and Associate Director of CSERGE (Centre for Social and Economic Research on the Global Environment).

Jean-Louis Weber, DES of Economy, University of Paris, 1970, has worked as a national accountant at INSEE (the French statistical institute), was Secretary General of the Interministerial Committee for Natural Patrimony Accounting and was head of the Unit of Statistics and Economic Studies of the French Ministry of Environment. Since 1992 he has been Director of International Affairs of IFEN (the French Institute of Environment).

VII   DISPERSION OF TOXIC SUBSTANCES

Professor Aristeo Renzoni was born in Siena, Italy, some seventy years ago, and has a life-long experience as a researcher in the field of environmental biology. Starting his carreer as a specialist with a degree in Veterinary Medicine in the early 1950s, he has also earned a reputation as a generalist in environmental issues. After working as a researcher in Italy, Holland, Germany, Wales and the USA, he held full professorships in Hydrobiology (1973–89), Ecology (1989–92), and currently in Conservation of Natural Resources, at the University of Siena.

A very large international contact network has led Professor Renzoni to research and teach in a great many parts of the world. He has also been responsible for and/or coordinator of projects within the frameworks of UNEP, ERASMUS, TEMPUS, NATO, INTAS, as well as the Socrates programme. Professor Renzoni has also been president and/or member of a large number of scientific committees of different laboratories and institutes. His list of national and international publications is extensive.

Dr Heidelore Fiedler obtained a master's degree in Chemistry and a Ph.D. at the University of Saarland in Saarbruücken, Germany. She has been a senior scientist in environmental chemistry at the University of Bayreuth since 1985. Her research focuses on sources, fate, and environmental exposures of organic chemicals, and risk assessment.

Professor Otto Hutzinger was born in Vienna, studied chemistry in Canada and held post-doctorate positions at the University of California. He was the Director of the Environmental Chemistry Laboratory in Amsterdam from 1974 to 1983. Since 1983, he has been a Professor and Chair of Ecological Chemistry and Geochemistry of the University of Bayreuth, Germany.

VIII   URBAN ENVIRONMENTAL PROBLEMS

Professor Colin Fudge is Dean of the Faculty of the Built Environment, University of the West of England, Bristol; he is also Urban Environment Adviser to the European Commission, Adviser on Research (DG XII), European Commission, chair of the EU Urban Environment Committee; chair of OECD Urban Indicators International Panel, and Director of the WHO Collaborative Research Centre on Healthy Cities and Urban Policy. He formerly held the post of Director of Environmental Services, Bath City Council, and was Honorary Professor in the Department of City and Regional Planning, University of Cardiff (UK). He was Deputy Permanent Secretary, Ministry for Planning and Environment, State of Victoria, Australia from 1983 to

1986; and was Senior Lecturer in Public Policy and Management at the School for Advanced Urban Studies, University of Bristol, for 13 years. He has extensive experience of working internationally, for various countries and organizations. He has written several books on public policy, government and planning.

IX   WASTE

Dr Donald Huisingh has been Professor of Environmental Sciences at Lund University, Sweden since 1997. From 1989 to 1997 he was Professor of Environmental Sciences, Cleaner Production and Sustainability at the Erasmus University in Rotterdam, The Netherlands. He has published more than 140 articles and has worked with many national and international organizations and companies. His main field of interest is cleaner production, environmental management and progress towards sustainability.

Karin Jordan has worked with the Berlin-based consultancy ARGUS since 1993 and has extensive experience on a series of studies on waste management and waste statistics for the EC Environment DG and for Eurostat. For the City of Berlin, Karin Jordan has undertaken a research study to formulate the specific requirements for a comprehensive soil protection strategy, including aspects of land-use as well as pollution of soil. In Germany she has carried out several investigations on the amount and composition of various waste types and prepared guidelines for waste prevention and recycling.

Peter Gössele has been Director for the statistical institute ARGUS at the Technical University of Berlin since 1987. He has been project manager for many studies concerning waste analysis, landfill monitoring and waste statistics, such as the LIFE-REMECOM project concerning development of a network for monitoring the quality of household refuse with a view to strengthening environmental legislation. He has been a member of the Board of Directors of the German Society of Waste Management since 1993 and leader of the Society Working Group Europe.

Professor Franco Cecchi is full professor of Biochemical Plants and of Biotechnological Environmental Processes at the University of Verona (Italy), Faculty of Sciences, Science and Technology Department. He is referee for several international scientific journals and member of the scientific committees of the Environmental Ministry and of the National Environmental Agency. He is author of more than 200 scientific papers including international reviews, books and conference reports. Main research topics include: energy and material recovery from organic waste through biological stabilization;

monitoring methodologies for sanitary landfills; biodegradation of aromatic compounds; mathematical models for simulation of chemical and biological processes; control of biological processes; fluid dynamic parameters in biological reactors; flue-gas cleaning; treatment processes for industrial and urban wastewater; and production reduction techniques for waste activated sludge.

Dr Paolo Pavan is a researcher at the University of Venice (Italy), Faculty of Sciences, Environmental Sciences Department. He is author of more than 120 publications, including articles for international scientific reviews, books and conference papers. His research is mainly concerned with advanced waste and wastewater treatment, in particular, the anaerobic digestion process applied to the organic fraction of solid waste, the anaerobic fermentation of putrescible wastes to produce light alcohols and volatile fatty acids (VFA), and the biological nutrient removal from wastewater considering also the integration with the organic waste treatment cycle.

X   WATER POLLUTION AND WATER RESOURCES

Dr Joan S. Davis is an aquatic chemist and until 1999 held posts as a researcher and directorial staff member at the Swiss Federal Institute of Environmental Science and Technology (EAWAG) in Zürich, and as lecturer at the Swiss Federal Institute of Technology and the University of Basel. As emerita, she now cooperates with the EAWAG on evaluation of Swiss river studies. She formerly had held posts also at the Technical University of Berlin, Gesamthochschule Kassel and University of Zürich. Her main research areas are the anthropogenic impacts (chemical and physical) on Swiss surface waters, and the technical and societal changes required for sustainable water management. She is a board member of a number of committees, research institutes, organizations and foundations associated with environmental issues, and has published papers on subjects including river water studies; correlation between resource consumption, economic growth and quality of life; sustainable use of resources; and technologies and risks.

Dr Klaus Lanz is an aquatic chemist and was involved in water research at the University of Minnesota (1986–87) and the Swiss Federal Institute of Environmental Science and Technology (EAWAG, 1987–88). He was a water campaigner for Greenpeace Germany (1988–92) and is author of the Greenpeace Book of Water (Newton Abbot, 1995). He is director if International Water Affairs, an independent institute focusing on interdisciplinary water research and is based in Hamburg, Germany. Current research topics include the potential environmental and social effects of European Union water legislation and the ongoing privatisation of water services.

Josefina Maestu is an economist and obtained a master's degree in Planning in the UK. She carried out studies for a Ph.D. degree in the Massachusetts Institute of Technology, and has worked for the Water Quality Directorate of the Spanish Ministry of Environment. She is currently the Director of the Spanish Office of ECOTEC Research and Consulting, and Associate Professor of Environmental Economics at the University of Alcalá de Henares. She specializes in the economic and institutional aspects of water management and has co-authored chapters in several books.

Jose Maria Gasco is a Doctor in Agricultural Engineering and a Professor of Edaphology in the School of Agricultural Engineering of the Madrid Technical University. He has extensive experience in field work related to salinization of land and water resources and the effect of pesticides and fertilizers on water-related habitats and agricultural production. He has recently carried out the Water Accounts for Spain using a revised OECD methodology.

Jose Manuel Naredo has a Ph.D. in Economic Science and is a member of the statistical profession. He has broad experience in macroeconomic studies combining concrete analysis of agrarian systems with more general reflections on economic science in relation to natural resources. He has written books on economic thought and on agriculture in Spain. He is currently the Director of the Argentaria Foundation Programme on Economics and Nature.

Federico Aguilera is an economist and Professor in Applied Economics in the University of la Laguna in Tenerife, where he has been teaching the economics of natural resources for the past ten years. He did postgraduate studies in agricultural economics in Montpellier (France) and has been visiting researcher at the University of Arizona. He has written books and articles on water economics and the economics of natural resources.

PART I

Air Pollution

1. Introduction

A. Markandya and N. Dale

1. THE AIR POLLUTION POLICY FIELD

The Air Pollution policy field covers the gaseous pollutants existing in the atmosphere as a result of human activities. This includes the release of primary pollutants such as sulphur dioxide, nitrogen oxides and volatile organic compounds, which result from the combustion of fossil fuels, industrial processes and agricultural practices, and the formation of secondary pollutants, such as ozone, resulting from the reaction of some primary compounds in the atmosphere. This policy field also includes the issue of acidification, which is the result of emissions of sulphur dioxide and nitrogen oxides reacting in the atmosphere with water, oxygen and oxidants to form acidic compounds, thus causing acidic deposition. The impacts of these various types of air pollution, as explained in the chapters in this part of the volume, include adverse effects on human health, natural ecosystems, agriculture and forestry, and historic buildings. Since current levels of many air pollutants are above accepted national and international standards in most European countries, this policy field is of great relevance to Europe.

Within the above definition of the Air Pollution policy field a wide range of pressure indicators was suggested by experts in the first-round questionnaire. For the second-round questionnaire this list was reduced to the 27 that were considered to be most relevant and the indicators were divided into four groups covering emissions, agriculture, energy-related activities and transportation.[1]

2. RESULTS OF THE SECOND-ROUND QUESTIONNAIRE

Figure 1.1 shows the top 15 core-ranked indicators for the Air Pollution policy field, along with the corresponding rankings for the three quality questions. The top five rankings for the four questions were as follows:

Air pollution

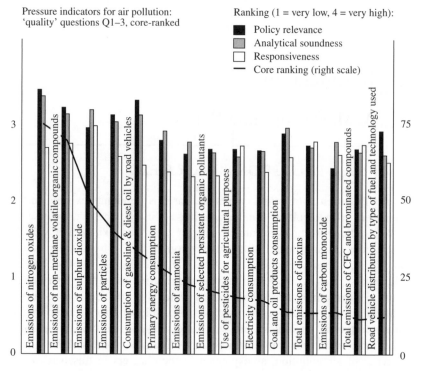

*Figure 1.1   Results of second-round questionnaire for the Air Pollution
                  policy field*

- Core-ranked indicators: emissions of nitrogen oxides (NO$_x$), emissions
  of non-methane volatile organic compounds (NMVOCs), emissions of
  sulphur dioxide (SO$_2$), emissions of particles, gasoline and diesel oil
  consumption by road vehicles.
- Policy relevance indicators: emissions of nitrogen oxides (NO$_x$), gasoline and diesel oil consumption by road vehicles, emissions of
  non-methane volatile organic compounds (NMVOCs), emission of particles, emissions of sulphur dioxide (SO$_2$).
- Analytical soundness indicators: emissions of nitrogen oxides (NO$_x$),
  emissions of sulphur dioxide (SO$_2$), emissions of non-methane volatile
  organic compounds (NMVOCs), gasoline and diesel oil consumption
  by road vehicles, emissions of particles.
- Response elasticity indicators: emissions of sulphur dioxide (SO$_2$), emissions of dioxins, emissions of non-methane volatile organic compounds
  (NMVOCs), emissions of CFC (chlorofluorocarbon) and brominated
  compounds emissions, use of pesticides for agricultural purposes.

These results show a high correlation between the top five rankings for all four questions with indicators for emissions of NO_x, SO_2, NMVOCs and particles featuring in at least three of the top five lists. This indicates the high level of agreement in the scientific community about the primary responsibility for pollution occurrences such as photochemical smog and acid rain. There is less consistency between the responsiveness rankings and those of the other questions. There is also less consistency between the quality question rankings and the core rankings for indicators below the top five. However, this does not represent a substantial difference in importance attached to indicators between the questions since, for positions 6 to 15, there is very little difference between the actual level of expert responses given for each question.

3. RELATIONS TO OTHER POLICY FIELDS

There are strong links between the Air Pollution policy field and several of the other policy fields, and some of the pressure indicators relevant to air pollution have been ranked relatively highly in other policy fields. For example, emissions of selected persistent organic compounds and emissions of dioxins are included in the Dispersion of Toxic Substances policy field core rankings, and use of pesticides for agricultural purposes is included in the Loss of Biodiversity and Dispersion of Toxic Substances policy fields core rankings.

Some indicators have been excluded from the final ranking because they are particularly relevant to other policy fields, for example, emissions of carbon dioxide are considered in the Climate Change policy field. The relationship with the Climate Change policy field is important because measures taken to reduce carbon dioxide emissions will influence the emissions of other air pollutants as well. A further link exists due to the cooling effect of aerosols resulting from emissions of sulphur dioxide and soot (causing acid rain). Reduction of emissions of these aerosols will result in a decrease of the regional cooling effect and make the warming of the atmosphere more apparent in highly industrialized regions. This means that an improvement in the pressures related to acid rain and regional air pollution results in a worsening in pressures related to climate change.

Links to the Ozone Layer Depletion policy field exist because tropospheric pollution (ozone and particles) in industrial regions has partly masked the effects of ozone depletion in these regions. An indicator for emissions of CFCs and brominated compounds is included in the core rankings for the Air Pollution policy field.

There are particular associations with the Urban Environmental Problems policy field and some air pollutant emission indicators are ranked relatively highly in the results of the second-round questionnaire. In order to avoid overlap, the Air Pollution policy field considers the regional scale (for example Mediterranean countries or Nordic countries, or Europe as a whole) as opposed to the urban context.

Treatment of waste (for example, incineration) can cause air pollution, depending on the waste type and the technology applied. However, highly ranked waste indicators relate to types of waste and waste treatment rather than emissions from waste. Air pollution indicators concentrate on the total emissions of various pollutants and include, for example, 'emissions of dioxins', which is related to waste incineration.

4.   APPROACH OF THE CONTRIBUTORS

The chapter by Professor Papagiannakopoulos gives a clear overview of the important pressures in the Air Pollution policy field, the actions required to reduce these pressures and the role of pressure indicators. He starts by identifying the main impacts of air pollution and acidification as those on human health and air quality, natural ecosystems, agriculture and forestry, and cultural heritage. Short- and medium-term actions to reduce these pressures are outlined as: (i) reduction in emissions of air pollutant gases (described by sector), (ii) improvement of materials, (iii) reductions in acidity, (iv) control of transboundary atmospheric pollution, and (v) improvements in scientific knowledge. A framework of long-term strategies is also presented. Professor Papagiannakopoulos concludes by giving an explanation of the benefits of pressure indices in general terms. He stresses the importance of a scientific consensus about the relative weighting of pressure indices, and warns that statistical information often fails to follow and describe the rapid changes in the environment.

Bjarne Sivertsen starts his chapter with an explanation of the concept of air quality indicators and discusses the selection of these indicators in his outline of problems related to urban air quality and acidification. Along with Professor Papagiannakopoulos, he points to the changing nature of the main air pollutants in recent years. Formerly these were linked to the burning of fossil fuels, but in recent years pollutants such as nitrogen dioxide, ozone and 'a reactive mixture of secondary air pollutants originating from road transport and other mobile sources' have become increasingly important. Therefore, actions recommended in Sivertsen's chapter stress the need to reduce the impact of road transport, and the importance of international cooperation in reducing the impact of the most common air pollutants on the environment. He also outlines the steps needed for a cost–benefit analysis of measures aimed at reducing a specific air quality indicator.

David Guinnup and Christine Sansevero from the US Environmental Protection Agency (USEPA) begin by outlining what they regard as the eight most common air pollutants, namely, carbon monoxide, lead, ozone, nitrogen dioxide, sulphur dioxide, volatile organic compounds and fine and coarse particulate matter. They then focus on these eight pollutants when addressing actions needed to reduce pressures and the benefits of such reductions. Their list compares reasonably closely with the core-ranking results for the Air Pollution policy field. Differences between the lists can be partly accounted for by the inclusion of source-based indicators, particularly related to energy consumption, in the PIP questionnaire. In their list of actions the EPA authors stress the need to reduce primary pollutants by subjecting emissions from electric utilities, road transport and various industrial processes to control programmes which could include installation of pollution control devices, increasing process efficiency and introduction of alternative raw materials. They point out that it is more difficult to develop control strategies for secondary pollutants because the mixtures of primary emissions that cause these are often location-specific. In conclusion, they argue that in the long term it is not enough to develop pollution control actions. Instead, pollution prevention measures must be developed to reduce expanding environmental pressures generated by worldwide growth.

5. INTERNATIONAL FRAMEWORK

The major international agreement relating to air pollution is the UNECE Convention on Long Range Transboundary Air Pollution (LRTAP), which was first adopted in 1985 and commits signatories to reductions in emissions of transboundary fluxes within agreed timetables and to present national emission data annually. The LRTAP includes protocols for sulphur dioxide (1985 and 1994), nitrogen oxides (1988) and volatile organic compounds. The need to comply with this convention has helped to drive the development of international integrated emission inventories such as the CORINAIR90 inventory for European countries.

The Protocol on Long Term Financing of the Cooperative Programme for Monitoring and Evaluation of the Long Range Transmission of Air Pollutants in Europe (EMEP) was adopted in 1984 and ratified by 30 countries. Over 100 monitoring stations are now part of the EMEP monitoring system.

As noted above, measures taken to reduce carbon dioxide emissions will influence the emissions of other air pollutants. Therefore, the Framework Climate Change Convention adopted at the UN Conference on Environment and Development in 1992 is likely to have important impacts on Air Pollution indicators even though it is primarily aimed at reductions in greenhouse gases.

A series of EC directives has been aimed at reducing emissions of air pollutants. In particular these have included directives concerning transport and industry.

In the case of transport, the original directive (70/220/EEC) on vehicle emissions laid down technical standards for emissions of carbon monoxide and unburned hydrocarbons. This has been amended and updated nine times to include NO_x emissions (77/102/EEC) and particulate emissions (88/436/EEC) and to lower limits in a number of ways.

In the case of industry, the Air Pollution from Industrial Plants Directive (84/360/EEC) was the first framework directive in the Air Pollution policy field. It required that Member States set up a permit system for air emissions from certain industrial activities, establish a procedure for the Council to adopt emission limits, and take steps to identify and improve air quality in particularly polluted areas or those which needed special protection. Subsequently, the Limitation of Emissions of Certain Pollutants from Large Combustion Plants Directive (88/609/EEC) was adopted for combustion plants for the production of energy with a thermal input of 50 megawatts (MW) or more. The goal was to achieve a 58 per cent reduction in SO_2 emissions in the Community as a whole by 2003 and a somewhat lower reduction in NO_x emissions.

Other relevant directives include those for Prevention of Air Pollution from New Municipal Waste Incineration Plants (89/369/EEC), Reduction of Air Pollution from Existing Municipal Waste Incineration Plants (89/429/EEC) and Air Quality Standards for Nitrogen Dioxide (85/203/EEC).

The 1996 Ambient Air Quality Assessment Directive (96/62/EC) provides a new framework for controlling the most serious air polluting substances and ensuring that the European Commission and the Member States monitor and assess air quality in a consistent way.

In conclusion, it should be noted that the traditional approach of policies to reduce emissions of air pollutants has been through national programmes and regulations focusing on specific pollutants. However, in the last 20 years this approach has been criticized for not recognizing the cross-medium nature of environmental problems, resulting in pollution prevention actions that simply transfer the problem to another medium. Therefore, a move towards integrated pollution control has occurred in some European countries and the Integrated Pollution Prevention and Control (IPPC) EC directive will further advance this process.[2]

NOTES

1. First questionnaire: December 1995; second questionnaire: October 1996. See Editors' introduction.
2. See targets set at European level on TEPI Web page (http://e-m-a-i-l.nu/tepi//what's new/ the documents/download example).

2. Air pollution and acidification

P. Papagiannakopoulos

1. THE PROBLEM AND ITS IMPACT

Air Pollution

The first signs of the postwar air pollution problem became apparent over thirty years ago, mainly in the large urban and industrial centres. This problem was closely related to the enormous postwar economic growth. Initially, the 'conventional' air pollutants were sulphur dioxide, black smoke and lead, which were usually connected with the combustion of fossil fuels. However, in recent years new classes of air pollutants, which include nitrogen monoxide, nitrogen dioxide and ozone, have appeared. These are especially evident in the urban atmosphere and are responsible for the well-known phenomenon of photochemical smog. This phenomenon was first noticed in the greater Los Angeles area, but it is currently present in many large European cities, such as Athens and Paris. Today's catalogue of harmful air pollutants has grown to a large number, which includes both primary (for example VOCs – volatile organic compounds) and secondary air pollutants (for example Peroxyacetylnitrate (PAN) carbonyl compounds). Finally, aerosols, several heavy metals and particulate matter are significant air pollutants in both urban and industrial environments.

Acidification

Since the early 1960s there has been growing evidence that the chemistry of precipitation over northern Europe is changing, along with the first negative impacts of acid rain on the environment. The emissions of anthropogenic sulphur and nitrogen compounds (mainly as SO_2 and NO_2 gases) are causing a critical chemical transformation of the atmosphere that results in the problem of acid rain or acidification. These gases are also transported over large distances in the atmosphere, and are eventually converted into acid substances through heterogeneous chemical reactions either in clouds (wet deposition), or on surfaces (dry deposition). The negative environmental effects of acidification have been evidenced in many ecosystems, such as lakes, vegetation, crops and forests. Moreover, acidification has caused substantial deterioration of stoneware and building materials, producing severe damage to historical buildings and monuments that constitute part of the European cultural heritage. These effects have been more pronounced during the last 40 years, and have mainly been produced by sulphur acid compounds. The deposition of oxidized or reduced nitrogen has made a lesser contribution to acidification, but becomes relatively important in areas where deposition exceeds critical loads. However, the trends in sulphur emissions have shown a continuous decline over the last decade, and nitrogen deposition now plays an equally important role in the acidification problem.

The main impacts of air pollution and acidification are:

1. *Impact on human health and air quality* Increasing levels of air pollutants, especially in heavily populated urban areas, result in adverse effects on human health. Furthermore, many air pollutants enhance the photochemical reaction mechanism that leads to the drastic increase of ozone and photo-oxidant levels.
2. *Impact on natural ecosystems* Aquatic and terrestrial ecosystems face significant consequences as a result of air pollution and acidification. The impact on various ecosystems depends on the type and degree of acidification. The rates of acidification are often faster than the ability of species to respond, while in other cases such responses may be sudden or gradual. Some species could be lost owing to increased stress, leading to a reduction in biological diversity.
3. *Impact on agriculture and forestry* Sufficient evidence is now available from different studies to indicate that air pollution and acidification has an important effect on agriculture and forestry. However, there are major uncertainties regarding likely effects in specific regions, and this should be a cause for concern.
4. *Impact on cultural heritage* Air pollution and acidification is causing severe corrosion and damage to historical buildings, statues and monuments, which are made of stone, marble and metal, and constitute part of the cultural heritage of Europe.

2. NEED FOR POLITICAL INTERVENTION

The existing levels of anthropogenic air pollutants in most European countries are above the acceptable national and international standards. However, these compounds are also transported over great distances in the atmosphere and export the problem to remote places, far away from the primary source of emissions. It is estimated that about 50–70 per cent of oxidized sulphur and nitrogen emissions, as well as approximately 80 per cent of reduced nitrogen emissions, are deposited within Europe. Thus air pollution and acidification is a European issue and an effective response requires a joint effort which may have considerable impact on the welfare of our societies.

The air quality in many urban areas of Europe is continuously deteriorating, and the subsequent impact on human health is an urgent issue, of growing public concern, that should be addressed in a proper manner. Several recent studies also indicate that health effects and health symptoms may be present at levels of exposure that have been previously considered as safe.

The main health risks from air pollution exposure are primarily concentrated on respiratory problems. However, there is a very poor understanding of the relationship between conventional air pollution levels and acidification, expressed as pressure indicators, and final human health effects. Thus it is important to establish the necessary air quality and acidification indicators that will assist in the application of the optimal solutions leading to a reduction in pressure on human health.

Furthermore, the high levels of acid deposition, well above the critical levels for soil and freshwater acidification, are causing severe ecological problems. Transboundary air pollution is also an essential factor in undermining the forest ecosystems, by impairing nutrient uptake, increasing soil acidification and reducing base elements.

Finally, the severe damage to historical buildings and monuments due to acidification is becoming a serious problem in many large cities of Europe. It is therefore urgent for governments and local authorities to undertake drastic measures and abatement strategies to combat acidifying compounds.

3.   ACTIONS TO REDUCE AIR POLLUTION AND ACIDIFICATION

There are several actions to be taken on regional, national and European levels, which can help to tackle the air pollution and acidification problems. These actions can be distinguished as short- and medium-term and long-term.

Short- and Medium-term Actions

Reduce emissions of air pollutant gases
This action can be achieved by interventions in several economic sectors.

1.   In the energy sector energy efficiency must be improved, thereby reducing emissions of sulphur and nitrogen compounds and improving overall

economic performance, and at the same time reducing emissions of other air pollutants. The use of cleaner energy sources and cleaner technologies will also reduce emissions of sulphur and nitrogen compounds, and other air pollutants. Further measures should include the installation of filters in power plants for the capture of sulphur and nitrogen dioxides in the flue gases, and the use of low-sulphur fuels that reduce emissions of sulphur compounds.

2. In the transportation sector traffic in large urban areas must be reduced, resulting in the reduction of air pollutants. There should be a transfer from use of private vehicles to other means of transport and improvements in vehicle design by use of clean-car technology that causes far less air pollution and is more friendly to the environment. Other actions include improving fuel quality, switching to more environmentally friendly fuels, the introduction of three-way catalytic converters for all new motor vehicles and the introduction of obligatory testing of exhaust gases in motor vehicles.

3. In the industrial sector it is essential to introduce clean production technologies that generate fewer pollutants, and increase productivity. Improved energy efficiency will reduce emissions of sulphur, nitrogen and volatile organic compounds, improve overall economic performance, and reduce the emissions of other pollutants.

4. In the agricultural and forestry sectors it is essential to alter use and formulation of fertilizers, and introduce best agricultural practices in order to reduce emissions of ammonia. Other actions should be to reduce other agricultural uses of land without affecting food security, improve forest management and reduce deforestation and forest degradation, improve management of landfills and improve management of livestock wastes, thus reducing emissions of ammonia.

Improve materials
This action can be achieved by developing alternative construction materials that resist air pollution and acidification, and by developing new coating treatments for historic monuments and materials that offer protection.

Reduce acidity
This action can be achieved by restoring the chemical balance of agricultural soils affected by acid rain by the addition of lime, and by treating acidified lakes with a buffering agent, for example lime, to achieve temporary neutralization effects.

Control transboundary atmospheric pollution
This can be achieved by a number of actions:

1. By establishing and strengthening regional agreements for transboundary atmospheric pollution control and cooperation, particularly with transition countries, in the areas of systematic observation and assessment, modelling and development, and exchange of emission control technologies for mobile and stationary sources of air pollution.
2. By establishing or strengthening early warning systems and response mechanisms for transboundary atmospheric pollution resulting from industrial accidents and natural disasters.
3. By facilitating training opportunities and exchange of data, information and national and/or regional experiences of air pollution control.
4. By enhancing cooperation on regional, multilateral and bilateral bases to assess transboundary atmospheric pollution, and elaborate and implement programmes to reduce atmospheric emissions.

Improve scientific knowledge in air pollution and acidification
This action can be achieved:

1. By developing better emission estimates for all air pollutants and acidifying gases (sulphur and nitrogen dioxide gases, volatile organic compounds, ammonia and so on), including biogenic species.
2. By developing and applying pollution control and measurement technologies for stationary and mobile sources of air pollution.
3. By validating chemical transport models for acidifying compounds on regional and continental scales.
4. By developing validated models for regional and continental air pollution and deposition of acidifying compounds.
5. By developing methods and models to provide a more quantitative description of air pollution and deposition of acidifying compounds.
6. By developing a better understanding of the heterogeneous processes in clouds that are responsible for the production of acidity.

Long-term Actions

The main long-term actions to reduce air pollution and acidification can be achieved in the following ways:

1. By promoting the development of appropriate methodologies for making integrated energy and environment policy decisions.
2. By promoting the research, development, transfer and use of improved energy-efficient technologies and practices, and of technologies and practices for environmentally sound energy systems, including new and renewable energy systems.

3. By encouraging industries to increase and strengthen their capacity to develop technologies, products and processes that are safe, less polluting and make more efficient use of all resources and materials.
4. By promoting efficient use of materials and resources, taking into account the life cycles of products.
5. By observing and systematically assessing the sources and extent of transboundary air pollution resulting from natural processes and anthropogenic activities.
6. By developing strategies aimed at the reduction of emissions causing transboundary air pollution and their effects.
7. By strengthening regional and continental systematic observation networks for land degradation and effects on crop production caused by acidification.
8. By supporting national, regional and continental programmes for integrated data collection and research networks carrying out assessment of soil and land degradation.
9. By encouraging beneficial behavioural and structural (for example, transportation and housing infrastructure) changes.
10. By expanding the number of the observation and monitoring systems.

4. BENEFITS OF PRESSURE INDICES

At present, there are many human activities that are harmful to the environment and a complete description and understanding of all these undesirable activities is rather difficult to communicate and diffuse to our society. However, it is possible to develop several pressure indices for the various environmental issues which may provide some scientific evidence and the overall picture to the general public and policy-makers.

The introduction of several pressure indices is an effective way to engender harmonization of guidelines and policies within the European Union, and also to assist in the adoption of common measures and efforts in the field of acidification. Furthermore, it is possible to carry out comparisons with similar efforts within the international community.

In addition, pressure indices constitute a set of parameters which reveal the apparent relationship between all negative human activities and the changes in the state of the environment.

The successful preparation of pressure indices will give the opportunity to perform statistical analyses and correlate the different variations in those indices with the apparent changes in the state of the environment. However, the collection of several such pressure indices requires a scientific consensus about their relative weighting. It should also be emphasized that statistical information is rather absolute, and very often fails to follow and describe the rapid changes in the environment. The development of a database for each issue will also require the implementation of particular methodologies and data collection systems.

The implementation of pressure indices is a new approach to monitoring negative impacts on the environment. It may also expose ways of avoiding the limitations of existing monitoring systems. Finally, it may be an excellent tool in the effort to quantify the extent and significance of various human activities.

3. Air quality indicators

B. Sivertsen

1. INTRODUCTION

Indicators for air quality have been identified and used within the pressure–state–response framework (PSR). The PSR framework is based on a concept of causality whereby human activities exert *pressures* on the environment and change its *state*, that is, quality and quantity of natural resources, and society makes a *response* to these changes through environmental, general economic and sector policies.

One important tool in judging the state of the environment is to establish environmental pressure indicators linked to human activities and natural sources. These indicators should also be used for identifying the state of the environment and should be simple and easily understandable for policy-makers and the public.

In general terms, an indicator can be defined as a parameter, or a value derived from parameters, which provides information about a phenomenon. The indicator has significance that extends beyond the properties directly associated with the parameter value. Indicators possess a synthetic meaning and are developed for a specific purpose. This points to two major functions of indicators. First, they reduce the number of measurements and parameters which would normally be required to give an 'exact' presentation of a situation. Second, they simplify the communication process by which the results of measurements are provided to the user.

The air quality indicator should be a parameter or a value derived from parameters which provides information about the state of the environment. It should give a general picture, and be easy to interpret. It should also be able to respond to changes, provide international comparisons and show trends over time.

Available measurement techniques should be reasonably accurate and within acceptable cost limits. The effect of the selected indicator on health, building materials, vegetation and on fauna should be adequately documented and linked to public awareness. Selected indicators should respond to actions mitigating man-made negative impacts on the environment. The indicators should also have a threshold or reference value against which to compare actual values, so that users can assess the significance of these values.

2. THE PROBLEM

The criteria for the selection of indicators should be two-dimensional. On the one hand they should be representative of certain groups of emission sources (such as transport, personal cars, trucks, industries, energy, use of solvents, waste burning, construction work and so on) and on the other hand they should represent different types of effects (such as on health, materials, flora and fauna). Ideally the indicator should represent the link between the source and the exposure to end-effects.

Urban Air Quality

It is normally impossible to measure all the air pollutants present in the urban atmosphere. We therefore have to choose some indicators that should represent a set of parameters selected to reflect the status of the environment. They should allow the estimation of trends and developments, and should represent the basis for evaluating human and environmental impact. Further, they should be relevant for decision-making and they should be sensitive to environmental warning systems.

Many national and international authorities are at present working through the process to select environmental indicators. The selected parameters for air quality are strongly related to air pollutants, for which air quality guideline values are available. The interrelationships between the indicators and other related compounds may, however, vary slightly from region to region due to differences in emission source profiles.

Urban air pollution has traditionally been linked to the burning of fossil fuels and to 'classical air pollutants' such as sulphur dioxide (SO_2), soot or black smoke (BS) and lead (Pb). In recent years the indicator for suspended particles in air has changed from BS to particles of less that 10 micrometre (PM_{10}). During the last decade there has also been a significant change in the composition of air pollution. SO_2, BS and Pb have been decreasing in large parts of Europe, while other pollutants such as nitrogen dioxide (NO_2) and ozone (O_3) have been increasing. The most harmful substances in the urban environment may at present be a reactive mixture of secondary air pollutants originating mainly from road traffic and other mobile sources.

Within the PSR framework human activities are the most important pressure factors in urban environments. They are linked to air pollution emission

Table 3.1 Indicators selected for different types of air pollution in Europe

Pollution type	Indicator	AQG (mg/m^3)	Cities with observed exceedance (%)*	Effects
Short-term effects				
Summer smog	O$_2$	150–200 (hour)	84	Decreased lung function, respiratory symptoms
Winter smog	SO$_2$+PM	125+125 (day)	74	Decreased lung function; increased medicine use for susceptible children
Urban traffic	NO$_2$	150 (day)	26	
Long-term effects				
Traffic/industry	Lead	0.5–1.0 (year)	33	Effects on blood formation, kidney damage; neurologic cognitive effects
Combustion	SO$_2$	50 (year)	13	Respiratory symptoms
	PM	50 (year)	0	Chronic respiratory illness

Note: * European cities in which Air Quality Guideline (AQG) values are exceeded.

Source: Sluyter (1995).

sources such as traffic and transportation, energy production (heating and cooling), industrial activities, waste burning, agriculture and other activities.

High concentration levels of local air pollution, especially in large urban areas, cause health disorders such as asthma and other respiratory complaints. They can also cause damage to vegetation, and deterioration of building materials and historic monuments.

In Europe different indicators have been established to characterize different air pollution types, as shown in Table 3.1.

The most commonly selected air quality indicators for urban air pollution are carbon monoxide (CO), nitrogen dioxide (NO_2), sulphur dioxide (SO_2), PM_{10} (or $PM_{2.5}$) and ozone.

3. ACIDIFICATION

Emission of sulphur dioxide and nitrogen compounds leads to deposition of acidifying compounds. The main contributing factors are energy production, energy transformation and consumption, as well as some industrial processes. In the atmosphere the gases and aerosols emitted from these activities are transported hundreds of kilometres away from the source areas. Chemical reactions and deposition (dry and wet) cause acidification problems in lakes, water courses and vegetation in areas where the soil has little capacity to neutralize the acidity so that critical loads are exceeded.

Sulphur has been the main cause of the acidification while, so far, acid nitrogen compounds have made only a moderate contribution to acidification (in the Nordic countries). This is because a large share of the nitrogen is absorbed as nutrient by the vegetation or accumulated as organic nitrogen in the soil. In southern Scandinavia, however, nitrogen deposition has almost reached the upper limit of what the vegetation can absorb, and the acidification status could easily deteriorate.

The pressure indicators used by international organizations and for international agreements and conventions are the emission rates of SO_x and NO_x and their changes since 1980, as well as emission intensity expressed as quantities emitted per unit of GDP and per capita (OECD, 1994).

The deposition of oxidized sulphur (dry and wet) has decreased considerably in recent years (~30 per cent from 1985 to 1992). This has not been the case for nitrogen compounds; for example, in southern Norway the total deposition of acid equivalents has decreased by only 10 per cent. An indicator of acid deposition is the acidity of wet deposition (precipitation) in selected regions. The total annual amount of sulphate and nitrate deposition is estimated as an indicator to evaluate changes in time.

The effect of acid precipitation varies with the properties of the water and land concerned. Critical loads express how much pollution the natural environment can withstand without becoming damaged or changed. The critical load is the highest level that does not cause damage, and is defined on the basis of information about pollution loads (exposure) and adverse effects. The state of acidification of the environment will thus be more directly reflected through the indicator showing by how much critical loads are exceeded in soils and waters. Such maps have been established for the Scandinavian countries and for parts of Europe.

4. WHY IS INTERVENTION NECESSARY?

Ambient air pollution in urban areas of Europe and the subsequent effects on human health has been a topic of increasing interest in recent years. Recent findings have also indicated that health effects and health symptoms can occur at levels of exposure previously considered safe.

Most specific studies examining the health risks from air pollution exposure have focused on respiratory problems. The links between fundamental air pollutants and ultimate health effects are complex and poorly understood. However, it is agreed that, based on the study of air quality indicators, it will be necessary to find optimal solutions (cost-effective measures) to reduce the pressure on human health. This work, based on systematic and quantitative methods, has barely started.

The cost–benefit analysis used for improving the air pollution situation as related to specific air quality indicators usually comprises several steps:

1. Identification and cost analysis of measures needed to arrive at the goal. Typically, such measures will be different emission abatement scenarios.
2. Assessment of air quality and exposure, both with and without additional abatement measures.
3. Defining the scope of benefits by identifying types of benefit categories (such as health effects, damage to ecosystems and material damage), and valuation of these benefit categories.
4. Comparison of effects to target objects (humans, ecosystems, buildings) with and without additional abatement measures.
5. Comparison of the estimated costs and benefits.
6. Sensitivity analysis.

Deterioration of our cultural heritage (buildings and monuments) has also focused attention on the need to reduce air pollutants and improve the general air quality in our cities. Again, expert assessments applying pressure indicators together with cost–benefit or cost-efficiency analyses are needed to obtain optimal abatement strategies as a basis for the political decision-making processes.

The UNECE Convention on Long-Range Transboundary Air Pollution has decided that new agreements on emission reductions in Europe should be based on nature's critical loads rather than on the principle of equal percentage reductions of emissions in all countries. This will also require expert assessment and further studies on indicators and indices. The OECD has suggested that the amount by which critical loads of pH in water and soil are exceeded should be a medium- and long-term indicator for the condition of acidification.

5.   CONCRETE ACTIONS

Some concrete actions for improving the urban environment relate to traffic planning, traffic reduction through taxation, green areas, green belts and various economic and regulatory instruments. Encouraging increased use of public transportation and bicycles, reducing private driving by building physical obstacles, improving combustion technology and gradually introducing electric vehicles have been used as alternative measures. Material research has led to the use of alternative materials and coatings for the protection of buildings and monuments.

The measures available for reducing emissions of those compounds that influence concentrations of given air pollutants are well known. Different abatement strategies for the direct reduction of emissions or for reduction of impact exist. The direct measures taken to comply with legislation are measurable in monetary terms. Such measures must take into account the secondary formation of pollutants in the atmosphere and thus include implementation of emission abatement strategies for more compounds than those under primary consideration.

International cooperation is important in order to reduce the adverse effects of SO_2 and NO_x emissions on the natural environment. A series of protocols on measures to reduce the emissions of SO_2, NO_2 and VOCs have been negotiated, including those in Oslo in 1994. Latest protocols for defining emission ceilings for sulphur, NO_x, VOCs and ammonia were negotiated in Gothenburg in 1999.

REFERENCES

Larssen, S., K.E. Grønskei, M.C. Hanegraaf, H.M.A. Jansen, F.H. Oosterhuis and A.A. Olsthoorn (1995), *URBAIR. Guidebook for urban air quality management strategy in Asia*. Kjeller (NILU OR 64/95).

OECD (1994), *Environmental indicators* (Paris: OECD).

Sluyter, R.J.C.F. (ed.) (1995), *Air quality in major European cities. Part I: Scientific background document to Europe's environment*. Bilthoven/Kjeller, RIVM/NILU (RIVM report no. 722401004).

4. Air pollution and acidification

D. Guinnup and C. Sansevero

1.   INTRODUCTION – HEALTH AND ENVIRONMENTAL EFFECTS OF EIGHT POLLUTANTS

Air pollution can induce a variety of adverse health effects in human beings and damage the natural environment by attacking plants, animals, vegetation and entire ecosystems. There are eight pollutants most commonly found in the ambient air: carbon monoxide, lead, ozone, nitrogen oxides, sulphur dioxide, volatile organic compounds, and fine and coarse particulate matter. Further, some of these pollutants are significant contributors to acidic deposition.

Acidic deposition, or acid rain as it is commonly known, occurs when emissions of sulphur dioxide and nitrogen oxides react in the atmosphere with water, oxygen and oxidants to form various acidic compounds. The formation of these compounds is enhanced by the presence of ozone in the lower atmosphere. These compounds then fall to the earth in either dry form (such as gas or particles) or wet form (such as rain, snow, and fog). Acidic pollutants can damage lakes and streams to the point where they cannot support fish life. Forests can also be affected by acidic compounds, which can directly impact trees at high elevations and can indirectly influence forest soil chemistry. In addition, before falling to the earth, acidic compounds contribute to visibility degradation and can pose certain adverse human health effects when inhaled.

The following paragraphs describe the specific health and environmental effects associated with exposure to the eight pervasive pollutants listed above.

Carbon Monoxide

Exposure to carbon monoxide can reduce the amount of oxygen delivered to the body's organs and tissues. Significant exposure can result in visual impairment, reduced manual dexterity and poor learning ability. Automobiles are a large source of emissions of carbon monoxide.

Lead

Lead can accumulate in the blood, bones and soft tissue. Because it is not readily excreted, lead can also affect the kidneys, liver, nervous system and other organs. Excessive exposure to lead may cause neurological impairments and, at low doses, foetuses and children often suffer from central nervous system damage. Historically, automobiles have been the largest source of emissions of lead. However, the widespread use of unleaded gasoline has dramatically reduced the contribution from automobiles worldwide. Industrial processes (for example metals processing) are another significant source of lead emissions.

Ozone

Ozone is not emitted directly into the atmosphere. It is formed when emissions of nitrogen oxides and volatile organic compounds react with sunlight. While beneficial in the upper atmosphere, ozone in the lower atmosphere can cause a variety of health problems as it damages lung tissue, reduces lung function and sensitizes the lungs to other irritants. Ground-level ozone also interferes with the ability of plants to produce and store food, making them more susceptible to disease, insect attack and other pollutants.

Nitrogen Dioxide

Nitrogen dioxide belongs to a family of poisonous, highly reactive gases called nitrogen oxides. Exposure to nitrogen dioxide can irritate the lungs and lower the body's resistance to respiratory infections such as influenza. The regional transport and deposition of nitrogen oxides can result in adverse environmental effects such as acidic deposition and eutrophication. The latter occurs when a body of water suffers an increase in nutrients that reduce the amount of oxygen in the water, producing an environment that is destructive to fish and other animal life. Nitrogen oxides also contribute significantly to the formation of ground-level ozone. Automobiles and fuel combustion (for example from electric utilities) are a significant source of emissions of nitrogen dioxide.

Sulphur Dioxide

Exposure to sulphur dioxide can adversely affect breathing and limit the ability of the lungs to fight infection. Sulphur dioxide can also aggravate existing cardiovascular disease and respiratory illness. Asthmatics and individuals with existing cardiovascular disease are most sensitive to sulphur dioxide. Additionally, along with nitrogen oxides, sulphur dioxide is a primary precursor to acidification. Fuel combustion (for example from electric utilities) is a significant source of emissions of sulphur dioxide.

Volatile Organic Compounds

Volatile organic compounds include a number of toxic pollutants such as benzene, acetaldehyde and formaldehyde that are associated with a variety of adverse health effects including cancer. Volatile organic compounds also play a significant role in the chemical reactions that produce ozone. Automobiles and industrial processes (for example metals processing) are significant sources of emissions of volatile organic compounds.

Particulate Matter

Particulate matter is the general term for solid or liquid particles found in the atmosphere. Emissions of coarse particles (larger than 2.5 microns in diameter) come from a variety of sources including windblown dust and grinding operations. Emissions of fine particles (less than 2.5 microns in diameter) often come from fuel combustion, power plants and diesel buses and trucks. Exposure to particulate matter (especially fine particles) can result in acute respiratory aggravation, chronic bronchitis, aggravated asthma, decreased lung function and, in some cases, premature death.

This list of the most pervasive air pollutants compares reasonably closely with the results of the second expert questionnaire for the Air Pollution policy field of Eurostat's Pressure Indicators Project.[1] Emissions of nitrogen oxides, sulphur dioxide, volatile organic compounds and particulate matter all feature in the top five of the core indicator list. Carbon monoxide emission is ranked outside the top ten. Lead and ozone have been considered in the related policy fields of Dispersion of Toxic Substances and Urban Environmental Problems although they have not been highly rated. Differences between the lists can be partly accounted for by the inclusion of source-based indicators, particularly related to energy consumption, in the PIP questionnaire. The list in this chapter concentrates on emissions of pollutants.

2.   WHY THE CONCERN ABOUT THESE POLLUTANTS?

As described above, there is a myriad of adverse health effects associated with exposure to these eight pollutants. In some cases the health effects can be as serious as premature death. For example, the US Environmental Protection Agency estimates that in moderately polluted areas, long-term exposure to fine particles may account for between 5 and 12 per cent of total deaths. This amounts to millions of deaths annually throughout the world. Furthermore, there are numerous other irreversible effects imposed on the environment as a result of exposure to these pollutants. Ground-level ozone alone is responsible for 1 to 2 billion dollars worth in reduced crop production in the USA each year.

As population, economic growth and vehicle activity continue to expand worldwide, so will emissions of these eight pollutants. We must work to control these increases. We must make every effort to combat the unfavourable environmental consequences resulting from expanding human activities.

3. HOW TO REDUCE THE PRESSURES IMPOSED ON THE ENVIRONMENT?

The primary sources of emissions of the eight major air pollutants are automobiles, industrial processes and fuel combustion. In order to relieve the pressures that these pollutants impose on the environment, we must make strong efforts to reduce or control emissions emanating from the above sources.

It is relatively straightforward to reduce emissions of primary pollutants (those that are emitted directly into the atmosphere): we must simply determine the major sources of emissions of these primary pollutants and target them for emission reduction efforts. For example, because both nitrogen oxides and sulphur dioxide contribute significantly to acidic deposition, in order to reduce acid rain we must target sources of sulphur dioxide as well as nitrogen oxides. Not only will this reduce acid rain; it will also protect human health against the adverse effects associated with direct exposure to these pollutants. Therefore, in order to reduce emissions of these pollutants, we must target emissions from electric utilities, automobiles and various industrial processes, and subject them to control programmes. Such programmes could include the installation of pollution control devices, the development of improved and more efficient processes to reduce or eliminate emissions, or the introduction of alternative raw materials.

It is more difficult, however, to develop control strategies to reduce emissions of secondary pollutants (those that are formed in the atmosphere as a result of various mixtures of pollutants). In many cases, the mixtures of emissions that ultimately result in the formation of these secondary pollutants are specific to particular geographical locations. Therefore, not only is it necessary to determine the major sources of emissions of the primary pollutants that contribute to the formation of these secondary pollutants; it is also necessary to determine the types of mixtures that occur in particular areas.

For example, ozone is a secondary pollutant that is formed when nitrogen oxides and volatile organic compounds react in the presence of sunlight. In some areas, we will only achieve ozone reductions by targeting emissions of nitrogen oxides, whereas in other areas we will achieve reductions by targeting emissions of volatile organic compounds. Even more challenging, some types of particulate matter are also formed secondarily in the atmosphere. Because particulate matter can consist of organics, metals, minerals or other substances, it is more difficult to identify the specific contributing components (as they tend to vary from location to location and season to season) and develop strategies to control the emissions of these components.

Currently, we can (and do) achieve significant emission reductions through the use of air pollution control devices. If these devices are installed and properly operated, they can significantly reduce emissions. For example, a control device known as a scrubber installed at a coal-fired power plant can reduce emissions of sulphur dioxide by more than 95 per cent; another, known as a selective catalytic reduction control device, can reduce emissions of nitrogen oxides by more than 80 per cent. Further, we can (and do) set concentration-based air quality standards that encourage facilities to find innovative ways to reduce emissions. If the air quality in a particular area cannot meet the level of the standard, the area will have to look to different types of pollution control to reduce the emissions that produce poor air quality. For instance, areas can implement other pollution reduction strategies such as car-pooling, alternative work hours and mass transit. Additionally, we can (and do) practise pollution prevention techniques (for example recycling industrial solvents, implementing extended combustion, using alternative chemicals and so on) that can reduce waste, conserve resources and in some cases actually reduce costs.

4.   BENEFITS ASSOCIATED WITH REDUCING THE PRESSURES ON THE ENVIRONMENT

As time progresses, we will continue to develop innovative technologies to reduce the pressures imposed on the environment by these pollutants. Nevertheless, it is important to understand that the same factors that ensure new pollution control technologies will also yield continued worldwide growth and development. Hence it is likely that this growth will impose further pressures on the environment and its resources. Some may argue that because of human ability to innovate, we do not need to be concerned with the available amount of a particular natural substance. For example, if the world exhausts its supply of oil, we will simply develop alternatives to oil. While this may be true, the same conditions that foster innovation also tend to increase the demand for resources. Therefore, even though technological advances may reduce environmental pressures, they also may result in new environmental hazards.

If we rely on innovation alone to solve our environmental problems, eventually we may exhaust our natural resources and find ourselves living in an over-polluted world. It will be very difficult (and perhaps impossible, given limited environmental and economic resources) to undo the effects that increased and uncontrolled pollution can have on the environment. As we begin the twenty-first century, we will be forced to become less reliant on current forms of energy, automobiles, manufacturing and other activities. In some cases, we will be forced to eliminate the sources of emissions of certain pollutants completely. In order successfully to meet this type of challenge, we need not only to investigate new alternatives, but also to change our behaviour. For example, because automobiles are a primary source of many types of air pollution, at some point in the future the automobile industry will have to go through some kind of major transformation. This transformation may be to electric vehicles, to solar-powered vehicles, or perhaps to other alternatives. Whatever transformations we may undergo, we will have to think differently about our needs as individuals and as a society, about the resources available to satisfy those needs, and about the environmental consequences associated with our actions. It is not enough to develop ways to control pollution; we also need to develop ways to prevent pollution. This will involve using economic resources to conserve natural resources.

If we begin to make changes now, we will be able to gradually (and economically) protect the environment while we continue to grow. If we fail to reduce the pressures imposed by these pollutants on the environment, we will ultimately be forced to live in an abused and unpleasant environment that can no longer provide an acceptable quality of life. If we are successful in identifying and controlling the sources of emissions of these eight pollutants, we will provide immeasurable benefits to society and the environment. People will live healthier lives and be less likely to have respiratory problems, contract cancer or die prematurely. Ecosystems will flourish more naturally, and vegetation will become less susceptible to disease, insect attack and other pollutants. Natural landmarks (for example rock formations and caverns) and human-made landmarks (for example monuments and statues) will be better preserved for generations to come. If we desire a healthy and clean environment, we must pursue actions that will reduce the expanding environmental pressures generated by continued worldwide growth.

NOTE

1. First expert survey: December 1995; second survey: October 1996. See Chapter 1 and Editors' introduction.

REFERENCES

US Environmental Protection Agency, Office of Air Quality Planning and Standards (1995), *National Air Quality and Emissions Trends Report, 1994*, EPA-454/R-95-014, Research Triangle Park, NC, October.

US Environmental Protection Agency, Office of Air Quality Planning and Standards (1995), *National Air Pollutant Emission Trends, 1900–1994*, EPA-454/R-95-011, Research Triangle Park, NC, October.

PART II

Climate Change

5. Introduction

J.F. Feenstra and P.E.M. Lammers

1. THE CLIMATE CHANGE POLICY FIELD

Naturally occurring gases (water vapour, carbon dioxide, methane, nitrous oxide and ozone) in the earth's atmosphere create a (natural) greenhouse effect on the earth, resulting in the earth's climate as we know it. Increase of the concentrations of these gases results in an enhanced greenhouse effect and thereby changes the earth's climate.

Since the beginning of the Industrial Revolution the atmospheric concentrations of most of the greenhouse gases have increased dramatically and are expected to increase even more in the decades to come. The largest emission sources of carbon dioxide, methane and nitrous oxide are the combustion of fossil fuels, deforestation and agriculture. Expected impacts of (future) climate change include those on agriculture and food security, coastal zones due to sea-level rise, ecosystems and human health, and water resources and human infrastructure. Policy-makers have started to acknowledge the necessity of adaptation to climate change impacts.

The chapters in this part of the volume provide an overview of the main issues related to climate change. Each has been written by a recognized expert (see Introduction to the contributors).

2. RELATIONS TO OTHER POLICY FIELDS

The Climate Change policy field is closely related to the policy fields of Ozone Layer Depletion, Air Pollution, Urban Environmental Problems and Loss of Biodiversity. The chapter by Grassl specifically highlights these relationships.

The relation with the Ozone Layer Depletion policy field is the most direct of those mentioned above. Ozone is a naturally occurring greenhouse gas, and therefore a decrease of the stratospheric ozone concentration will result in radiative cooling. However, the ozone-depleting substances (for example

CFCs and halons) are effective greenhouse gases which enhance the greenhouse effect.

The relationship with the Air Pollution policy field is important due to the cooling effect of aerosols. Emissions of sulphur dioxide and soot (causing acid rain) result in atmospheric aerosols that reduce the incoming solar radiation and thereby have a cooling effect. In contrast to the *global* warming effect of greenhouse gases, the cooling effect of aerosols is *regional*. Reduction of emissions of these aerosols will result in a decrease in this regional cooling effect and make the warming of the atmosphere more apparent in highly industrialized regions. This means that an improvement in the environmental situation with regard to acid rain and regional air pollution results in a worse situation as far as global warming/climate change is concerned. In practice, it is hard to identify how climate has been changed at regional level by the opposing effects of aerosols and greenhouse gases.

Another link between the Climate Change and Air Pollution policy fields is related to the measures to reduce emissions of air pollutants. Measures taken to reduce carbon dioxide emissions will influence the emissions of other air pollutants as well. Therefore emission reduction measures should be focused on these win–win situations.

Since air pollution is a major component of urban problems, the above relation with the Air Pollution policy field means that there is also a relation between the Climate Change and Urban Environmental Problems policy fields.

A relation between the policy fields Climate Change and Loss of Biodiversity exists in the areas of deforestation, reforestation and afforestation. Deforestation is one of the main contributors to climate change. By decreasing the forest areas, the existing sinks of carbon dioxide are reduced. The burning of wood gives rise to emissions of greenhouse gases such as carbon dioxide, methane, nitrous oxide, nitrogen oxides. Reforestation and afforestation increase the sinks of carbon dioxide and have thereby a positive effect on climate change. Since tropical forests are the largest source of biodiversity, any changes in the area of tropical forests will have effects on biodiversity. Therefore, measures to protect biodiversity are likely to have a positive effect in the Climate Change policy field as well.

3.   INTERNATIONAL FRAMEWORK

At the Earth Summit (Second UN Conference on Environment and Development) in Rio de Janeiro in June 1992, the United Nations Framework Convention on Climate Change (UNFCCC) was agreed and signed by 154 countries. The convention came into force on 21 May 1994 after 50 countries ratified the convention. The main objective of the UNFCCC is given in Article 2:

> The ultimate objective of this convention ... is to achieve... stabilisation of greenhouse gas concentrations in the atmosphere at a level that would prevent dangerous anthropogenic interference with the climate system. Such a level should be achieved within a time frame sufficient to allow ecosystems to adapt naturally to climate change, to ensure that food production is not threatened and to enable economic development to proceed in a sustainable manner.

As Houghton states in his chapter, 'the best way to meet the demands of this objective will require a great deal of debate and discussion'. Grassl illustrates this point by mentioning the inability of the first Conference of Parties (CoP 1) to the Convention to agree on even a weak CO_2 protocol and the subsequent postponement of such a protocol to the CoP in Kyoto in December 1997. Further intense debate surrounded the Kyoto Conference and the agreement reached was viewed by many as containing many loopholes.

Research Activities

Climate change research is carried out in numerous national and international programmes, including the Environment and Climate Programme of the European Union. Results of climate change studies are combined and assessed by the Intergovernmental Panel on Climate Change (IPCC). This panel, in which 1500 scientists from all over the world participate, was initiated by UNEP and WHO in 1988. The first scientific assessment of this intergovernmental panel was published in 1992 and can be seen as the precursor to the UNFCCC.

The Second Assessment report, published in 1996, was clearer on the impacts of human activities on climate. This report stated in the summary for policy-makers that: 'the balance of evidence suggests a discernible human influence on global climate'. This statement makes clear that human activities are already influencing global climate. Political measures are needed to prevent further influences, which could have irreversible effects.

4. OVERVIEW OF PRESSURE INDICATORS FOR CLIMATE CHANGE

Figure 5.1 provides an overview of the key indicators for the Climate Change policy field. The selection of the indicators and corresponding scores are the results of the second-round Eurostat Pressure Indicators Project expert questionnaire. The figure provides the ranking of each indicator for policy relevance,

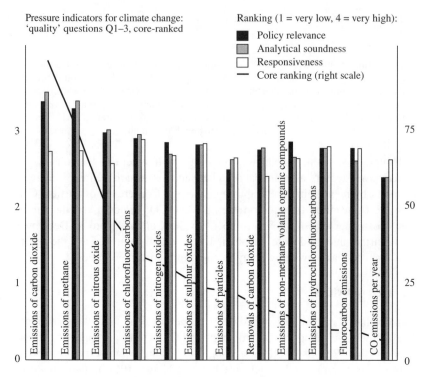

Figure 5.1   Results of second-round questionnaire for the Climate Change
policy field

analytical soundness and responsiveness expressed as a score from 1 (very low) to 4 (very high). Also, the core ranking of the indicators is presented, expressed as a percentage of experts who included the indicator in their top five list of essential indicators.

The indicators for the direct greenhouse gases CO_2, CH_4 and N_2O score highest for policy relevance, analytical soundness and core ranking. However, for responsiveness they score lower (although differences are not large). This indicates that emissions of these direct greenhouse gases are believed to be more difficult to reduce than emissions of halocarbons or sulphur dioxides.

The indicator for CFC emissions scores fourth, except for responsiveness where it scores first. This can easily be explained by the fact that the Montreal Protocol calls for a complete phasing out of CFC emissions. However, since this target has led to a drastic reduction of CFC emissions, it can be argued that CFCs should not score high in the set of top five core indicators.

The detailed discussion on this issue in Part V on Ozone Layer Depletion is also applicable to the Climate Change policy field.

In section 6 of his chapter Grassl discusses the results of the second questionnaire. In his opinion, the indicators for N_2O and CFC emissions are highly overrated and should not play a role in an integrated climate change index. In the case of N_2O, there is a lack of knowledge about the sources of emissions and, moreover, only limited possibilities exist to reduce emissions. In the case of CFCs, Grassl agrees with the point made above that since the most important CFCs are already phased out in the EU, they are not relevant to the list of climate change indicators.

Although Grassl is correct on the limited possibilities of reducing N_2O emissions, this argument alone is not a sufficient reason to remove the N_2O emission indicator from the set of climate change indicators. In international research and policy-making, N_2O (together with CO_2 and CH_4) is considered to be one of the major greenhouse gases. This can be illustrated by the fact that, at the minimum, emissions of CO_2, CH_4 and N_2O should be included in the national emission inventory as part of a National Communication.[1] As shown in the scores on responsiveness, the European experts agree with Grassl that N_2O emissions will be hard to reduce. Nevertheless, they rank the indicator in third place as a core indicator.

According to Grassl, the indicator for NO_x emissions should score higher than in the results of the second questionnaire. His reasoning is that NO_x contributes to many environmental problems and should therefore be considered more important. However, it should be noted that NO_x is ranked highest as a core indicator in the Air Pollution policy field.

Houghton states that climate change indicators should relate to a wider context (sustainable development, other environmental problems). Indeed, some environmental pressures may play a role in several policy fields and have a large impact on total environmental quality, even though they may not be considered as a priority in any of the policy fields. If the effects in all policy fields were combined, the reduction of such a pressure might have a greater overall impact than the reduction of a priority pressure. This indicates an inherent disadvantage of dividing environmental pressures into different policy fields. The suggestion of valuing the importance of the indicator to other policy fields within the ranking of one particular policy field will lead to overvaluing the importance of the pressure indicator to that field.

The development of an additional set of core indicators to mirror the integrated environmental quality may be a solution to the points made by Grassl and Houghton. Based on the importance of a specific pressure indicator in each policy field where it is considered, an overall importance of this indicator for the environment as a whole could be estimated. This extra set of core indicators for the total environment could supplement the specific indicators for each policy field.

An issue not addressed in the chapters that follow is the policy relevance of the indicators for SO_x and aerosol particles. Due to the regional cooling effect of these emissions, reductions will lead to a worsening of the climate change index. However, since emissions of SO_x and aerosol particles have other negative environmental effects (acidification, human health), emission reductions are justified for reasons other than climate change. Therefore, the policy relevance of inclusion of these indicators into a climate change index is highly disputable.

5. DISCUSSION AND CONCLUSIONS

In general, the indicators for climate change are well defined and consensus between scientists is relatively high. However, there is discussion on the relative importance of indicators and the best set of core indicators. This relates to four particular indicators. First, N_2O, which is an important greenhouse gas, but whose emissions are hard to reduce; second, NO_x, which has a relatively limited importance for climate change, but may be a very important indicator for total environmental quality; third, CFCs, for which emissions have been reduced drastically due to the implementation of phasing-out actions under the Montreal Protocol, and finally, SO_x and aerosol particles, for which the policy relevance of inclusion in a climate change index is highly disputable.

An issue not addressed in the chapters that follow is how to aggregate the indicators into one climate change index. Partly, the concept of global warming potentials, a measure of the relative radiative effects of greenhouse gases, can be used for this aggregation. However, global warming potentials have not been quantified for all greenhouse gases. The chapter on climate change in the TEPI publication on *Indicator Definition*[2] provides a more detailed discussion on the various aspects of aggregation.

NOTES

1. A National Communication is a report on greenhouse gas emissions and mitigation policies and options that every party has to submit to the secretariat of the UNFCCC.
2. See Foreword.

6. Indexing climate change

J. Sweeney

1. THE PROBLEM OF CLIMATE CHANGE

Changeability is an inherent component of climate on all time scales of variation. The importance of this changeability for people has largely been experienced through its influence on food production. For almost all of human history the harvesting of food has been the single most crucial determinant of well-being and socio-cultural development. It is even possible to speculate that the ecological dominance of the human species owes a great deal to its capability to survive and adapt to the swings of the climatic pendulum. The vital harvest surplus on which so much depended has always been largely determined by the vagaries of temperature and rainfall. Today, despite technological advancement – perhaps even more so because of it – humans remain highly susceptible to the jolts of a climatic system the functioning of which is only imperfectly understood. The lessons of history, however, demonstrate that climatic variability is ignored only at the cost of compromising the well-being of ourselves or our children, an unsustainable situation that runs counter to any principles of intergenerational equity.

Public sensitization to the problems of climate change has grown with the realization that, while for most of recorded history humans have been the prisoners of climate, today the converse may be true. The future course of global climate seems increasingly likely to be determined by the aggregation of individual assaults on the composition of the atmosphere by people and nation states acting in their own self-interest and armed with the technologies of the Industrial Revolution. In the most recent report of the Intergovernmental Panel on Climate Change, the considered opinion of some 2500 scientists was that 'the balance of evidence suggests a discernible human influence on global climate' (Houghton et al., 1996). Such impacts on the atmosphere necessitate a radical change in approach in terms of managing the atmospheric environment. The norms of the 30-year climate average, for so long used to build bridges, dams, sea walls and drainage systems, and to help manage the technological fabrications of modern life, are now more unsound than ever as awareness of the complex mix of natural and human-induced climatic variability has increased. The long-term planning necessary for modern agriculture, urban settlement, coastal management, industry and a host of other endeavours has become fraught with difficulty as the future course of climate threatens a change more rapid over this century than over the ten millennia since the end of the last glaciation. This rate of change, increasing global temperature averages by 0.25°C per decade, and altering a multitude of other climatic variables in a similar fashion, may be rapid enough severely to stress natural as well as human ecosystems.

Environmental hazards, such as those associated with climate change, always most affect the margins of society. The climatic extinction of early European settlers on Greenland is a good example of this vulnerability. As the Medieval Warm Period, in which their initial colonies had been established, waned and the increased sea ice and storminess of the northern ocean beckoned the approach of the Little Ice Age, their inability to adapt and respond to climate change ultimately sealed their fate. On the margins of viable precipitation in semi-arid zones such as the Sahel, a similar hardship has been evident in more recent times. Those most vulnerable to climate change are frequently those with fewest resources and those who have been least instrumental in causing climate change. It is incumbent therefore on the scientific community to provide the best possible advice to decision-makers to enable mitigation of possible adverse effects, or indeed to capitalize on some of the new advantages climate change will confer on certain areas. In keeping with the principles of sustainable development espoused by the World Commission on Environment and Development (1987), such a 'no regrets' or 'precautionary principle' approach will ensure that the positive as well as the negative opportunities of climate change are grasped.

Climate change leads to a complex mixture of associated environmental impacts, not capable of being addressed piecemeal. The precise magnitudes of these impacts are not yet fully understood, since it is not yet possible to project confidently the regional scale of climate change from computer-based global circulation models. In addition, since climate-related systems tend to be non-linear, certain impacts may not materialize until a critical threshold is crossed, by which time recovery may be extremely difficult. However, as models tend to converge increasingly in their predictions, the assessment of impacts may be more confidently carried out. It is clear that there will be 'winners and losers' both between and within countries should climate change as suggested by most models occur. For individual countries, especially in the developing world, where dependence on the annual harvest is still of crucial economic importance, the stakes are high.

In the first instance, it may be suggested that extra warmth and extra CO_2 for photosynthesis will benefit agriculture in many areas. Yield increases of over 20 per cent can be expected in many grassland areas of north-western

Europe for example, while a poleward expansion in agricultural potential will occur. New crops will become viable beyond their present latitudinal and altitudinal limits, and additional growth periods will mean greater productivity, especially for wheat and barley in the higher mid-latitude regions. A poleward advance of 150–200 km per one degree centigrade rise in mean annual temperature is suggested by the models, with corresponding altitudinal changes of 150–200 metres. However, some new regions, such as northern Scandinavia, may be unsuitable for accepting new agriculture by virtue of their soil endowments. Upland and high-latitude regions with legacies of intensive glacial erosion are not going to be able to achieve the yield potential which their changed climate might suggest. Elsewhere, especially in the interiors of the continents, decreased soil moisture levels will similarly limit projected yield increases. Overall, reductions in the principal 'breadbaskets' of the mid-latitudes may outweigh increases elsewhere. In the developing countries of the lower latitudes, changes in the frequency and severity of such hazards as floods, droughts, storms, heatwaves, agricultural pests and diseases may make it difficult for food production to keep pace with population growth.

Similar geographical changes in productivity in ocean fisheries may occur, with cold-water species retreating polewards to be replaced by species from warmer waters, often less palatable to the consumer. Inland, salmonids may be less productive in warmer, less oxygenated, watercourses. Projected drier summers in many developed temperate regions will also create problems for the maintenance of water quality as dilution water for effluent is reduced. However, future rainfall changes are least confidently projected at present by global circulation models, mainly because of the difficulties of incorporating feedback effects due to cloud and ice-cover changes. Resolving such difficulties as they relate to precipitation holds the key to better assessment of a number of potential impacts of climate change. Certainly, new challenges will be posed for the husbanding of freshwater resources, in particular in coping with seasonal changes in water availability for hydroelectric power, irrigation, and domestic and industrial, as well as agricultural, uses.

Sea-level rise has for long been the touchstone of concern regarding climate change. As projected increases have diminished over recent years, now down to 0.5 m by the end of the twenty-first century, and as confidence in such estimates has grown, so more sober assessments of impacts have been made. Due to the slower time scale on which ocean systems respond to atmospheric changes, this sea-level change may be considered inevitable, and the areas under threat may be quite confidently delimited.

First, there is the probability of a gradual inundation of low-lying lands: deltas, marshes and coastal wetlands, estuaries and reclaimed lands in the coastal zone. In some cases these are among the most densely populated zones in the world, and their problems may be exacerbated by local land subsidence.

Second, there is the more general problem of storm frequency and storm track changes which may accentuate wave attack on exposed coastal areas. Sea defences built in former times may need considerable strengthening to cope with higher and more frequent storm surges. Greater expanses of warmer water may also extend the ranges of tropical disturbances, posing a threat to areas further polewards of their present influence, while greater latent heat release may also increase the vigour and damage potential of mid-latitude depressions. Even under conditions of a slight sea-level rise, dramatic changes in the statistical recurrence intervals of marine incursions and coastal erosion may occur. Destabilization of dune and coastal barriers, and mobilization of coastal sediments will pose problems for the management of coastal zones.

Third, as sea level rises, coastal groundwater tables will rise, making for drainage difficulties and also increasing the risk of aquifer salinization. Public fear of coastal inundation cannot often be assuaged rationally, and 'hard' engineering schemes are frequently demanded to protect coasts. These will often not be practical outside of heavily urbanized areas. Planned retreat and precautionary planning in relation to infrastructure and settlement will be the only options available in many rural locations.

A final set of impacts relates to transformations of treasured landscapes and wildlife habitats. These are not easily quantifiable or amenable to traditional cost–benefit analysis. Peatlands, for example, can be considered as 'cultural' resources and the few raised bogs remaining intact in Europe are particularly vulnerable to drying out in 'greenhouse' summers. Sand dunes, fens, salt marshes and machair can likewise be considered environments under threat. All these ecosystems have often unique flora and faunal assemblages which society in general is loath to see disappear and which current EU policies are designed to protect.

2. THE NEED FOR CENTRAL POLITICAL INTERVENTION

The atmosphere is the last of the 'free' resources. Throughout history, ownership and utilization rights for natural resources, such as land, water, forests, minerals and so on have gradually become institutionalized and regulated as societies have recognized that freedom of access to 'common' resources leads to over-utilization and ruin. The assimilative capacity of the atmosphere for greenhouse gas emissions appears to have been exceeded, with reductions in anthropogenic emissions of over 60 per cent for carbon dioxide and 15–20 per cent for methane required to stabilize atmospheric concentrations at present-day levels. This poses global as well as local problems since the consequences of failing to reduce such emissions may ultimately produce warmer climates beyond human experience, and accelerate and accentuate the impacts discussed above.

One appropriate analogy is that of a common area of pasture, open to all the herders of a particular village, where the positive marginal return to each individual of increasing his/her stocking level beyond its carrying capacity is achieved at the negative cost of impairment of the resource for the entire community. It will always be in the individual's and even in the nation state's interest to use the free dispersive capacity of the atmosphere as a sink for waste. It will always be economically easy to justify unilateral increases in greenhouse gas emissions either because an individual's relative contribution is small, a country is developing rapidly to catch up with its competitors, or a 'special case' applies for some reason.

Accordingly, a consensus at a global level can only be achieved by supranational bodies. Climate change is thus no different from other global environmental issues such as acid rain or ozone depletion in requiring international management. In the case of regional economic groupings, such as the European Union, international management is also necessary to standardize emission control costs between Member States in order to ensure the cost burden is equitably distributed. For an emergent problem, such as climate change, where the evidence is as yet uncertain and the natural variability of the climate system is similar to possible anthropogenic changes observed to date, a judgement must also be made on when to take action and over what time scale the burden of inconvenience should be spread. A judgement must also be made on what is technically and economically feasible, that is, a best practicable means/best available technology approach. Such management decisions require organizations with the capability of placing global priorities above national interests. Central political intervention is thus necessary in the climate change problem at a scale above that of national governments. This thinking underlies the formation of the Intergovernmental Panel on Climate Change in 1988 as a joint creation of the World Meteorological Organization and the United Nations Environment Programme.

It is the judgement of the IPCC that the time has come to set limits on emissions of the major greenhouse gases. The emission rduction commitment of the EU under the Kyoto Protocol is 8 per cent on 1990 levels, to be achieved by 2010. A primary focus on carbon dioxide, methane and nitrous oxide is apparent in seeking to achieve this objective. Annual emissions of these three gases constitute the three leading core pressure indicators identified in the EU Pressure Indicators Project. There is scientific consensus on the belief that changes in annual emissions of these three gases will provide the best criteria against which progress in slowing human-induced climate change in the twenty-first century can be monitored. A fourth greenhouse gas family, chlorofluorocarbons, is now considered less influential as an indicator of global warming, and 'Annual CFC emissions' rank fourth in the core pressure indicators list. This is a reflection of the reductions in emissions already under way as a result of the Montreal Protocol to address the problem of stratospheric ozone depletion.

It is important to note, however, that the UN Framework Convention on Climate Change ultimately seeks to achieve stabilization of greenhouse gas *concentrations*, a much more difficult objective to realize, entailing reductions in greenhouse gas emissions in excess of 50 per cent. It is appropriate that the lead, both for short- and medium-term actions, should be taken by industrialized countries, since the bulk of emissions has emanated from such areas, and their scope for reductions without hardship is greater. Developing countries should also, within the limits of their economic circumstances, take steps to decouple energy growth from economic growth where possible. Only by a dual-track approach can political intervention forge the partnership of all nations that is necessary to provide an effective attack on the problem.

3. ACTION TO SLOW AND STABILIZE GREENHOUSE-GAS-LED CLIMATE CHANGE

There is no prospect at present of shifting the direction or magnitude of natural trends in climate. It is unclear what direction this natural trend is currently taking, either to reinforce or mitigate human forcing of climate change. Equally, because of the long atmospheric lifetime of some greenhouse gas emissions, such as carbon dioxide (100–200 years), a commitment to increasing concentrations presently exists. This means that, even if all anthropogenic emissions had been halted in 1990, about 50 per cent of the increase in atmospheric concentrations due to human activities would still be evident by 2100. These considerations, augmented by political difficulties especially between the developed and developing countries, such as those which have surfaced at recent Conferences of the Parties to the UN Framework Convention on Climate Change, suggest that a 'business-as-usual' scenario must be considered for greenhouse gas emissions for the immediate future at least.

Short-term actions to stabilize emissions should focus first on methane emissions, which have a relatively short lifetime in the atmosphere (11 years). Improvements in methane concentrations would thus be noticeable almost immediately. This explains the strong emphasis given to methane emissions per year as a core pressure indicator. A modest reduction of only 10 per cent in emissions would stabilize methane concentrations and this is readily achievable in the short term. First, action to reduce biomass burning by discouraging deforestation would considerably curtail the 40 million tonnes emitted to the atmosphere from this source each year. It would, in addition, have a beneficial effect in increasing CO_2 removal processes. Second, repair and better ongoing maintenance of natural gas pipelines should be undertaken throughout Europe and in countries such as Russia to eliminate leakages as far as possible. Although considerable improvements appear to have occurred in tackling this problem in recent years, there is still scope for improving the performance of such installations, which may contribute similar amounts of methane as biomass burning on an annual basis. Design standards for new landfill sites should also be introduced as a matter of urgency so as to enable collection or flaring of the gas. This could reduce emissions from this source by up to 90 per cent. Increased recycling would of course further reduce gas production as well as saving on fossil fuel energy expenditure. Finally, new research indicates that methane emissions from rice paddies can be greatly reduced by regulating the irrigation water more carefully. Such low-cost, low-technology solutions should be extensively implemented without delay. Ultimately, reductions in methane emissions could amount to 5 per cent of total greenhouse gas emissions.

Stabilizing carbon dioxide concentrations before the end of the twenty-first century is probably unrealistic, and therefore no stabilization of human-induced climate change can be expected. Only draconian economic measures could achieve carbon dioxide stabilization at today's concentrations and short-term measures to slow the rate of growth are, therefore, all that is practical. Foremost among these must be aggressive energy conservation measures. These should focus on improved insulation, lighting and electrical appliance efficiency standards in housing, industry and commerce. New homes and offices could be at least twice as energy-efficient as at present, while in industry the present-day capability for reducing energy consumption is in the order of 15–40 per cent. Short-term measures should also focus on developing and transferring technology relating to energy-saving devices, and energy-saving power generation technologies, to developing countries. This is particularly true for cooking and heating technologies. Improved private and public transport systems, especially in urban areas, would reduce emissions considerably, as would the immediate incorporation of presently existing vehicle energy efficiency technology. A rapid expansion in renewable energy generation is also possible with present-day technology. The fact that a 40 per cent increase in the energy efficiency of the US economy occurred between 1973 and 1990 confirms that there is scope for development and energy use to be successfully decoupled in the years ahead.

Looking further ahead, continued improvements in energy efficiency must be sought. Structural changes in settlement patterns will be required to lessen the requirement for mobility based on the private car. Compact cities, workplaces accessible by public transport, walking or cycling, and energy technologies based on hydrogen or safe nuclear fusion hold the best prospect for success. These will all, however, entail major changes in infrastructure and lifestyle, and will need implementation on time scales which may exceed the public's patience.

4. COMMUNICATING THE PROBLEM TO THE GENERAL PUBLIC

Global warming is now perceived by the general public as an important issue facing society. This sensitization has occurred on the back of the ozone depletion problem, which stirred the public consciousness on a global environmental problem for the first time. Indeed, blurring of the two problems has become so entrenched that it is difficult to envisage climate change ever being seen by the general public for the separate and more intractable problem that it is. The fact that the seven warmest years in the global instrumental temperature record occurred in the 1990s assisted with this process of sensitization. However, society's collective memory is short and the 'post-Pinatubo' years have seen climate change slip down the political agenda. Galvanizing events, such as the spectacular satellite imagery of ozone depletion, are required to mobilize public sentiment and by its nature climate change cannot provide the catalytic instances when definite links are apparent between climatic aberrations and greenhouse-led climate change.

One way of addressing the communication difficulty is by modelling the environmental problem concerned using indices which simplify the complexity of the interacting processes. Such a procedure provides the general public, and policy-makers, with a tool whereby 'what if' questions may be answered at a rudimentary level. This is particularly important for providing initial information on the relative merits of alternative mitigation strategies. For example, the relative impact of reforestation versus energy savings from insulation might be compared, or the impact of fuel switching from coal to natural gas. Such an approach may also be integrated with other index systems currently becoming established, for example indices relating to sustainable development as part of general health indicators for the global environment.

Communicating with the public via indices is already commonplace in financial and economic matters. Such indices are in some cases the results of a complex calculation, but convey an impressionistic message which can be easily grasped. This is a desirable objective in communicating the interrelated issues of climate change to the public and to decision-makers. However, caution is required when simultaneously employing several indices. The public may get confused when an action causing a positive response in one environmental index causes a negative response in a seemingly related one. For example, a reduction in stratospheric ozone in polar regions may slow global warming. A reduction in an air pollution/acidification index may result in an opposite movement in a global warming index. Such divergences are difficult for the public to rationalize at first and it may be necessary, in the methodology of preparing an index system, to give greater consideration to presentation. Indices are essentially a new approach to bridging the gap between complex scientific interactions and complex socio-political interactions. If consistent, they are transferable between nations and perhaps ultimately between the developed and developing world. They may thus ultimately provide a 'single currency' for negotiating an accommodation between nations to limit human impact on the functioning of the atmosphere and thus assist human transition on to the path to a sustainable world.

5. CONCLUSION

Europeans have historically been both winners and losers as climate has fluctuated in past times. In the coming decades, the direction of climate will be shaped both by natural and, increasingly, by human influences, posing new threats and opportunities for inhabitants of the continent. Indeed, it is probable that, by the end of the twenty-first century, much of Europe will be warmer than at any time during the Quaternary Period. Responding to the challenges posed by this scenario of climate change will require new skills and novel management techniques; indeed, it presently necessitates an urgent marriage of scientific and political approaches. The Pressure Indicators Project represents such an innovation, a first step to ensuring that the adverse consequences do not render Europe, and indeed the world, once more a prisoner of the climate system.

REFERENCES

Houghton, J.T., Meiro Filho, L.G., Callander, B.A., Harris, N., Kattenberg, A. and Maskell, K. (eds) (1996), *Climate Change 1995: The Science of Climate Change*, (Cambridge: Cambridge University Press).
World Commission on Environment and Development (1987), *Our Common Future*, (Oxford: Oxford University Press).

7. Climate change

J. Houghton

1. THE MAIN IMPACTS OF CLIMATE CHANGE

Since the last Ice Age, generations of human beings have organized their activities to take advantage of locally available resources of food, fuel, fibre and forage. Human settlements, their agriculture, water use and commercial activities have adapted to the current climate (that is, temperature and rainfall, including their variability). Any large, rapid change in climate will affect these activities and the resources on which they depend and will require rapid, and probably costly, adaptation to re-establish the match between climatic resources and human needs.

Climate extremes are an important manifestation of the natural variability of climate. During recent decades, different parts of the world have experienced extreme temperatures, record floods, droughts and windstorms. There is no strong evidence that these events are outside the range of the variability of the natural climate that has been experienced during the last few centuries. However, their impact serves to emphasize the vulnerability of human communities to climate variation and extremes. In particular, during the later years of the 1980s and into the 1990s, the insurance industry has experienced unparalleled losses due to extreme weather events, which well illustrate the increased vulnerability.

Significant climate change over the twenty-first century is expected because of the increase in 'greenhouse gases' (especially carbon dioxide and methane) which is occurring as a result of human activities (especially fossil fuel burning and deforestation). This increase is leading to an average warming of the earth's surface, such that, if no controls are introduced for environmental reasons, an increase in global mean temperature of about 2.5°C (range 1.5°C to 4°C) can be expected by the year 2100. This would represent a change of climate more rapid than has been experienced by the earth at any time during the last 10 000 years.

Estimation of the likely future climate change is complicated by the effects of anthropogenic aerosols (microscopic particles in the atmosphere), which originate especially from the sulphur-containing gases emitted from power stations (effluents which also give rise to the acid rain problem). These aerosols reflect sunlight and so tend to cool the earth's surface. However, they are very short-lived (a few days), and are therefore concentrated near industrial regions (for instance, in North America, Europe and industrial regions of Asia). Nevertheless, their effects on the climate, even far from these regions, can be considerable. Because of the acid rain problem, emissions of sulphur-containing gases are being severely controlled, especially in North America and Europe. However, they are growing rapidly in Asia, although controls can also be expected there in due course. Some of the results quoted below would be significantly changed if aerosol concentrations over Asia grew substantially.

The main impacts of the expected climate change are a rise in sea level, and changes in rainfall and temperature extremes.

The expected rise in sea level of about 0.5 m (range from 0.2 m to 1 m) by the year 2100 arises mostly from the expansion of water in the oceans because of the increased temperature and from the melting of glaciers. The contribution from changes in the ice sheet in the Arctic and Antarctic is expected to be small. Adaptation, at a cost, to such a rise will be possible in many coastal regions. However, adaptation will be extremely difficult, if not impossible, in some vulnerable areas such as the delta regions of large rivers in Bangladesh, Egypt and southern China, and the many low-lying islands in the Indian and Pacific oceans. The situation in many of these areas will be exacerbated because the land is sinking at a similar rate to that expected from global warming for other reasons, for instance tectonic movement and the extraction of groundwater. Substantial loss of land will occur in these areas and many millions of people (for instance, 6 million live below the 1 m contour in Bangladesh) are likely to be displaced.

The changes in rainfall are likely to be manifest particularly through increased tendencies to both droughts and floods in some places. For instance, in continental areas at mid-latitudes in the northern hemisphere, such as North America and southern Europe, summers are likely to be warmer, with increased evaporation from the surface and possibly with less average rainfall. Drought conditions can therefore be expected to occur more frequently and sometimes be more prolonged. In southern Asia, more intense monsoons can be expected, with increased tendency to floods (although if large anthropogenic aerosol concentrations were present over Asia, this effect could be reduced). As the demand for water increases in nearly every country, substantial tensions can be expected, especially in regions where the water from major river systems is shared between nations. The Secretary General of the UN has suggested that wars in the future are likely to be about water rather than oil.

Studies of global food supplies in a globally warmed world tend to suggest that the global quantity of available food supply might not be affected by very much. Some regions might be able to grow more while others grow less. However, the regions likely to be most affected with reduced food production are those in developing countries in the sub-tropics, where there are rapidly growing populations. In the areas most seriously affected there could be large numbers of environmental refugees.

Other impacts of the likely climate change are on human health (increased heat stress and more widespread vector-borne diseases such as malaria) and on the health of some ecosystems (for example forests), which will not be able to adapt rapidly enough to match the rate of climate change.

These impacts of anthropogenic climate change will have substantial social and political implications, and also implications for world security. Of special concern are some developing countries which will be substantially disadvantaged and in which a large number of environmental refugees will be created (studies have suggested 150 million by the middle of the twenty-first century).

2. THE NEED FOR A CENTRAL POLICY INTERVENTION AND/OR A SOCIETAL DISCUSSION

The increased greenhouse gases of most importance emitted from any anthropogenic source have a relatively long life in the atmosphere (10 to 100 years or more) and so a have a global effect on the climate. The impacts of any given emission are therefore very widely distributed. Further, the areas of activity involved in any mitigating action are concerned with the energy industry or large-scale forestry, both of which tend to be organized internationally. International agreements for action are therefore essential.

The main problems concerning what action to take arise because of the large degree of uncertainty associated with the projections of the likely magnitude and distribution of anthropogenic climate change, and with the assessment of the impacts of the projected change. More scientific research will remove some of the uncertainty, although, because natural climate variability is large, especially on regional scales, considerable uncertainty will always remain.

The Framework Convention on Climate Change (FCCC) agreed at the Earth Summit at Rio, in its Objective stated in Article 2, puts action regarding climate change in the context of sustainable development. It states:

> The ultimate objective of this Convention ... is to achieve ... stabilisation of greenhouse gas concentrations in the atmosphere at a level that would prevent dangerous anthropogenic interference with the climate system. Such a level should be achieved within a time frame sufficient to allow ecosystems to adapt naturally to climate change, to ensure that food production is not threatened and to enable economic development to proceed in a sustainable manner.

To find the best way to meet the demands of this objective will require a great debate and discussion, based on the best scientific and technical information from all scientific (including social scientific) disciplines.

The European Union has been playing a significant role in the international discussions concerning the FCCC. As the relevant industries (for example those concerned with energy and transport) are strongly connected across Europe, the EU also needs to be involved in some of the detailed technical and industrial developments which will enable the objective of the FCCC to be met.

3. CONCRETE ACTIONS REQUIRED TO REDUCE THE 'PROBLEM PRESSURE'

The actions required to mitigate the effects of global warming are to increase the sinks which remove carbon dioxide from the atmosphere, and to reduce the emissions of both carbon dioxide and methane from anthropogenic sources.

Short-term Actions

It is difficult to argue for drastic action in the short term, because of the uncertainty which exists in the magnitude, the timing and the impacts of global warming. However, the uncertainty is not an argument for no action at all, as has already been agreed by the FCCC in its Article 3. But as that article also states, the measures taken need to be cost-effective. In fact, there is much action which has significant benefits other than those of mitigating global warming and which can be taken at little or no cost. Two areas of important action concern forestry and energy efficiency.

Regarding forestry, tropical deforestation is currently contributing to anthropogenic emissions of carbon dioxide. Because of the current scale of deforestation, it is also contributing to local climate change and to other environmental problems. A large reduction in deforestation is an appropriate short-term action which possesses general benefit both to those countries where deforestation occurs and on a global level.

Afforestation is also an appropriate short-term action which can act as a temporary sink for carbon dioxide and slow down the rate of increase of carbon dioxide in the atmosphere. There is much suitable available land for afforestation.

Regarding energy efficiency, studies show that in developed countries, in all energy sectors, large increases in energy efficiency are possible at little or no cost, or in a significant number of cases with an overall cost saving. This is particularly the case in the building and industrial sectors. The transport sector has rapidly growing energy use, and the opportunities for increased efficiency could help to stem this growth. For instance, technology now exists for acceptable motor vehicles with fuel consumption per km less than 50 per cent of the current average. Technical improvements under development could cut fuel consumption in due course by a further 50 per cent.

In developing countries, energy demand will increase with increased industrialization and improved standards of living. It is important that increases in energy supply are provided in efficient ways that take proper account of environmental concerns.

Long-term Actions

Most of the actions mentioned above under the short term need to continue into the long term.

The most important long-term action for which planning needs to begin now is for reappraisal of energy sources and supply in the light of environmental concerns such as global warming. One clear requirement is for improvements in the efficiency of energy generation from fossil fuel sources. A second requirement, if the reduction in fossil fuel use which is likely to be required is to be achieved without economic disruption or excessive cost, is for the development of appropriate renewable energy sources. Both of these need urgent attention and require not only planning but necessary investment.

4.   EXPECTED BENEFITS OF A PRESSURE INDEX FOR COMMUNICATING THE SUCCESS OR FAILURE OF SUCH ACTIONS TO THE GENERAL PUBLIC AND TO POLICY-MAKERS

The FCCC places the problem of climate change firmly in the context of sustainable development, which means that the cost and impact of action regarding the mitigation of climate change must be balanced against the likely impact of that change. Other balances that must be maintained and which are mentioned in the FCCC are the impact on developing countries against that on developed countries, and the impact locally on any given country (which in some cases could be beneficial) against the impact globally. Yet a further consideration, again brought out in the FCCC, is the action that is appropriate in the face of the scientific uncertainty as to just what the damage due to anthropogenic climate change will be. In this context we have seen the importance of action concerning climate change, which may also address other environmental problems or which is beneficial for other reasons.

Other global problems related to climate change are those of world population growth, world resource use and world poverty.

In addressing climate change, the public and policy-makers need to be presented with the detailed actions which are possible and necessary. They also need to be aware of how these actions fit into the wider context of sustainable development and how they relate to the wider considerations we have mentioned. Indices used for addressing decisions regarding climate change therefore need to be carefully defined and to relate to these wider contexts if they are to be of value.

8. Climate protection as the key to sustainable development

H. Grassl

1. INTRODUCTION

With the intense and still accelerating use of fossil fuel, mankind started an unprecedented rapid development. The average life span of an individual has doubled since 1800 in industrialized countries and is still growing. Our number has quadrupled since 1800, and mankind is increasing by roughly 85 million heads per year, that is, growing exponentially at 1.5 per cent per year. Democratic, market-oriented societies using fossil fuels more efficiently at high throughput have reached unprecedented levels of personal wealth for the majority of citizens, and agriculture in these 'fossil fuel countries' is more productive per hectare than ever before. There are also high levels of carbon dioxide in the atmosphere as a consequence of fossil fuel burning and defor-estation.

Why should we then reduce emissions of greenhouse gases, foremost carbon dioxide, in order to decelerate a potential global warming, possibly disrupting economic development in some industrialized countries and caus-ing increased poverty in developing countries?

This chapter will first, in section 2, describe global environmental change problems caused by the above-mentioned developments, and the close inter-actions between them and climate change, thereby pointing both to the strong links to fossil fuel use and the potential synergies of action. In section 3, the reasons for a central policy intervention with a synergistic view are given. Section 4 contains my priority list for concrete goals before section 5 will argue for a combined assessment of measures by the use of aggregated indices. This last section has to take into account that the parties to the UN Framework Convention on Climate Change (FCCC) are forced to take meas-ures while the implementation of the non-binding Agenda 21 will only be stimulated through the recommendations of the Agenda's Commission for Sustainable Development (UNCSD).

2. CLIMATE CHANGE IN THE CONTEXT OF GLOBAL ENVIRONMENTAL CHANGE

The four major global environmental trends, often called global change, are population growth, degradation and loss of soils, loss of biodiversity, and atmospheric composition change. These trends are all related to or caused by fossil fuel use, and are strongly interacting, mostly by positive feedbacks, that is, enhancing each other. For the last two trends, three UN conventions have been agreed to try to reverse the trends.

The Vienna Convention for the Protection of the Ozone Layer (first signed in 1985) has resulted in the first successful global environmental protection through its Montreal Protocol (signed in 1987, enacted in January 1989 and strongly enhanced in 1990 and 1992). Clearly, it has helped to reduce the anthropogenic greenhouse effect increase and thus is of relevance here.

The respective UN convention on biodiversity, first signed at the Second UN Conference on Environment and Development (UNCED) in Rio de Janeiro in June 1992 was enacted in December 1993. The obvious dependence of biodiversity loss on population growth but also on soil degradation, acid rain, photochemical smog, eutrophication and climate change shows the strong interrelations of environmental problems and is a good argument for a synergistic approach in political measures, but also points to major difficulties in finding near-optimum strategies. Therefore, any political measure concerning environmental protection needs both close cooperation between political decision-makers and scientific bodies, as well as flexibility for changes in measures.

The UN Framework Convention on Climate Change (UNFCCC), first signed in Rio de Janeiro in June 1992 and enacted on 21 March 1994, has attracted a great deal of public attention. Because global climate change will affect all countries, funding of climate research increased strongly in the 1980s and the scientific base is clearer, although many uncertainties remain. This base is assessed by a globally coordinated scientific body, the Intergovernmental Panel on Climate Change (IPCC). The necessary measures seem straightforward with respect to climate parameters, as laid down in paragraph 2 of the convention: stabilization of the concentrations of greenhouse gases in the atmosphere within a time frame which is sufficiently short in order that ecosystems can adapt to climate change, general food supply is not endangered and sustainable economic development remains possible. This goal means, in the long run, even allowing an unprecedented climate change for *homo sapiens* – reduction of greenhouse gas emission rates as compared to present rates. In other words, the UNFCCC fosters, in the long run, the transformation of the industrialized fossil fuel burning societies into solar energy societies and it prolongs the more sophisticated use of fossil fuels in industry, avoiding the mere burning at low efficiency.

The second scientific assessment of the IPCC has recently shown that we do already have an impact on global climate by stating in the Summary for Policy-makers that 'The balance of evidence suggests a discernible human influence on global climate'. This statement became possible because two further pathways of human influence on global climate were better assessed. First, a temperature decrease in the lower stratosphere mainly due to depletion of stratospheric ozone, especially in the mid- and high latitudes, and second, a regional reduction in masking of global warming by the fossil-fuel-related sulphate aerosols over and downwind of industrialized areas. Thus the combination of latitude-dependent stratospheric ozone depletion, tropospheric sulphate aerosol plumes and global increases in greenhouse gases has allowed the detection of the anthropogenic climate change. In this context, earlier environmental protection measures, such as desulphurization of coal- and oil-fired power plant flue gases in Germany and other countries, have accelerated global warming, since no throughput regulations were imposed as well.

Additionally, the Second Assessment of IPCC has pointed to tropospheric ozone increase as contributing the same mean global radiative forcing to climate change as accumulated anthropogenic methane emissions. Hence photochemical smog, although a continental-scale phenomenon, has reached global significance through continental-scale plumes over both industrialized areas of the northern hemisphere and biomass-burning areas in the tropics. Since any deforestation (often driven by population growth) and any intensified use of artificial fertilizers moves carbon stored in soils into the atmosphere as carbon dioxide or methane, climate change is also caused by land use changes. In turn, rapid climate change reduces biodiversity. Thus climate protection by reducing emissions of long-lived greenhouse gas emissions also reduces many other environmental problems such as acid rain, eutrophication of rivers and marginal seas, photochemical smog, intensified UV-B radiation and loss of biodiversity. It is thus a key element in the difficult path to sustainable development which is the consensus goal of UNCED but which lacks a clear definition.

3.   WHY WE NEED A GLOBALLY CONCERTED EFFORT

The global (environmental) trends are caused by all countries. While the changed composition of the atmosphere is mainly due to the industrialized countries, degradation and loss of soils by overgrazing, unsustainable irrigation, harmful agricultural practices and deforestation is, at present, more intense in developing countries, but is by no means absent in industrialized countries. Biodiversity loss, although especially strong in the humid tropics as a consequence of deforestation, is still an issue in industrialized countries and is driven there mainly by monocultures in agriculture and more transport infrastructure. Many countries have had some success in reducing population growth rates, but there are still many that have not made such an effort despite the problems caused by this growth.

There are four main reasons for the necessity for global rather than bilateral or multilateral action as a means of approaching sustainability.

1. UN conventions are binding and misconduct will be known globally, although there is no punishment. A sign of the high pressure for compliance with a convention is the intense discussion needed for even small enforcements of existing commitments. A recent example was the inability to get even a weak CO_2 protocol at the first Conference of the Parties to the FCCC in Berlin and its postponement until the Kyoto Conference in 1997. Although agreement was reached at Kyoto for more binding constraints on emissions, this was surrounded by further fierce debate and the existence of many loopholes in the new agreements.
2. Negotiations for implementation of conventions raise awareness of problems by dissemination of scientific results and by sharing of knowledge about the difficulties encountered in other countries. Without the IPCC, we would have neither the UNFCCC nor the Kyoto Protocol.
3. Long-lived pollutants cross borders and often affect non-polluters more strongly. An example is the chlorine which is depleting ozone over the Antarctic and which was emitted mostly in the form of CFCs (more than 90 per cent) in the northern hemisphere over decades. As a consequence the daily erythemal UV-B dose on a sunny day in summer no longer has a gradient from the equator to the South Pole. South Australians and Argentineans now get sunburnt more rapidly than some decades ago.
4. Equity must be a basis: that is, all calculations of allowed emissions should be per capita. On the way to tolerable emissions per capita, joint implementation of measures is just one first step forward, to be followed by others, such as certificates.

The FCCC points to sources and sinks of several long-lived greenhouse gases, while the new Second Assessment of the IPCC points to sulphate aerosols and tropospheric ozone and their precursors as short-lived climate change agents. This difference in emphasis allows for strongly differing approaches to climate protection procedures, depending on the peculiarities of a region or country. Therefore, we need an aggregated climate change index, taking into account not only sources and sinks of several gases and their climate change potential, but also aerosols and the lifetime of all trace substances, as well as a time frame within which the effects of all agents are integrated. In this context, global warming by long-lived greenhouse gases and regional cooling by sulphate aerosols should not be seen as partly compensating, since effects of a regionally differing radiative forcing might well lead to additional circulation changes, causing strong regional climate change.

4.   TOWARDS A LIST OF CONCRETE ACTIONS

The anthropogenic substances released into the atmosphere, which are directly or indirectly climatically relevant, are numerous. These have been listed in Table 8.1, ranked roughly according to their importance to present radiative forcing of climate, relative to pre-industrial times. Most of these substances are also part of natural cycles and therefore enhanced sinks, if existing at the surface, must be considered in principle since the concentration on emission reduction is not sufficient. This argument is especially valid for carbon dioxide, since this greenhouse gas does not react chemically in the atmosphere and is the leading anthropogenic climate gas. Most of the substances in Table 8.1 are related to the burning of fossil fuels, and therefore several emissions can be reduced by a single measure affecting primarily CO_2.

Table 8.1 points to key measures for climate protection. The highest priority should be the reduction of CO_2 emissions, because of the many positive side effects which would result. There will be a concomitant reduction of other long-lived emissions accompanying fossil fuel use (CH_4, N_2O), leading to a larger reduction of the greenhouse effect increase as compared to the CO_2 emission reduction alone. There will also be equivalent reduction of SO_2 emissions, with stronger effects in countries without strong desulphurization measures, leading to less sulphate aerosols, and thus less acid deposition. Equivalent reduction of NO_X and non-methane hydrocarbon (NMHC) emissions with stronger effects in countries at present without strong denoxification measures will lead to less tropospheric ozone (photosmog), less nitrate in aerosols and thus less acid deposition, and less recycled nitrogen in the form of long-lived nitrous oxide (N_2O) emanating from soils. Equivalent reduction of carbon monoxide emissions with stronger effects in countries with weak measures against CO emission will result in less tropospheric ozone, thus reducing the anthropogenic greenhouse effect growth rate further. Equivalent reduction of soot emissions with stronger effects in countries without strong controls on soot emissions will lead to less absorption of solar radiation in the atmosphere and more heating of the surface. At the same time many health problems caused by air pollution would also be reduced.

Another high priority action is the relatively simple task of stabilizing methane concentration. This could be attained by using methane emanating

Table 8.1   Climatically relevant substances with strong anthropogenic sources

Substance	Causes	Lifetime of an anthropogenic addition	Convention concerned plus measures implemented	Type of radiative forcing		Emission rate reduction needed for stabilization
				Direct	Indirect	
Carbon dioxide (CO_2)	Oil, coal, gas burning	100–200 years	UNFCCC, emissions of 1990 to be reached in 2000 for ANNEX I countries	Global		~60%
Methane (CH_4)	Agriculture	12.5 ± 3 years	UNFCCC, no commitments	Global	Regional by tropospheric ozone and stratospheric water vapour increase	~10%
Chlorofluoro-carbons (CFCs)	Industrial applications, cooling, foams	50–200 years depending on compound	Vienna Convention, phase out by Montreal Protocol	Global	Regional by stratospheric ozone depletion	50–80%
Sulphur dioxide (SO_2)	Coal, oil burning	A few days	UNECE agreement for −30% for European countries. More efficient regulations exist in several EU countries		Regional to continental by sulphate aerosols increase	None
Nitrogen oxide (NO_X)	Oil, coal, gas burning	Days	UNFCCC, no commitments: regional reductions implemented for cars and power plants mainly in OECD countries		Regional to continental by tropospheric ozone increase and nitrate in aerosols	None
Nitrous oxide (N_2O)	Agriculture, fossil fuels	120 years	UNFCCC, no commitments	Global	Regional by stratospheric ozone depletion	~65%
Non-methane hydrocarbons (NMHCs)	Fossil fuels	Hours to several days	UNFCCC, no commitments; regional regulations exist in OECD countries		Regional by tropospheric ozone increase	None
Carbon monoxide (CO)	Cars, industry, power plants	A few months	UNFCCC no commitments; reduction implemented for cars and aeroplanes	Hemispheric (weak greenhouse gas)	Continental by increased tropospheric ozone	None
Ammonia	Agriculture	A few days	Not mentioned in UNFCCC		Regional by increased tropospheric aerosols mass	None
Soot	Diesel engines	A week	Not mentioned in UNFCCC; reductions for cars and jet engines implemented widely		Regional by absorption of solar radiation	None

from coal mines and landfills, which has been demonstrated to be technically feasible and even partly economically viable in some industrialized countries. Agriculture (animal husbandry and rice paddies) could also contribute strongly to lower methane emissions by changing to practices which reduce methane emissions while keeping crop yields at high levels.

An important action for climate protection is the enlarging of CO_2 sinks by reforestation, which also contributes to soil protection, water management and biodiversity conservation. However, these new sinks are active only for some decades, after which the use of the forest for energy supply is necessary to keep the sink active and to replace fossil fuels. Furthermore, agriculture can contribute to climate protection by reducing soil erosion, which leads to at least a partial release of the removed soil carbon into the atmosphere, and by reducing the loss of humus caused by over-fertilization. European programmes exist for all these carbon sink enhancement measures, although they were started due to other environmental concerns.

It is inefficient to reduce the concentration of a distinct climatically relevant trace substance in an exhaust plume without imposing a reduction on the entire exhaust mass. A prominent example of this is the desulphurization of power plants in Germany and other European countries which, although effectively reducing acid deposition, accelerates regional warming. Another example is the large regulated reduction of CO emissions from aircraft exhaust without concomitant reductions (or even with an increase) of NO_x emissions.

The UNFCCC goal of stable greenhouse gas concentrations, to be reached in a time frame sufficiently short to avoid dangerous interference with the climate system, still needs basic research efforts to define, for example, the adaptability of ecosystems to climate change. Therefore, the reduction of greenhouse gas emissions finally needed is still unknown. However, since any global reduction of greenhouse gas emissions is a very big challenge, an immediate start, especially in view of so many 'no-regret' points (see above), is the best way to proceed. The agreements at the 1997 Kyoto Conference provide the basis for tackling the challenge; however, there is much debate about whether the agreement goes far enough.

5. WHAT SHOULD A PRESSURE INDEX ON CLIMATE CHANGE CONTAIN?

The concept of the global warming potential (GWP), that is, the calculation of the equivalent CO_2 increase for other long-lived greenhouse gas increases, is only applicable to CH_4, CFCs and N_2O since they are globally distributed. The integration of regional direct radiative forcing of climate by tropospheric aerosols in cloudless parts of the atmosphere, the indirect effect via changed radiative properties of clouds or the forcing by tropospheric and stratospheric ozone changes into a pressure index is difficult. It is still not discussed in sufficient detail by scientists for it to be put forward, like the GWP, to policy-makers and the general public. Here, only some guiding principles can be given.

First, tropospheric aerosols (SO_2, NO_x and NH_3 emissions) should not be seen as a mere partial offset of the enhanced greenhouse effect despite the opposite direction of their radiative forcing. The reason for this is their different height profile as well as their regionalization, which creates locally strong gradients of radiative forcing to which the climate system might respond differently than to a more uniform forcing of a long-lived greenhouse gas. Second, increased tropospheric ozone is also confined to regional scales, but wider ones than for aerosols and partly overlapping with the aerosol pattern. Therefore, similar problems apply to a mere addition of these two factors because of the strong horizontal gradients of the radiative forcing by tropospheric ozone. Third, for stratospheric ozone depletion a somewhat simpler integration into a climate change pressure index could exist. The mainly latitude-dependent and thus rather zonal forcing can be transformed into a changed stratospheric temperature stratification, which can be taken into account for the calculation of radiative forcing of the surface/troposphere system by ozone depletion.

If carbon sinks are enhanced, then any pressure index should be lowered, thus creating an incentive for reforestation and afforestation as well as soil protection measures. It would, at the same time, help to reduce some of the other pressure indices related to biodiversity loss and soil degradation.

Because the problem of the changed composition of the atmosphere has not only the necessary basic legal framework for action, but also enough scientific understanding for more practical action, climate protection could well become the first big step towards sustainable development, long before other equally important or even more acute trends receive the proper attention. An easy step towards proper handling of other problems should in this context be a global soil convention into which the UN convention to combat desertification could be embedded. Then all nations would have to act to secure global food production.

6. COMPARISON WITH THE RESULTS OF THE SECOND SURVEY

The ranking of core indicators as given in the questionnaire results section (see Chapter 5 and Annex I), taking into account answers by European experts, differs at several points from my personal assessment. These differences are as follows. First, N_2O emissions are overall ranked fourth although knowledge on its sources and possible measures is rather limited. Second, most fluorocarbons are extremely long-lived greenhouse gases; thus any emission today will accumulate and cause climate change for thousands of years. Therefore, their rank is not too low. Third, CFCs are regulated by the Montreal Protocol and the most important have already been phased out in the European Union. CFCs could therefore be removed from the list while HCFCs (hydrochlorofluorocarbons) should remain. Finally, NO_x emissions are contributing to many environmental problems (photosmog, eutrophication, acidification, ozone depletion in high latitudes and so on) and should be ranked higher.

In view of the above points my ranking would be: CO_2 emissions per year, CH_4 emissions per year, NO_x emissions per year, fluorocarbon emissions and HCFCs, CO_2 removals per year, SO_x emissions per year, particle emissions, and NMVOC emissions per year.

PART III

Loss of Biodiversity

9. Introduction

A. Markandya and N. Dale

1. THE LOSS OF BIODIVERSITY POLICY FIELD

Biological diversity is defined by the Convention of Biological Diversity (UNEP, 1992) as:

> the variability among living organisms from all sources including, *inter alia*, terrestrial, marine, and other aquatic ecosystems, and the ecological complexes of which they are a part; this includes diversity within species, between species and of ecosystems.

The importance of maintaining this diversity can be summed up as follows: (i) it is the basis for the stability and sustainability of natural ecosystems, (ii) it has a great range of potential and unexplored uses for humans, and (iii) it has existence values such as the amenity values of protected areas.

The available evidence on species numbers and stress on ecosystems within Europe points to a decline of biodiversity within ecosystems (loss of habitats), within habitats (loss of species) and among species (decline of species abundance) (EEA, 1995). The causes of these declines are wide-ranging and complex, and this was reflected in the variety and number of proposed pressure indicators received in the first PIP expert questionnaire.[1] This list of proposed indicators covered a range of 38 'sub themes' such as habitat fragmentation, agricultural practices, loss of genetic resources, pollution and urban development. For the second-round questionnaire the list was reduced from an original total of 258 proposed Loss of Biodiversity indicators to the 28 that were considered to be the most relevant and compatible with established sources of data.

2. RESULTS OF THE SECOND-ROUND QUESTIONNAIRE

Figure 9.1 gives the top core-ranked indicators expressed as percentages of experts who included the indicator in their top five list, together with the

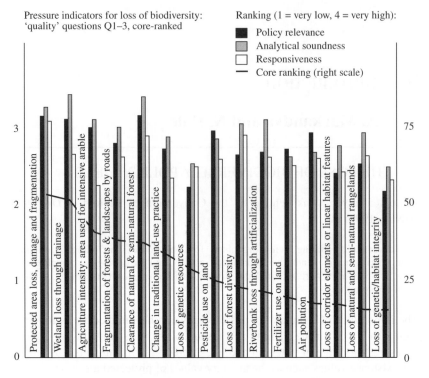

*Figure 9.1   Results of second-round questionnaire for the Loss of
             Biodiversity policy field*

corresponding rankings for the three quality questions. The top five rankings
for each question were as follows:

- Core-ranked indicators: protected area loss, damage and fragmentation,
  wetland loss through drainage, agricultural intensity: area used for intensive arable agriculture, fragmentation of forests and landscapes by roads/
  intersections, clearance of natural and semi-natural forests.
- Policy relevance indicators: protected area loss, damage and fragmentation, clearance of natural and semi-natural forests, wetland loss through
  drainage, agricultural intensity: area used for intensive arable agriculture, pesticide use on land.
- Analytical soundness indicators: wetland loss through drainage, clearance of natural and semi-natural forests, protected area loss, damage
  and fragmentation, riverbank loss through artificialization, agricultural
  intensity: area used for intensive arable agriculture.

- Response elasticity indicators: protected area loss, damage and fragmentation, loss of forest diversity, clearance of natural and semi-natural forests, loss of natural and semi-natural rangelands, wetland loss through drainage.

In general, there is quite close correlation between the quality question rankings and the core rankings. Protected area loss, damage and fragmentation, clearance of natural and semi-natural forests and wetland loss through drainage are ranked highly in all four questions, while agricultural intensity is ranked highly in all questions except for the response elasticity question. In common with other policy fields, the main differences in top five rankings exist between the response elasticity question and the other three questions.

3. RELATIONS TO OTHER POLICY FIELDS

The broad nature and complexity of issues covered by the Loss of Biodiversity policy field means that it has strong links with a number of the other policy fields. Since overlaps are inevitable, the following delimitations were applied to avoid double counting in very closely related policy fields. First, biodiversity issues related to marine and coastal areas were included in the Marine Environment and Coastal Zones policy field. Second, forest ecosystem issues were included in Loss of Biodiversity while wood consumption was seen as a Resource Depletion issue. Third, in matters of land use, factors affecting the existence of biological systems were included under Loss of Biodiversity while factors affecting non-biological resources were grouped under Resource Depletion.

Particularly close links exist with the Climate Change policy field centred on the issue of deforestation. This issue is one of the main contributors to climate change as a result of the decrease in forest areas and reduction in the existing sinks of carbon dioxide, and the increase in emissions of greenhouse gases due to the burning of wood. However, any change in the area of tropical forests also has effects on biodiversity. Therefore, measures to protect biodiversity are likely to have a positive effect on climate change.

Biodiversity is also affected by air pollution and acidification. In particular, acidification often occurs at a rate faster than the ability of species to respond, thus resulting in the loss of some species. A further close interrelationship exists with the Water Pollution policy field since issues such as eutrophication and soil degradation are clearly relevant to biodiversity.

4.   APPROACH OF THE CONTRIBUTIONS

The chapter by Pierre Devillers gives an enlightening general overview of
'The biodiversity crisis' structuring his contribution to address the central
questions set out in the editor's introduction to this handbook. The introduction explains the human causes of the crisis and potential consequences. The
consequences are categorized as the destabilization of ecosystems, the loss of
vital resources and cultural amputation.

The chapter by Marianne Lefort concentrates on her specialist interest in
the consequences of the loss of genetic diversity for domestic species, and the
actions needed to reduce this loss. She explains that the concentration of
selection efforts on a very limited genetic base is often associated with the
lack of interest in, and loss of, that genetic diversity which is not exploited.
The chapter argues that the maintenance of genetic diversity, more than
biological diversity, is indispensable for the maintenance of the adaptive
potentials of species, and to provide for the future needs of mankind, whether
social, cultural, agricultural or industrial. Lefort's chapter is structured to
address the same central questions as the Devillers chapter.

Role of Central Political Intervention

Devillers stresses the importance of central political intervention for conservation of biological diversity at the scale of the European Union, stating that
'Nature conservation is clearly a matter in which Community competence is
indispensable to insure fulfilment of common goals and reciprocal responsibilities'. He explains that the nature of biological diversity means that
conservation policy objectives are best set at international conventions, and
that European legislation and policy should encapsulate these and establish
the minimum results for Member States to achieve. It is then for the Member
States to establish the framework and create the necessary instruments for
implementation of the directives. However, the disparity of biological diversity between northern and southern Europe makes cash flows from north to
south indispensable if the whole of the Union is to participate in the preservation of the natural heritage.

Lefort argues that a concerted European approach to the conservation of
genetic resources is necessary for technical, political and socio-economic
reasons. In particular, since the erosion of genetic diversity is not contained
within national boundaries, it makes sense for intervention to be at the EU
level.

Actions

Devillers stresses that, since the main threats to biodiversity are habitat destruction, fragmentation and degradation, short-term conservation strategies should concentrate on the establishment of 'coherent networks of areas under diverse levels of protection, adapted to the conservation of the biological values targeted'. These networks may be supplemented by overall conservation measures applied in the rest of the environment, protecting less sensitive species and less fragile communities. In the longer term, however, networks of protected areas will not be capable of fulfilling their role as reservoirs of biological diversity if the environment that surrounds them continues to degrade. Devillers points to two approaches to conserving the biological diversity of the surrounding environment: rational exploitation of natural resources and land stewardship.

The chapter by Lefort makes a number of technical proposals for short- and medium-term action and identifies some indicators to allow the monitoring of these actions.

For plants, she urges the establishment of a genetic reserve comprising a collection of genetic resources to be maintained in long-term *ex situ* conditions. This should be complemented by the establishment of networks of genetic resources that are of interest to agriculture, preserved in *in situ* conditions. Actions to favour the diversification of production by increasing numbers of cultivated species and genetic variability are also outlined.

For animal species traditionally selected by humans, Lefort recommends actions including: monitoring the number of races, the genetic diversity between these races and the evolution of genetic diversity within major races, and the establishment of stocks of semen and embryos for the most endangered races.

Lefort recognizes that, in the long term, for both plants and animals, we should consider establishment of production systems involving a less intensive and more balanced use of agricultural and forest lands.

Pressure Indicators

Devillers explains that, in the case of both protected area networks and non-protected areas, the need to orientate action and ensure its acceptance makes monitoring and communication to the decision-makers and the public concerned indispensable. Indicators of environmental pressure are a useful tool for such monitoring and communication functions. They have the advantage of a direct relation to corrective action and many of them can be relatively easily calculated from existing administrative statistics.

He concludes that, whether based on pressures, habitats or indicator species, indicators do yield results that are timely, compatible and comparable.

Moreover, he argues that the recent trend towards multiplication and redistribution of levels of decision-making has made the availability of easily
understood and transparently developed common measuring standards all the
more necessary.

In her chapter Marianne Lefort argues that pressure indicators related to
genetic diversity can be beneficial for a number of reasons. The wide distribution of indicators for genetic diversity in agriculture will raise the awareness
of the public and politicians about the risks of the erosion of genetic resources, lead to a better management of these resources within Member
States and inspire collective EU action. An analysis of the evolution over
time of the indicators should, moreover, help to target legislation and regulation towards a better long-term preservation of genetic resources.

Lefort stresses the importance of the 'intensification of agriculture' indicator (LB-1) which, in time, could have significant impacts on the environment.
She recognizes that there are difficulties in envisaging concrete actions to
reduce this indicator, as well as the 'changes in traditional land-use practice'
indicator (LB-2). However, the chapter concludes that there are now some
positive examples in the agricultural field where the importance of conservation in order to achieve sustainable development is now emphasized.

5.   INTERNATIONAL FRAMEWORK

International policies on biodiversity have, in general, concentrated on the
protection of species and sites through the agreement of international conventions and programmes, and within EU legislation. The principal international
initiatives of relevance to Europe are outlined below.

- The Ramsar Convention on Wetlands of International Importance was
  signed in 1971 and includes 70 countries. Under the convention 362
  wetlands sites have been designated in Europe.
- UNESCO's 'Man and the Biosphere' programme (MAB) has developed Biosphere Reserves which aim to combine preservation of
  ecological and genetic diversity with a viable local economy, and
  research and education functions. Since its inception in 1971 the MAB
  programme has established over 120 reserves in Europe.
- The Convention on International Trade in Endangered Species of Wild
  Fauna and Flora (CITES) was signed in 1973. It aims to restrict such
  commercial trade in order to prevent extinction of endangered species.
  Most European states have now joined the convention and it has been
  ratified by over 110 countries worldwide.
- The Convention on the Conservation of European Wildlife and Natural

Habitats (Berne Convention) was signed in 1982, and includes EU countries and some other European and African states. It aims to protect flora and fauna and their habitats and promote international cooperation in resolving transboundary issues, especially those concerning the protection of endangered and vulnerable species.

- The Convention on Biological Diversity was signed at the 1992 UN Conference on Environment and Development (UNCED) in Rio de Janeiro, and enacted in December 1993. Nearly all European states have signed the convention, which requires signatories to prepare national plans for the conservation of biodiversity and sustainable use of biological resources. The convention is seen as a major step forward in efforts to structure international action for preservation of biodiversity.

There are a number of European Union-based initiatives which promote biodiversity across Member States. These include: Biogenic Reserves (promoted since 1975), The Bird Directive (1979), and The Habitats Directive (1992). Other recent European initiatives include the European Ecological Network (EECONET) and the IUCN Action Plan for Protected Areas.

NOTE

1.　First questionnaire: December 1995; second questionnaire: October 1996. See Editors' introduction.

REFERENCES

EEA (1995), *Europe's Environment: The Dobříš Assessment* (Copenhagen: European Environment Agency).

UNEP (1992), *Convention on Biological Diversity* (Nairobi, Kenya: United Nations Environment Programme).

10. Biodiversity

P. Devillers

1. THE BIODIVERSITY CRISIS

The expression 'biological diversity' or 'biodiversity' refers to 'the variability of living organisms of all origins, including the diversity of species as well as between species and that of ecosystems' (Glowka et al., 1994). Three fundamental components can be recognized. First, the diversity of species, and therefore of all independent manifestations of the evolutionary process. Second, the diversity of populations, and therefore of the capabilities of species to adapt to a changing environment and to colonize new niches. Third, the diversity of communities, and therefore of the network of interactions between species that is the basis of small- and large-scale landscape mosaics.

The first two components decrease with global extinctions of species or populations and with loss of intrapopulational genetic diversity, and increase as a result of speciation or incipient speciation phenomena and with gain of genetic diversity. The third component decreases with local extinctions which impoverish, simplify and uniformize communities, and increases with local colonization or recolonization successes.

The global evolutionary phenomenon resulting from the interaction of these events is a historical process, unique and non-predictable. In the course of this process, the evolution of biodiversity is characterized by alternation between periods of relatively stable growth and short periods of massive extinction (Gould, 1989, 1993).

The growth periods are governed by the stochastic frequency of speciation and extinction events, largely controlled by local abiotic factors (Cracraft, 1982; Eldredge, 1989), and by the Darwinian determinism which underpins the evolution of populations. The periods of extinction, which may be triggered by exogenous or endogenous causes, decisively affect the qualitative course of evolution. The selection of the species that survive follows rules which, although probably not random, differ at any rate fundamentally from those that prevail during periods of growth (Gould, 1989, 1993); the orientation imparted to the evolution of lineages after the periods of extinction results both from that selection and from the limitations imposed by the genetic heritage accumulated in the previous epochs, so that there is never a return to the starting-point.

The present times are a period of considerable prevalence of biodiversity losses over biodiversity gains. For the species component, net extinction rates have been evaluated at approximately 0.001/year, a rate which, extrapolated to the level of resolution available for past extinctions (0.1 to 1 million years) leads to a loss at least as large as that of the most severe events (Simberloff, 1984; Devillers and Chaline, 1989; Wilson, 1992; Ramade, 1993). The origin of this extinction event is endogenous, in that it results from the proliferation and behaviour of one species produced by the evolutionary process itself. This characteristic is also shared with at least some of the documented palaeontological examples. This biodiversity crisis, however, differs from previous vicissitudes in that a conscious species is both a witness to it and an actor in it, and is capable of influencing its outcome in response to a perception of its undesirability.

Evaluation of the impact of the biodiversity crisis depends on the time scale at which it is considered. Placed in its historical context and regarded from a purely quantitative point of view, the biodiversity crisis is not a threat to the long-term future of life on earth. There is no reason to think that, even if biological diversity were severely reduced, it would not later resume a growth comparable to that of previous epochs, leading to a new radiation and proliferation, differing from that of today, and with or without the conscious species. This restoration would, however, entail time scales incommensurable with our affective interests and is thus, for the human observer, irrelevant.

At the scale of a few human generations, the only one compatible with our perception, our concern and our responsibilities, the biodiversity crisis leads to an irreversible deterioration of the biological heritage, with consequences that can be broadly organized into three classes: destabilization of ecosystems, loss of vital resources and cultural amputation.

Complex ecosystems offering multiple pathways for the flow of energy from one trophic level to the next are more stable than simple ones. Thus, as biodiversity decreases, systems become increasingly vulnerable to external perturbations of abiotic, biotic or anthropogenic origin. Small oscillations are more likely to grow into large-scale catastrophes leading to further decreases in biodiversity, a feedback process with potential for a snowball effect, and to human disasters, such as soil erosion, floods, desertification, epidemics and crop failures. Concern for ecosystem stability is a reformulation of the long-held preoccupation with the 'balance of nature'. It focuses conservation attention on keystone species the disappearance of which is most likely gravely to upset the communities to which they belong.

Biodiversity constitutes an enormous reservoir of 'unmined riches' in the words of Wilson (1992), of as yet undiscovered material for technological innovations in feeding or equipping humans and protecting or improving their health. Several examples exist of rare, threatened and newly discovered organisms offering considerable potential for the development of new, more advantageous domestic strains, or for treatment of previously incurable diseases (Wilson, 1992). Many others undoubtedly exist and may, at the current rate of diversity loss, disappear before they are discovered, or their potential known. This concern, which can generally be expressed in economic terms because of the obvious industrial gains connected with the development of new technologies, places emphasis on the numerical strength of diversity *per se*, as the carriers of potentially useful traits cannot be identified *a priori*. Attention to individual species is then channelled towards indicator species as a measure of the overall health and richness of communities.

Besides its roles as stabilizer of the environment or provider of economic wealth, biological diversity has an immense intrinsic value as part of the cultural heritage of mankind. Curiously, its significance in this respect is less readily recognized than that of the other resources on which culture and civilization rest, in particular, the monuments of past artistic achievement and the written sources of knowledge, although it is perhaps even more fundamental and irreplaceable. In this light, the loss of biodiversity is felt as an irremediable deprivation of sources of intellectual, sentimental and sensual inspiration and satisfaction for this generation and the subsequent ones. This approach places the main emphasis on the species that speak most to the human conscious and unconscious, often called flagship or umbrella species.

2. THE ROLE OF CENTRAL POLITICAL INTERVENTION

Sustaining the three components of biological diversity imposes the interdependence of all efforts and all requirements of conservation at the scale of the European Union. The preservation of any local population of a species is an integral part of the essential conservation strategy for that species and thus of the legitimate aspirations as well as of the obligations of all, and not only of the inhabitants of the region concerned. Similarly, the preservation of the full spectrum of diversity of biocoenoses makes the conservation of a unique habitat, present in a single region, the concern and the responsibility of all, even if the concrete measures decided have to be implemented by local authorities. Thus no nature conservation matter arising in one region of Europe should leave the rest of the Union, its neighbours or the international community, indifferent or inactive. Nature conservation is clearly a matter in which Community competence is indispensable to ensure fulfilment of common goals and reciprocal responsibilities.

To manage nearly all semi-natural habitats, in Europe at least, in order to ensure their durability necessarily entails substantial costs. It is only possible to meet those costs by the systematic recourse to incentive programmes rather than by coercive measures and integral financing of management needs. It is indispensable also to recognize that the considerable disparity of biological diversity between regions inevitably leads to higher costs in some regions than in others. Mechanisms of financial transfers must be installed to guarantee the needed and normal solidarity in the sharing of charges. In particular, orography, climate, history of biocoenoses and human action concur to give to southern Europe a biological diversity very much superior to that of the north. A flow of resources from the north to the south is thus indispensable if the whole of the Union is to participate in the preservation of its most precious natural heritage.

The distribution of responsibilities between the various jurisdictions that would best favour the harmonious conduct of these conservation policies leaves the definition of the objectives and of the results to be attained to the highest decision-making levels, and the choice of the means to the lowest of these levels. International conventions should thus define general goals; European legislation and policy should encapsulate them and establish the minimum results that the Member States pledge to reach. It is the Member States that best establish, in accordance with their particular legal systems, the framework of implementation of the directives, and impose conservation targets extending beyond those required by the directives. The Member States or, where relevant, their subordinate entities, create the necessary instruments to attain the targets required by higher jurisdictions and those that they additionally impose on themselves.

3.   CONCRETE ACTIONS

The main and most active threats to species, populations and biocoenoses are habitat destruction, habitat fragmentation and habitat degradation. In the short term it is thus inescapable that conservation strategies should be centred on the establishment of coherent networks of areas under diverse levels of protection, adapted to the conservation of the biological values targeted. These networks may be supplemented by overall conservation measures applied in the rest of the environment and which bring a complement of protection to less sensitive species and less fragile communities. This approach has been increasingly resorted to, and is embodied, for instance, in Directive 79/409/EEC on the preservation of wild birds, in the Berne Convention, in Directive 92/43/EEC on the preservation of fauna, flora and habitats. It also underlies the data-collecting methodology within the European Community's (now

EEA) CORINE Biotopes project referred to below and is the only workable approach to the implementation of the Biodiversity Convention.

Networks of conservation areas may contain areas of small dimensions with a high level of protection, suited for very fragile species with concentrated distribution, as well as areas of large dimensions with a relatively low level of constraints, needed for the preservation of species of diffuse distribution or large spatial requirements. In the selection of sites two approaches can be used concurrently. The application of individual site qualification criteria is the most established one (Grimmett and Jones, 1989; Moss et al., 1991). In particular, very large expanses of natural or semi-natural habitats, now extremely rare in Europe, should, by virtue of their very size, qualify for preservation in their entirety. Most other sites should rather be selected on the basis of their contribution to integrated species, population and community-level conservation objectives, an approach which has the advantage of basing decisions on pre-established algorithms rather than expert opinions.

Of the integrated objectives of the conservation area networks, those related to the preservation of species diversity are the easiest to define. It can, for instance, be reasonably proposed that the strength of the populations of a species included within a network of protected areas should constitute a proportion of the total population of the species that increases with the vulnerability of the species; indeed, the greater the fragility of a species, the smaller the contribution of unprotected space to its survival.

The requirement of preserving intraspecific diversity can likewise be roughly met if the proportionality between protected population and total population is satisfied not only at the global or continental scale but also at an appropriate local scale. Finer selectivity is in general not feasible nor probably desirable, as it is impossible to predict which genetic material or which populations will be the material of the future successful evolution of a species and the origin of its branching into new entities or lineages. In this context the preservation of peripheral populations has no more or no less importance than that of central ones. All the regional populations of a sensitive species must be protected.

These species-oriented approaches have, however, a limitation in that they can realistically be applied only to a limited number of taxa, in general to those species that relate most to human perception. The conservation of other species and populations, and thus of the overwhelming majority of the specific and intraspecific diversity, is generally better achieved through a community approach. Indeed, the preservation of ecosystem diversity, besides achieving the conservation of webs of species interactions and the intrinsic aesthetic and exemplary value of the biocoenoses they compose, is also the only possibility of ensuring with some success the conservation of the less obvious and less understood species for which particular efforts are unrealistic. Here again, the first prerequisite is that all distinctive regional manifestations of any sensitive type of habitat be identified and conserved.

The knowledge and understanding of communities needed for such action is unfortunately not as available as that which concerns species or even populations. As a very first step, a catalogue of the recognizable communities formed by the flora and fauna in response to the abiotic environment and to each other's influence is a prerequisite to any attempt to characterize sites in terms of their importance for nature conservation, of inventorying such sites, of constituting coherent networks of protected sites, or of monitoring the evolution of such networks (Devillers and Devillers-Terschuren, 1993).

Habitat conservation measures within the components of the networks of protected areas are generally sufficient to ensure the survival of the majority of the species that inhabit them provided of course that all characters of the biotopes are preserved and that the areas are sufficiently large to harbour viable populations. For a few species, however, those measures are not enough. Species with very large space requirements, dependent on the conjunction of several habitats and with an unfavourable conservation status resulting not only from habitat deterioration but also from harvesting, disturbance or competition pressures, require the preparation and implementation of large-scale conservation strategies and restoration plans (Maguire et al., 1987; Beudels, 1991). Species dependent on one or several very specific constituents of the habitat may not be retained on a site if their particular ecological requirements are not taken into account in detail in management plans (Gutierrez and Carey, 1985).

In the longer term, networks of protected areas will not be capable of fulfilling their role as reservoirs of biological diversity if the environment that surrounds them continues to degrade. There is indeed an inevitable erosion of their value with time. Increasing effective insularization of their components results in loss of species (Diamond, 1975, 1986). Natural evolutions of some communities towards more mature or more senescent types is not compensated by emergence of new sites in more pioneer stages. Encroachment on the sites themselves increases as time passes if the neighbouring human populations are fundamentally hostile or envious. Long-distance influences may progressively accumulate, in particular those related to wind transport or pollutants, long-range dispersal of epidemics, or exaggerated visitor pressure.

These effects can be minimized only if the overall harbouring capacity of the multiple-use environment for biological diversity is improved and the rate of loss of this diversity in non-protected areas is slowed down. Several approaches exist that offer interesting prospects in that respect. The two most important ones can be labelled rational exploitation of natural resources, on the one hand and land stewardship, on the other.

Particularly in areas of high biological diversity it has been suggested that a shift in the exploitation of natural or semi-natural habitats from the destructive quest for raw materials currently in use to the mining of higher-value products such as genetic material would lead to survival of much greater surfaces of wildland or restored landscape while augmenting considerably their economic value (Wilson, 1992). Although mostly applicable to tropical regions, the reasoning holds for alternative use of land destined for agriculture or urbanization in other parts of the world.

More specific to areas of intensive agricultural exploitation leading to unmanageable local surpluses, the opportunity of inflecting agricultural policies from exclusive goals of production towards a more integrated management of the land, taking into account quality of life and biodiversity requirements, is of major importance. Large-scale reversals in biodiversity trends could easily be achieved if systems of direct remuneration to farmers producing biological diversity on their land were established in lieu of compensations for loss of revenue because of de-intensification or non-intensification of their traditional agricultural production.

4. PRESSURE INDICES

The construction of protected area networks requires a process of site selection based on necessarily incomplete knowledge of the distribution and abundance of fauna, flora and habitats. The adequacy of the network sufficiently to protect key elements of biodiversity must be assessed.

Many habitats of great biological importance result from past agro-pastoral activities or represent stages of evolution that will no longer be attained by new sites in the highly regulated environment of today. Both kinds must be managed to mimic the effects of natural or exploitation-oriented cycles that no longer exist if they are to retain their significance for the specialized species that they harbour. Even in more natural sites management is often necessary to compensate an insularization-induced fragility that prevents communities or their most specialized components from surviving crises provoked by climatic vicissitudes. Such management is only possible if its effects can be evaluated so that it can be constantly corrected and reoriented.

Incentive instruments favouring rational use of non-protected space are effective only if their level of acceptance by targeted social groups is sufficiently high. This can rarely be fully evaluated *a priori* as it depends on a large number of economic, social, cultural, historical and psychological factors with complex interactions. Moreover, the expected effects of most of them on biodiversity are indirect. In practice, therefore, schemes can fall very short of their theoretical expectations if their impact is not closely watched, quantified and compared on a cost–benefit basis with other conservation approaches.

The design of conservation efforts in favour of species covering extensive spatial areas often entails substantial costs and interference with the activities of various interest groups. These efforts can be sustained only if their necessity, their adequacy and their success can be clearly and unambiguously demonstrated.

In all cases the need to orientate action and ensure its acceptance makes monitoring and its communication to both decision-makers and the public concerned indispensable. The size of the territory over which those monitoring systems must operate and the diversity of the phenomena they must reflect impose an economy of material, effort and manpower in their execution. Overall indices of the state of the environment are a satisfactory tool to this effect. Since the total biodiversity can never be inventoried, indices necessarily rest on surrogate variables. Conceptually they fall into three categories; those that measure the evolution of pressures or risk factors, those that monitor the fluctuations in range or population size of indicator species or groups of species (Devillers et al., 1990), and those that record the distributional or quality changes of communities (Devillers and Devillers-Terschuren, 1996a, 1996b). In practice, simultaneous, successive or complementary use of combinations of all three sets can probably not be avoided.

Pressure indicators have the advantage of a direct relation to corrective action. Many of them can be relatively easily calculated from existing administrative statistics. Reliance on them assumes, however, that the relation between a particular pressure and damage to overall biodiversity is strong and that the subset of pressure factors that are monitored is a good surrogate for the total set of existing pressures.

The first assumption is strongly dependent on the adequacy of the sample chosen to measure the pressure. Thus even an intuitively strongly relevant indicator, such as the loss, damage and fragmentation of protected areas, is only valid if the network of such areas adequately covers the regional biodiversity. This is less likely to be the case for a set of protected areas than for a parallel but usually larger set of areas identified as of great interest for nature conservation, such as the CORINE site set. Indeed, into the designation of protected areas have entered economic, social and political considerations not related to the conservation of biological diversity and potentially detrimental to it. In either case, the choice of the initial set has necessarily included the use of criteria based on indicator species or habitat-related indices.

The validity of the second assumption may greatly vary in time and space. It requires, in any case, that the subset monitored be relatively large. Both assumptions are more likely to be valid if the sample on which the pressures are measured is structured along the lines of a biotic community classification such as the CORINE habitat typologies (Devillers and Devillers-Terschuren, 1996a, 1996b).

Overall indicators, whether based on pressures, habitats or indicator species, do yield results that are timely, compatible and comparable. Comparability is a particularly arduous constraint at a time when growing awareness about the gravity and the immediacy of environmental problems, including those that concern biodiversity, has evolved in parallel with a transfer of powers previously held by nation states in two opposite directions, towards supranational entities or international organizations on the one hand, and towards their constituents on the other hand. The multiplication and redistribution of levels of decision-making which have resulted from that double migratory current have had considerable influence on the management of the environment and of natural heritage, and made acutely necessary the availability of easily understood and transparently developed common measuring standards.

REFERENCES

Beudels, R.C. (1991), 'The Monk Seal Register: its structure and organisation', *Proceedings, Séminaire sur la protection du phoque moine de Méditerranée. Aspects scientifiques et techniques* (Strasbourg: Conseil de l'Europe), pp. 61–72.

Cracraft, J. (1982), 'A nonequilibrium theory for the rate-control of speciation and extinction and the origin of macroevolutionary patterns', *Systematic Zoology*, **31**: 348–65.

Devillers, Ch. and J. Chaline (1989), *La théorie de l'évolution: état de la question à la lumière des connaissances scientifiques actuelles* (Paris: Bordas).

Devillers, P. and J. Devillers-Terschuren (1993), *A classification of palaearctic habitats and preliminary list of priority habitats in Council of Europe Member States* (Strasbourg: Council of Europe).

Devillers, P. and J. Devillers-Terschuren (1996a), *A classification of palaearctic habitats. Nature and Environment* no. 78. (Strasbourg: Council of Europe).

Devillers, P. and J. Devillers-Terschuren (1996b), *A classification of South American habitats. Report to the Commission of the European Communities* (Brussels: Institut Royal des Sciences Naturelles de Belgique).

Devillers, P., R.C. Beudels, J. Devillers-Terschuren, Ph. Lebrun, J.-P. Ledant and E. Sérusiaux (1990), 'Un projet de surveillance de l'état de l'environnement par bio-indicateurs', *Naturalistes belges*, **71**: 75–98.

Diamond, J.M. (1975), 'The island dilemma: lessons of modern biogeographic studies for the design of natural reserves', *Biological Conservation*, **7**: 129–46.

Diamond, J.M. (1986), 'The design of a nature reserve system for Indonesian New Guinea', in M.E. Soule, (ed.), *Conservation Biology. The science of scarcity and diversity* (Sunderland, Sinauer Associates),pp. 485–503.

Eldredge, N. (1989), *Macroevolutionary dynamics* (New York: McGraw-Hill).

Glowka, L., F. Burhnne-Guilmin and H. Synge (1994), 'A guide to the Convention on

Biological Diversity', IUCN, *Environmental Policy and Law*, Paper no. 30, pp. 1–192.

Gould, S.J. (1989), *Wonderful Life. The Burgess Shale and the Nature of History* (Harmondsworth: Penguin).

Gould, S.J. (ed.) (1993), *The Book of Life* (London: Ebury-Hutchinson).

Grimmett, R.F.A. and T.A. Jones (1989), *Important Bird Areas in Europe*, ICBP Technical Publication 9, pp. 1–888.

Gutierrez, R.J. and A.B. Carey (1985), 'Ecology and Management of the Spotted Owl in the Pacific Northwest', *US Foreign Service General Technical Report* PNW 185.

Maguire, L.A., U.S. Seal and P.E. Brussard (1987), 'Managing Critically Endangered Species: The Sumatran Rhino as a Case Study', M.E. Soule (ed.), *Viable Populations for Conservation* (Cambridge: Cambridge University Press), pp. 141–58.

Moss, D., B. Wyatt, M.-H. Cornaert and M. Rockaerts (1991), *CORINE biotopes. The design, compilation and use of an inventory of sites of major importance for nature conservation in the European Community* (Luxembourg: Commission of the European Communities).

Ramade, F. (1993), *Dictionnaire encyclopédique de l'écologie et des sciences de l'environnement* (Paris: Ediscience international).

Simberloff, D. (1984), 'Mass extinction and the destruction of moist tropical forests', *Th. Obschch. Biol.*, **45**: 767–78.

Wilson, E.O. (1992), *The Diversity of Life* (Harmondsworth: Penguin).

11. Genetic diversity in agriculture

M. Lefort

1. EROSION OF GENETIC DIVERSITY AND CONSEQUENCES FOR AGRICULTURAL DEVELOPMENT

Biological diversity is an essential factor for the maintenance of the living world's major balances. It is defined by the Convention of Biological Diversity (UNEP, 1992) as 'the variability among living organisms from all sources including, *inter alia*, terrestrial, marine, and other aquatic ecosystems, and the ecological complexes of which they are a part; this includes diversity within species, between species and of ecosystems'. In all cases, diversity is considered dynamic, and capable of evolution and adaptation under environmental constraints, thanks to a high variability at the three aforementioned levels. This chapter concentrates particularly on the consequences of a loss of genetic diversity for domestic species, and the short- and medium-term solutions which can be envisaged to reduce the loss.

For centuries, animal and plant species have dispersed from their centres of origin (Frankel, 1973; Lauvergne, 1989) and have progressively adapted to highly varied environments (Harlan, 1970). These adaptations have allowed the creation and the expression of an enormous amount of genetic variation through traditional races and cultivars, subjected to very different selection pressures depending on the surroundings and human impact with which they were confronted.

These cultivars evolved alongside their wild parents, allowing constant genetic exchange, either directly or via bridging species and spontaneous interspecific hybrids (Pernès, 1984). This evolutionary dynamic, the basis of peasant agriculture, allowed the long-term maintenance of a large genetic diversity, notably even within populations.

More recently, agricultural intensification has resulted in the homogenization of animal and plant production over a large area, but also in increased use of inputs. It has involved a notable reduction in the number of species used by man as well as a new type of exploitation of the potentially useful genetic diversity – replacement of local races and cultivars by élite forms.

These different elements, which have contributed to the development of agricultural progress and its worldwide extension, have probably contributed to the erosion of genetic diversity among the large number of species of interest to agriculture and food production. In fact, if genetic evolution of populations is a natural phenomenon, it should progress in a way that is compatible with the harmonious readjustment of the major biological, economic and social equilibria. However, agricultural evolution over recent decades, while undoubtedly important in economic terms, has been accompanied by an exploitation of biological resources which seems difficult to reconcile with the maintenance of such equilibria.

Intraspecific genetic diversity has been particularly affected by this evolution, and has started the current social debate on the necessity of maintaining genetic resources in the long term. For cultivated plants, there are several examples of the problems encountered following exploitation of a very narrow genetic base, including potato mildew, vine phylloxera and maize helminthosporiosis. However, agriculture is currently continuing to exploit genetic diversity at different levels by a reduction in the number of species cultivated, reduction of the range of intraspecific varieties, and promotion of variety homogeneity (FAO, 1996).

For domestic animals, similar phenomena can be seen. The focus of selection efforts has been on a few species of major economic interest, and there has been a restriction of the exploited intraspecific variability to a few dominant types (Lush, 1946; Bulmer, 1971). There has also been widespread use of artificial insemination and reduction of the number of producing animals, and for some species, such as chickens, an orientation of selection towards production of highly homogeneous genotypes (Bougler, 1989). The FAO estimates that 30 to 50 per cent of domestic animal races are currently under great threat (FAO/UNEP, 1993).

This concentration of selection efforts on a very limited genetic base is often associated with the lack of interest in, and even a loss of, that genetic diversity which is not exploited. However, the maintenance of genetic diversity, more than biological diversity, is indispensable for the maintenance of adaptive potentials of species, and to provide for the future needs of mankind, whether social, cultural, agricultural or industrial. Genetic resources will contribute, *inter alia*, to the development of a sustainable agriculture which will cover the food requirements of an uncertain future – a future that may include, for example, the appearance of new parasites, specific production requirements and new markets, the need to manage non-agricultural lands, and climate changes. It is therefore necessary to ensure the preservation of such resources in the long term, without hindering the biological, social and economic mechanisms which ensure their continued maintenance.

2. NEED FOR A CONCERTED APPROACH AT EUROPEAN LEVEL

Technical Level

With regard to cultivated and domestic species, several identical resources are being conserved by neighbouring states. It would be wise to get rid of the overlaps between Member States and to spread the responsibilities between them. This should be accompanied by a free circulation of the resources concerned within Member States.

With regard to wild species and in particular natural populations, the distributions are often not contained within the boundaries of any one country. In such cases, only a concerted approach by the countries concerned for the preservation of genetic diversity within these species can make any sense. A national directive would be useless in the long term, because it might not take into account all of the biological mechanisms that lead to the maintenance and the evolution of genetic diversity of species over the whole of their range.

Political Level

All countries are interdependent when it comes to genetic resources, and the erosion of genetic diversity is a problem which stretches beyond the national context. Even if the raising of awareness regarding this problem is a reality in several countries, this has yet to give rise to real political and financial support for this sector. However, the preservation of genetic resources comprises a real insurance for the long term, guaranteeing the availability of a genetic reservoir for an uncertain future.

Political support from the EU would have positive repercussions in the following ways. It would underline the willingness of the EU to act in this field, ahead of the international community and, in particular, the USA and Canada. Second, it would encourage states to live up to their obligations with regard to long-term conservation of genetic diversity. Third, it would allow the establishment of appropriate legislation within the EU, as has happened, for example, for international commercial agreements. Finally, it would stimulate cooperation between Member States in this field and could constitute an unprecedented example on the international stage.

Socio-economic Level

The management of genetic resources is not without cost. Its reason for existence is directly linked to the use which could be made of the resources, as much for agricultural and industrial production as for research and teaching, or for socio-cultural reasons. The management should therefore be agreed between the parties involved in these different uses, in order to be able to respond to the needs of all. A discussion on the ways to maintain a sustainable agricultural development, compatible with environmental conservation, is necessary within developed countries. It should also include the possibility of significant changes in current agricultural systems, with a view to shifting to a wider diversification of both animal and plant production, and associated agrarian systems.

In any case, it seems essential not to isolate the management of genetic resources from those who contribute directly or indirectly to its exploitation. In industrialized countries, it is probably the separation between these two types of activity and the absence of cooperation between those involved which has limited education in the case of genetic resources and consequently hindered their use. The development of a concerted approach to the management of genetic resources between those who conserve and those who evaluate the material will allow all actions to be firmly based on an ecological logic likely to endure over time.

3. ACTION IN THE SHORT AND LONG TERM TO STEM CURRENT EROSION

For those species which have been selected by humankind over a long period, it is important to put in place measures to ensure the long-term maintenance of those genetic resources which are still available and to characterize them well so as to promote their use. It would also be useful to promote the present evaluation and use of certain interesting resources through the diversification of agricultural production. With regard to those species for which the selection effort is recent, action must be taken to preserve the variability of natural populations as much as possible in the face of the dominant use of selected populations.

The measures proposed below are realistic in terms of their implementation in the short and medium term in developed countries. They involve technical proposals, for which some indicators are identified to allow their monitoring.

Plants

A genetic reserve needs to be established urgently in order to respond to the unforeseen needs of the agriculture of tomorrow. This reserve will comprise a collection of genetic resources to be maintained in long-term *ex situ* conditions. This means that a choice must be made as to which should be considered for inclusion in the collection according to their genetic originality. This requires a sound knowledge of the genetic diversity and its spatio-temporal structure for each of the species under consideration. Research in this field at the European level would allow a reduction in the overlap of activities between the countries concerned due to the maintenance of the same types of resources.

The establishment of the reserve has two requirements. First, we need to define the contents of all national collections of genetic resources maintained in *ex situ* conditions, and to encourage complementarity at European level. Second, we need to monitor periodically the status of these collections. This should include the number of resources, the number of representatives of each identified resource, the frequency of regeneration and germination quality, parental coefficients between genotypes in the collection (Malécot, 1948), and other indicators of genetic diversity estimated on the basis of interesting agricultural characteristics and genetic markers spread evenly throughout the genome.

The constitution of the genetic reserve should be completed by the establishment of networks of genetic resources of interest to agriculture preserved in *in situ* conditions (prairie and forest species, wild parents of cultivated species). This requires us to define and make clear the contents of all national reserves of genetic resources of interest to agriculture, maintained *in situ* (complementary to the larger European network for nature conservation), as well as the management methods used to preserve the diversity. Also, it is necessary periodically to verify the status of these reserves, and analyse the evolution of this diversity, the stability of the number and dimensions of initial sites, and the evolution of the genetic variability within and between them on the basis of agronomic and molecular criteria. The reserves should be modified and enriched, if necessary, on the basis of experimental results accumulated over time and space, following the completion of the first management cycle for the *in situ* reserves.

It also would seem essential to improve the characterization and evaluation of representative samples of genetic resources, to allow for a wider valuation at a later stage. This will require the production of catalogues describing the conserved resources in both *in situ* and *ex situ* conditions, and the monitoring of the progressive enrichment of the number of phenotypic and molecular descriptors of the resources, according to the needs expressed by the users.

In parallel, it is important to envisage ways in which to favour the diversification of production, either by an increase in the species cultivated or by an increase in the genetic variability exploited, at least in certain agricultural zones. This could be achieved by support for the diversification of cultivated species, the only guarantee of the dynamic maintenance of genetic variability for species of secondary economic interest. A larger diversity of commercialized species could also be encouraged by favouring the growing and valuation of traditional varieties, often well adapted to a given region, but also by stimulating the creation of modern varieties for regional use. Finally, this would also encourage the further study of non-homogeneous varieties at genetic level (mixed or composites) which are likely to show greater performance stability over time as a result of their potential to respond to multiple biotic and abiotic constraints.

This requires us periodically to monitor the number of species grown, their parentage and their associated agricultural or forestry surface areas. The number of commercialized varieties for any given species, their parentage and the associated agricultural areas should also be periodically monitored. Further, we should regularly quantify the genetic diversity really used for agriculture, on the basis of neutral and non-neutral characters with regard to natural selection.[1]

Animals

Species traditionally selected by man or raised in enclosed areas
The long-term maintenance of the genetic diversity of species of domestic animals in small and large numbers, in particular by sensible management, is a priority. It can be achieved in part by the maintenance of species which are highly endangered at the genetic level due to high inbreeding and, on the other hand, by the cryopreservation of semen and embryos taken from selected representatives of those races.

The maintenance of species on the hoof is a priority for different reasons. It ensures the transmission of learned behavioural attributes, but above all it allows one basis of value of the race to be put in place, whatever its size. In this way a contribution is made to the maintenance of employment in rural areas. In addition, it often contributes to the appreciation of local culture, and ensures a social and cultural role at regional level. It is therefore necessary rapidly to inventory those species under threat from the genetic point of view, and in particular the potential reproducers. If these data are already partially available at European level (European Zootechnical Federation Database, EEAP, 1993), it remains to be completed for certain species and needs to be refined for others. The collection of this information should allow the establishment and implementation of sound management plans to revive the species, with the participation of breeders. Further, knowledge of the genetic diversity between and within species should allow us to concentrate efforts on the species which are 'sources of genetic diversity' and limit all duplication of activity at European level, since several species are managed and used simultaneously by several countries.

This requires the monitoring and orientation of the development of the European Database to create a real decision-making tool. It should include number of threatened species, number of reproducing individuals within each race, coefficient of parentage (Malécot, 1948) and other indicators of genetic distance between and within races, estimated on the basis of neutral and non-neutral characteristics with regard to selection.

The establishment of stocks of frozen semen and embryos will allow long-term security, in particular, to help in the rational management of breeding plans for the revival of a species or its stabilization. This point, for which the priority requirements are for the species currently most endangered, should also be developed for the species with high numbers, mainly to maintain the outliers with respect to the selected dominant model.

This requires a periodic monitoring of the state of cryopreservation, including the number of species considered, the relationship between races and genetic diversity maintained globally for the species (genealogies, neutral and non-neutral selection criteria); number of reproducing individuals/race, genetic originality of the latter and potentially accessible intrarace diversity; number of doses conserved/reproductive individuals and quality of stocks conserved.

As with plants, it is important to stimulate the increase in genetic diversity exploited in agriculture, at least in certain agricultural zones. One way is to favour the breeding of ancient local races, often more rustic and better adapted, but also to support research into a better valuation of them. It is therefore wise to introduce criteria of adaptability to regional conditions within more classic selection schemes. Another way is to maintain a wide genetic base within those races of high population numbers, selected for highly targeted objectives (dominant model). In principle this means finding a compromise between making significant genetic progress in the short term and the maintenance of a certain genetic variability for each of the main races, and this at the scale of exploitation which is often distributed over several countries: the choice of relevant criteria to be taken into account remains to be defined.

Finally, the long-term economic impact of a non-uniform agricultural system (breeding of representatives of different races for differences uses, simultaneous husbandry of herds of different species) also has to be made clear. It will ensure a certain flexibility in the face of the uncertainties of the global economy but will be more restrictive for a farmer in comparison with a uniform system.

Thus the following actions are required:

- monitoring the number of races maintained on the hoof and the proportion which are valuable;

- monitoring the genetic diversity between these different races (parentage and other indicators) and their geographic distribution within the national territory for each species;
- monitoring periodically the evolution of genetic diversity within the major races, on the basis of neutral and non-neutral selection criteria, with a view to reorientation if necessary of the selection objectives in order to maintain diversity;
- establishing stocks of semen and embryos for those most endangered races and for the original genetic characteristics identified within the major races, monitoring their physiological quality to renew and enrich the stocks as required.

Species introduced or used by humankind in open areas

In this field, the inventory of available resources and the necessary biological basis for optimizing their management in the long term are still to be established.

For some species of economic interest, it would be useful to inventory the existing genetic diversity and to study the factors affecting its structure in space and time under the effect, notably, of anthropic constraints.

For these same species, it would be useful to specify the phenomena of genetic introgression of natural populations by selected populations and their impacts on the structure of genetic diversity. This would require the monitoring of the quantitative and qualitative evolution of the genetic diversity, on the basis of neutral and non-neutral selection criteria, with a view to better understanding the biological and socio-economic mechanisms which led to the spatio-temporal distribution of the species under consideration.

The preceding information would allow the establishment of key lines for actions to reinforce or to exploit natural populations, in order to preserve the maintenance and exploitation of their genetic variability over the long term by inscribing it in a sustainable socio-economic logic. These key lines should be regularly reviewed in the light of results from the first cycles of activity and as a function of the possible modifications of socio-economic constraints.

In the Longer Term

In both the animal and plant sectors it is essential to ensure the continuation of the measures allowing the management and conservation of genetic resources in both *in situ* and *ex situ* conditions in the long term. These measures are the guarantee of a permanent availability of an indispensable genetic reserve for future needs of agriculture and its partial valuation.

The above recommendations regarding the management and conservation of genetic resources all apply here. These could be linked to more analytical indicators, integrating the evolution over time of certain earlier indicators taking account of biological and socio-economic constraints. The construction of relevant indicators, however, remains to be studied, together with their integration into models and their validation in the light of a database of results accumulated over several years.

Moreover, the accumulation of quantitative and qualitative information on the use of genetic reserves over several decades would probably be one of the most effective demonstrations of the importance of measures for the long-term preservation and valuation of genetic resources.

In a wider perspective, we should begin to consider the establishment of production systems involving a less intensive and more balanced use of agricultural and forested lands. These systems, which would lead to a resource exploitation which was more respectful of the environment (more environmentally friendly resource exploitation), are the guarantee of a sustainable and economical agriculture. A global reorganization of the systems of agricultural management and production should contribute to:

- reducing the uncertainties of production in the face of biotic and abiotic variations;
- the more effective integration of sustainable environmental protection;
- facing up to the very rapid market and legislative changes in the agricultural domain;
- maintaining employment in agricultural zones.

4. COMMUNICATION OF PRESSURE INDICATORS TO THE MEDIA AND LEGISLATORS

The regular publication of qualitative and quantitative information on genetic diversity of interest to agriculture, and on its evolution over time depending on different management constraints, is needed for the education of the public, via the media, and politicians about the risk of genetic erosion. The level of risk is largely unknown or underestimated due to a lack of viable information. Wider distribution of objective information that the different parties will interpret according to their respective key interests is an indispensable stage in the raising of collective awareness of the real risks.

At EU level, the regular production of a series of indicators linked to genetic diversity should lead to a better rationalization of the management of this diversity within Member States. It should inspire collective reflection on the optimization of management methods and should lead to a progressive assignment of tasks between countries with a view to joint maintenance of a well-identified genetic diversity, according to norms defined together. This last idea assumes the free exchange of genetic resources within the system as a whole, as well as a solidarity between Member States in understanding the problems. It would allow each one to value specific resources better, while at the same time managing them within a wider genetic capital, allowing the maintenance and the evolution of the genetic diversity at a more worthwhile/ significant scale.

The accumulation of quantitative information on these questions, at both national and European level, should assist political decision-making in favour of the preservation of genetic resources. It would also help the debate about choice of priority actions, in a context where the financial means are limited, and aid the establishment of systems for warning when rapid interventions are necessary. It should, of course, be complemented by a finer analysis of the causes and consequences of obtaining this information, as well as a prospective analysis of the proposed changes in policy in a given socio-economic context. Such an accumulation of information would ensure a greater objectivity in the raising of media awareness of these questions, and would place the social debate on a more solid scientific grounding.

The summary analysis of the evolution over time of the different indicators should, moreover, help to target the legislative and regulatory needs for better long-term preservation of genetic resources. It is right to discuss and elaborate this type of regulation at EU level in the first instance, but it is also necessary to participate more actively in current international debates in this domain (Conference of the Parties to the Convention on Biological Diversity; FAO Genetic Resources Commission).

5. CONCLUSION

The proposed indicators for the Loss of Biodiversity policy field would be relatively simple to put into practice at the European scale. They would allow all social, economic and political parties to engage in a real dialogue on the measures needed for improved management and valuation of genetic diversity, which is the essential ingredient of biodiversity. The measures outlined in this chapter will only have an effect if they are embodied in and supported by regulation, which allows the maintenance of diversified and high-quality agricultural production while at the same time ensuring environmental preservation. They should be periodically reconsidered, taking into account the results of their impact on the agricultural system in its entirety, including the social and economic components.

The indicator 'intensification of agriculture', which is linked to a uniformity of production and intensive resource exploitation on agricultural lands, is an important one for politicians to take into account as it could, in time, lead to significant changes in the pressures on the environment. It is, on the other hand, important to stress the difficulty of envisaging concrete actions to reduce this pressure indicator, as well as the indicator linked to 'changes in traditional land use'. Some very positive examples do, however, exist in this respect, notably in the case of plans for sustainable development. The objective of these is to encourage farmers to reflect on their future exploitation of resources and to fulfil three major functions: those of producer, environmental manager, and player in the rural scene. This process has been undertaken collectively with state support and several players in the agricultural field now emphasize the importance of conservation in order to achieve sustainable development.

NOTE

1. The periodicity referred to in this paragraph should be defined according to the complexity and the cost of the proposed indicators: for example 3.5 to 10 years.

REFERENCES

Bougler, J. (1989), 'Les ressources génétiques animales françaises: situation actuelle et perspectives', in *La gestion des ressources génétiques animales domestiques* (Lavoisier Tec&Doc), pp. 19–27.

Bulmer, M.G. (1971), 'The effect of selection of genetic variability', *American Naturalist*, **105**, 201–11.

EEAP (1993), *Genetic diversity of European livestock breeds*; Wageninen Pers.

FAO (1996), *Rapport sur l'état des ressources phytogénétiques dans le monde* (FAO).

FAO/UNEP (1993), *World Watch list for domestic animal diversity*.

Frankel, O.H. (1973), *Survey of crop genetic resources in their centres of diversity* (Rome: FAO–IBP).

Harlan, J.R. (1970), 'The evolution of cultivated plants', in O.H. Frankel and E. Bennet (eds), *Genetic resources in plants – their exploitation and conservation*, (Oxford: Blackwell Scientific), pp. 19–32.

Lauvergne, J.J. (1989), 'Constitution des ressources génétiques animales de ferme: évolution des concepts les concernant', in *La gestion des ressources génétiques animales domestiques*, Paris: Lavoisier Tec&Doc, pp. 9–18.

Lush, J.L. (1946), 'Chance as a cause of change in gene frequency within pure breeds of livestock', *American Naturalist*, **80**, 318–42.

Malécot, G. (1948), *Les mathématiques de l'hérédité* (Paris: Masson).

Pernès, J. (1984), 'Gestion des ressources génétiques des plantes', Vol. 1: Monographies, Vol. 2: Manuel (Paris: Lavoisier Tec&Doc).

UNEP (1992), *Convention on Biological Diversity* (Nairobi, Kenya: UNEP).

PART IV

Marine Environment and Coastal Zones

12. Introduction

A. Markandya and N. Dale

1. THE MARINE ENVIRONMENT AND COASTAL ZONES POLICY FIELD

It is very difficult to define precisely or place clear boundaries around the Marine Environment and Coastal Zones, due to the complex and interconnected problems of this policy field. A useful working definition used by the US Commission on Marine Science, Engineering and Resources and quoted in the *Dobříš Assessment* (EEA, 1995), is:

> The part of the land affected by its proximity to the sea, and that part of the sea affected by its proximity to the land as the extent to which man's land-based activities have a measurable influence on water chemistry and marine ecology.

As an interface between land and sea, coastal regions are particularly valuable as ecosystems. Within Europe there is an exceptionally wide range of important and fragile natural coastal habitats covering arctic, temperate and subtropical climate zones. Pressure from human activities, including urbanization, industrialization, fishing, agriculture, energy generation and tourism has led to increasing degradation of the coastal environment and the necessity to produce pressure indicators for this policy field as an aid to the policy response.

The multidimensional nature of this policy field resulted in a diverse set of proposed pressure indicators in the first-round questionnaire launched by Eurostat.[1] The indicators included in the second-round questionnaire were primarily developed from those indicators that had been proposed at least ten times by the first-round questionnaire experts. These were grouped into four broad categories:

- pollution (for example, oil pollution at coast and faecal pollution)
- structural development (for example, wetland loss and loss of coastal green space)
- biodiversity/natural habitats (for example, priority habitat loss and accidents in coastal zone and at sea)
- unsustainable use (for example, overfishing and tourism intensity).

2.   RESULTS OF THE SECOND-ROUND QUESTIONNAIRE

Figure 12.1 shows the results of the second-round questionnaire for the three quality questions and the core-ranking question. The core rankings are expressed as a percentage of experts who included the indicator in their top five list of essential indicators. The top five rankings for these four questions were as follows:

- Core-ranked indicators: eutrophication, overfishing, development along shore, heavy metal discharges, oil pollution at coast and at sea.
- Policy relevance indicators: overfishing, eutrophication, oil pollution at coast and at sea, wetland loss, discharges of halogenated organic compounds.
- Analytical soundness indicators: eutrophication, heavy metal discharges, overfishing, development along shore, tourism intensity.

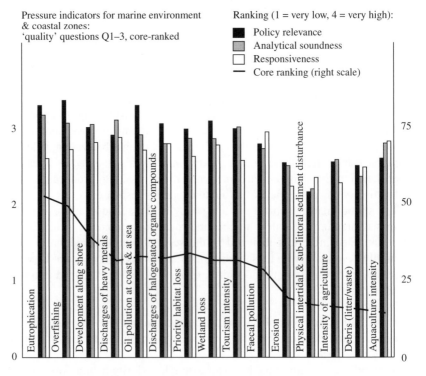

Figure 12.1   Results of second-round questionnaire for the Marine Environment and Coastal Zones policy field

- Response elasticity indicators: faecal pollution, heavy metal discharges, aquaculture intensity, development along shore, discharges of halogenated organic compounds.

From these results it is clear that there is a reasonable degree of agreement between the top five indicators for the core rankings and the three quality questions. Eutrophication, overfishing, development along shore and heavy metal discharges all feature in three of the four top five rankings. In line with most of the other policy fields, there is less agreement between the response elasticity indicator rankings and rankings for the other questions.

There is also a good level of agreement between question responses when the top ten rankings are compared. Along with the four indicators mentioned above, priority habitat loss, wetland loss, tourism intensity, discharges of halogenated organic compounds and oil pollution at coast and at sea all feature in at least three top ten rankings.

3. RELATIONS TO OTHER POLICY FIELDS

The Marine Environment and Coastal Zones policy field is intricately linked to a number of the other policy fields due to the broad-based nature of its definition. In common with the Urban Environmental Problems policy field it is defined by physical environment as opposed to environmental media, such as water, or specific issues, such as dispersion of toxic substances. Therefore, the principal pressure indicators cut across related policy fields such as Water Pollution, Dispersion of Toxic Substances, and Loss of Biodiversity.

Links with the Water Pollution policy field are highlighted by the prominence of the Eutrophication indicator in the rankings. As explained in Part X, the Water Pollution and Water Resources policy field section of this volume, these two ecosystems are in continuity with each other. However, they are delineated by considering continental aquatic ecosystems under Water Pollution and marine aquatic ecosystems under Marine Environment and Coastal Zones.

In Part VI, on Resource Depletion, it is suggested that marine resources may be perceived as a subset of natural resources. Interrelations between these policy fields are clear from the high ranking of the overfishing indicator in Marine Environment and the inclusion of the exceedance of fish catch quota indicator in Resource Depletion.

Overlaps with the Loss of Biodiversity policy field are evidenced by the inclusion of indicators for priority habitat loss and the wetland loss in the Marine Environment top ten core indicators. Similarly, the close relations to the Dispersion of Toxic Substances policy field are shown by high rankings for heavy metal discharges.

A further close relation exists in some coastal locations with the Urban Environmental Problems policy field in connection with issues such as tourism and coastal development. This is illustrated by the high ranking of Marine Environment policy field indicators for tourism intensity and development along shore.

Finally, sea-level rise as a consequence of climate change is forecast to result in potentially serious damage to unprotected low-lying areas of European coastal zones. Therefore, indicators such as erosion and flooding are linked to the Climate Change policy field and could be viewed as state indicators in that policy field. However, these were not ranked highly in the second-round questionnaire for Marine Environment and the primary climate change pressures are included in the Climate Change policy field.

4.   APPROACH OF THE CONTRIBUTIONS

The chapter by Professor Coccossis presents a view of the policy field from a sustainable management perspective. He stresses the complex nature of the pressures on coastal zones, pointing out that 'the ecological and socio-economic importance of coastal areas extends beyond a narrow geographical strip along the coastline'. The impact of a number of human activities are outlined, covering the areas of fishing, aquaculture, agriculture, industry, transport, tourism and urban development. Included among the range of particularly relevant pressures from these human activities are such pressures as overfishing, pollution from excessive use of fertilizers and pesticides, loss of natural habitat areas, and tourism intensity. These correspond to the highly ranked core indicators in the second-round questionnaire, even though definitions vary.

The main part of the chapter concerns the need for an integrated approach to coastal management so that environmental management is incorporated into socio-economic and physical development planning. In particular, it explains the need for coordination of coastal management above the regional and national levels, as envisaged by the 5EAP.[2] On the basis of this integrated approach the chapter outlines the phases needed for preparing a coastal management action plan, and explains the necessity of developing a coastal management information system to support this plan.

Professor Coccossis sees pressure indicators as important for raising awareness and support for the coastal management action plan by improving communication and understanding on coastal issues for both decision-makers and the public. At European level they can aid the development of common policy frameworks for similar contexts and help to communicate successful coastal management.

Margarida Cardosa da Silva gives a clear overview of coastal zone problems, policy actions and the place for environmental indicators in policy assessment and monitoring. The problems of coastal zones are categorized under the five headings of urban encroachment, pollution of estuarine and coastal waters, marine resource exploitation and nature conservation, coastal hazards and institutional problems. These connect closely to the core indicators given in the second-round questionnaire except for institutional problems, which are an interesting extension to the list of problem pressures on coastal zones.

The chapter outlines the reasons for adopting a strategy for conservation and sustainable management of coastal zones at EU level with reference to 'The Golden Fringe of Europe' document and defines tasks that can best be undertaken at EU level. It then gives examples of actions needed to address the five categories of problems given above but stresses that for these actions to be most effective the finer details of the actions can only be defined on a case-by-case basis because of the varying characteristics of problems between different regions.

Cardosa da Silva concludes by looking at environmental indicators within the pressure–state–response model, explaining their use as a tool for decision-makers and for assessing the effectiveness of policies. It is pointed out that the process of reaching agreement on standard indicators for coastal zones in Europe is a long and difficult one. This is partly due to information availability and compatibility problems, but also to the different characteristics of coastal zones across Europe.

5.   INTERNATIONAL FRAMEWORK

Responsibility for coastal management has historically rested with regional and national authorities, and this has not generally been based on an integrated view of coastal zone management. International progress in this area has been slow; however, as stated above, Professor Coccossis draws attention to the integrated approach taken by the 5EAP. Other important international and European coastal zone management initiatives have often been related to specific issues and have not embraced an integrated approach:

- Helsinki Convention on the Protection of the Marine Environment of the Baltic Sea Area (1974 and 1992) (HELCOM);
- Oslo Convention for the Prevention of Marine Pollution by Dumping from Ships and Aircraft (1974) and Paris Convention for the Protection of the Marine Environment of the North East Atlantic (1978) (OSPAR);

- Barcelona Convention for the Protection of the Mediterranean Sea against Pollution (1975). Under this convention the Mediterranean Action Plan has been developed, which includes a series of legally binding treaties, establishing a pollution monitoring and research network and a socio-economic programme for sustainable development. The Barcelona convention also has four related protocols related to dumping from ships and aircraft, pollution from land-based sources, pollution emergencies, and endangered species in marine and coastal areas;
- European Coastal Charter, established in 1981 at the Conference of Peripheral Maritime regions of the EEC;
- Joint Declaration on the Protection of the Wadden Sea, adopted in 1982 by Germany, The Netherlands and Denmark;
- North Sea Task Force established in 1988;
- Convention for the Protection of the Black Sea (1992).

There has also been a number of resolutions and directives adopted by the Council of Europe in the last 25 years. These include council directives on the quality of bathing water (1975), the quality required for shellfish (1979), the conservation of wild birds (1979), Environmental Impact Assessment (1985), and the conservation of natural habitats and wild flora and fauna (1992). Relevant council resolutions include: Resolution 29 of the Committee of Ministers on the protection of coastal zones (1973), Resolution of Planning Ministers on coastal areas (1983), Resolution on integrated management of coastal zones (1992) and the 5EAP (1993).[3]

NOTES

1. See Editors' introduction (first questionnaire: December 1995; second questionnaire: October 1996).
2. Fifth Environmental Action Programme (EU). See Annex IV.
3. See details on targets set at European level on TEPI Web page (http://e-m-a-i-l.nu/tepi/ what's new/the documents/download example).

REFERENCES

CEC (1993), *Towards Sustainability*, Fifth Environmental Action Programme (Luxembourg: Commission of the European Communities).
EEA (1995), *Europe's Environment: The Dobříš Assessment* (Copenhagen: European Environment Agency).

13. Coastal zone and marine area pressures

H. Coccossis

1. INTRODUCTION

Coastal areas are extremely valuable as they concentrate a rich diversity of natural habitat areas and a large variety of natural resources (Carter, 1988). As the interface area between land and sea, coastal areas are extremely important and fragile from an ecological perspective and should be carefully managed.

Coastal areas also provide opportunities for the development of a wide range of human activities, either exploiting local resources (for example fishing, recreation and so on) or taking advantage of favourable locations near the sea (mild climate, break of bulk transport and access to sea routes and so on). As a result there is an increasing concentration of people in such areas (WCED, 1987). These concentrations of population and activities present considerable threats to coastal ecosystems and resources. Four major categories of impacts can be identified.

First, there is an impact on the structure and function of natural ecosystems as a result of the construction and operation of facilities for human activities, and the associated development. This impact can be either direct, through loss of vital habitat areas or pollution, or indirect, for example, through noise or the presence of people.

A second impact is on the quality and quantity of natural resources (forests, soil, water and so on) as a result of increasing concentration of people and activities adding to the demand for their use and exploitation, and increasing disposal of waste.

A third category of impact is on land use, in terms of the spatial organization and function of the area as a consequence of the development of human activities and associated facilities, infrastructure and urban development.

Finally, there is an impact on the natural and man-made landscape as a result of the size and scale of facilities and associated development. The landscape can be a major tourist attraction.

From the above it is evident that the ecological and socio-economic importance of coastal areas extends beyond a narrow geographical strip along the coastline.

2. COASTAL ZONE(S)

The spatial extent of coastal areas depends on physical geographical factors (geomorphology, hydrology and so on), ecological factors (terrestrial and marine ecosystems), human activities and uses of land (type and intensity of development), as well as on institutional factors (administrative and legal framework regulating development and use of space).

From a management perspective, depending on the physical, ecological, human activity and development characteristics, several zones can be identified in coastal areas. These are, first, a critical zone or a narrow band of land and sea a few hundred metres wide, adjacent to the shoreline, usually of highest ecological value and subject to intense pressures for development. Second, there is a dynamic zone, which may extend inland and seaward, usually a few kilometres wide, where there is strong dependence and/or influence of human activities and natural processes on coastal features and resources. Third, a wider zone of influence can be identified, often several kilometres wide which influences in part, directly or indirectly, the other two zones.

3. COASTAL IMPACTS

Environmental deterioration can have a significant impact on the development prospects of coastal areas. Conflicts over the use of coastal resources, threats to natural habitat areas, pollution and resource degradation seriously affect the potential of coastal areas to support human activities (Table 13.1). The long-term future of coastal areas depends on a rational management of resources within the framework of ecologically sustainable economic development.

In the future these areas are likely to face increasing pressures, particularly on habitats, natural resources (land, water and energy) and infrastructures (transport and wastewater treatment facilities). Fishing, agriculture, industry, tourism, transport and urbanization are major forces of change.

Among the activities of the primary sector *fishing* is certainly the one that is tied to coastal locations. Although coastal (near-shore) fishing is gradually declining in relative importance in the European and world economy, it still has significant impacts on coastal marine resources, mainly due to overfishing or the following of certain practices, in most cases illegal, such as the use of small-size nets or dynamite. Another aspect of the fishing sector which has potentially negative impacts on the environment is *aquaculture*, which could compete for the use of sea space with other uses, mainly recreation, but also with traditional fishing activities, industry and so on. The impacts from

Table 13.1   Coastal impacts

Activity	Resource base	Effects	Impacts	Consequences
Fishing	Fish	Fish population	Depletion	
Agriculture	Land	Use of land	Open space reduction	Terrestrial ecosystem degradation Soil productivity decline
	Water	Use of water	Depletion Salinization	Scarcity Soil productivity decline
	Fertilizers/pesticides	Run-off	Pollution/eutrophication	Marine ecosystem degradation Fish productivity decline Loss of recreation opportunities
Industry	Land	Use of land Solid waste	Open space reduction Pollution	Terrestrial ecosystem degradation Terrestrial ecosystem degradation Underground water degradation Loss of recreation opportunities
	Material extraction	Aesthetics	Landscape degradation	Scarcity
	Water	Use of water	Depletion Pollution	Ecosystem degradation Loss of recreation, agriculture and fishing opportunities
Transport	Land/seawater	Use of space	Open space reduction	Disturbance of ecosystems
Tourism	Land/seawater	Use of space Wastes	Open space reduction Pollution	Terrestrial ecosystem degradation Ecosystem degradation Loss of recreation opportunities
	Public works	Use of land	Shoreline alterations	Coastal erosion

aquaculture installations are not restricted to the use of sea space but also include possible pollution from excessive use of fishfood, a problem which can be particularly important in enclosed bays, estuaries and the like.

The role of *agriculture* in changing coastal environments is indirect and primarily affects the dynamic and wider zones. Changes in agricultural practices (modernization and crop restructuring) affect the management of rural areas with possible impacts on the extent and intensity of the use of land (abandonment, conflicts with other uses or even over-utilization). This affects mostly open space and natural areas, but also both the use of coastal resources, that is, freshwater and soil (abandonment, depletion or degradation) or pollution from excessive use of fertilizers and pesticides, and the quality of the marine environment as a result of agricultural run-off.

The impacts of *industry* on coastal areas can be direct or indirect. Direct impacts refer to pollution problems at the site level, affecting underground water resources and the marine environment, in most cases through effluent emissions. Indirect impacts relate to the attraction or 'repulsion' that local industries (mostly the large-scale plants) have for other industries (economies of agglomeration) or activities (economies of urbanization), ultimately leading to concentration and urban development on the coast. The siting of agro-industries, refineries, thermal power plants and metallurgical and chemical complexes on the shore or on nearby up-river locations are potential threats to seawater quality. Land-use conflicts might also arise in this context as a result of locational incompatibilities.

The various facilities for sea *transport* (fishing, commercial, industrial ports or some special-purpose terminals) requiring coastal locations can also affect the marine environment through pollution or as a result of the coastal engineering works required. Coastal habitats can be severely affected due to loss of vital space and changes in coastal processes (water flow, sediment transport and so on).

Coastal *tourism* is strongly seasonal and is becoming increasingly intensive. This results in reduction of natural sites and open space, substantial alterations of coastal landscapes and conflicts over the use of land, water and other resources. These adverse effects are further exacerbated by the associated indirect effects of tourism-related urban development for trade, transport facilities, vacation houses, infrastructure, residences for those working in the tourism sector and so on. Recreation and leisure activities can also have adverse impacts on coastal ecosystems due to physical effects (for example trampling effects on sand-dune vegetation) or disturbances (noise and so on) from human presence. Pressures on the coastal zones are likely to increase in the future. It is estimated, for example, that coastal tourism-related development in the Mediterranean could double in 20 years (Batisse and Grenon, 1989). By far the largest share of such growth is expected within the parts of the European Union (EU) Member States which are already established as major destination areas.

The impacts of *urban development* on coastal resources include the following:

- the loss of natural habitat areas due to reduction of vital space, or pollution and waste disposal;
- the decline in biodiversity of species, ecosystems and interspecies variation as a result of losses in habitat areas;
- coastal erosion or accumulation as a result of marine engineering works to provide additional land for new facilities or to protect existing installations and facilities;
- the loss of forest land due to urban expansion and related hazards (forest fires);
- the decline in the quantity and quality of drinking water resources, and the increase in sea pollution as a result of waste disposal.

4. COASTAL MANAGEMENT

Coastal areas are characterized by complex patterns of interaction between natural and human ecosystems. Therefore, their problems are extremely complex to manage. An integrated approach is necessary whereby environmental management is incorporated in socio-economic and physical development planning (Coccossis, 1985). Such an approach requires strong coordinating mechanisms to ensure a balance between environmental conservation, economic efficiency and social equity in the framework of sustainable development.

There are several 'actors' who influence or have an interest in coastal areas and who have a multitude of goals and perspectives on their use and protection. In addition, administrative boundaries often transcend natural areas and functional regions. As a result there are considerable conflicts, overlaps and gaps in managing the coasts. In spite of some developed planning and management systems, there is a need for special attention and better coordination to manage coastal areas. Quite often the basic mechanisms exist, but what is lacking is a coordinating policy which links environmental protection to development policy, and seeks intersectoral coordination as well as coordination between the various geographical levels of administrative authority (local, regional and so on).

The multitude of interests in coastal resource use imposes the need to mobilize all those concerned through a participatory process of policy-making. In most cases the initiative of coastal management rests with regional or national authorities due to their statutory coordinating role (OECD, 1993). However, there is increasing concern that coordination should also be sought at other levels. The importance of developing an integrated policy for coastal management has already been asserted at EU level in the basic document of the Fifth Environmental Action Programme, *Towards Sustainability* (CEC, 1993).[1] On the basis of these guidelines, the Commission has prepared a communication on the management of coastal areas. The basic reasons for this EU approach are that there are problems in coastal areas which transcend national boundaries (that is, pollution, fish stock depletion, natural habitat areas and so on), there are EU policies which have an impact on coastal areas (agriculture, fishing, energy, Structural Fund interventions and so on), and the problems are of common interest, so it is beneficial to communicate at this level.

5. COASTAL MANAGEMENT ACTION PLAN

Once the necessity for coastal management is accepted, a plan of action can be adopted (at various spatial levels) to improve policy coordination in related matters. By its very nature coastal management is a process involving several actors, in the context of democratic policy planning, seeking better coordination of their actions (UNEP/MAP/PAP, 1995). Its character is basically anticipatory, although in the short term it can be of a predominantly corrective nature. The preparation of such a plan for most practical purposes can be considered to consist of a series of interlocking phases with strong feedback mechanisms. Such phases include the following.

Problem Identification

This is one of the most important activities as it sets the framework for the ones which follow and determines the scope (content and extent) of management. Information on the state of the environment is an essential component, as is information on the dynamics of the man–environment interface (trends, processes, assessment of impacts and so on). Information should extend not only to the state of the natural and man-made environment but also to existing actions (policies, plans, programmes, authority statutes and the like) as part of an assessment of the problems, constraints and opportunities in the coastal zone(s). An identification of the 'zone(s)' for management is essential at this stage.

Definition of Goals and Objectives

On the basis of the 'problems' (state of the coast) identified earlier, goals, objectives and targets can be identified. These can be in quantitative and qualitative terms.

Development of Strategy

Goals, objectives and targets can be linked into a coherent set of actions. This stage essentially includes the mobilization and allocation of resources (natural, human, financial, organizational and so on) to ameliorate coordination among interested 'actors' in coastal areas with a view to manage coastal resources in a rational way according to the principles of sustainable development. Actions can be regulatory (zoning, building regulations, prohibitions, standards, land use and the like), organizational (for example procedural), financial/economic instruments (say incentives or taxation) or physical interventions (that is, infrastructure or superstructure).

Implementation

Essential to this phase is a monitoring and evaluation system which is the basis of a periodic review process for gradual adjustment and modification of policy-making.

In the preparation of a coastal zone management plan certain preliminary activities can be envisaged. These include improvement of communication and exchange of experiences on coastal management actions at various spatial levels, development of information systems on the state of the coastal environment (on a geographical basis), and improvement of review procedures for projects, plans and programmes dealing with the coastal zones (specification of Environmental Impact Assessment, Strategic Environmental Assessment and so on).

Other short-term actions can include establishing procedures to incorporate environmental management into development programmes, and the development of pilot programmes for coastal problems using an integrated planning approach, along with concrete sustainable actions for key problems such as beach erosion protection/management, coastal habitat management (linking water basin management with ecosystem protection and so on), and management of coastal tourist resorts in 'crisis'.

Further to this there should be development of innovative management tools and techniques for sustainable development. This involves establishing thresholds for development on the basis of local resources and infrastructure constraints, while upgrading capacities through organizational or technological means, visitor flow management programmes. 'Demonstration' programmes can be developed to solve environmental problems, for example establishing waste treatment facilities, cleaning the beaches, and restoring natural processes.

Finally, such preliminary actions should involve measures for raising public awareness. Existing plans and programmes should be reviewed and revised on the basis of the principles of sustainable development, controlling for negative impacts on the quality of the environment, and respecting critical resources and ecosystem functions.

A tentative list of principles applicable to the above framework for coastal management is set out in Figure 13.1.

- Coastal areas are unique and require a special management approach.

- Coastal management should concentrate on the coastline and the critical area of interface between land, water and air.

- Coastal management should include an area on the seaside and an area on the landward side.

- The geographical boundaries of the area for coastal management should respect the function of coastal ecosystems and could reflect administrative boundaries as well.

- Special emphasis should be put on the protection of common-use resources such as the shore area and so on.

- Protection from natural hazards should be taken into consideration and combined with the protection of coastal resources.

- The approach to the development of the coastal areas should reflect and respect the functioning of natural ecosystems.

- A multiple use of coastal resources could be a good basis for coastal management.

- Traditional means to manage coastal resources should be incorporated to the extent possible in the coastal management scheme.

- Special forms of estimated costs and benefits of actions should be considered to incorporate the need to sustain the use of resources.

Figure 13.1 Principles for coastal management

6. COASTAL MANAGEMENT DECISION SUPPORT SYSTEM

Policy coordination is essential for coastal management. Key to effective coordination is a coherent strategy in which objectives are clearly stated and expressed in interrelated policy interventions (actions). As coastal management is a multi-objective and multi-actor policy activity based on consensus, communication and clear statement of scope and purpose is crucial. Information is therefore an essential component in coastal management. It is necessary for identifying problems (state of the environment), targeting actions, monitoring progress towards desired goals and periodic reviewing and revision of policies. Thus an information system is central to coastal management.

Given the strong spatial character of coastal problems (land–sea interface, different geographic scales of natural processes, different spatial distribution of human activities, fragmented interests and multiple authorities and so on) a coastal information system should be able to discriminate spatial distribution of phenomena and problems. Therefore a geographic information system is appropriate.

An essential aspect of any information system for effective management is clarity and simplicity. However, in coastal areas there are complex patterns of interactions between natural and human ecosystems occurring at varying scales and intensity in space and time. Summarizing a multitude of aspects and phenomena, and linking natural and human (socio-economic) phenomena is essential, and requires a set of indicators and/or indices.

As there is a multitude of interests and management objectives, a coastal geographic information system should reflect such concerns as much as possible, in order to link cross-impacts. Although some interactions are measurable (therefore quantifiable), a number of linkages and phenomena can only be expressed in a qualitative manner. Both kinds of information should be included.

Two basic types of information are essential for effective management: on the state of the system and measurable policy outcomes. The latter should preferably relate to the former in order to monitor and evaluate policy achievements. Information on the state of the system can concentrate on key coastal characteristics (resource capacities, ecosystem structure and so on) and problems/pressures (for example demands and conflicts). Policy objectives should relate to coastal characteristics but be expressed in terms of problems. A coastal management information system could therefore have a set of pressure indicators at its core. Outcomes can be expressed in terms of the achievement of objectives. However, as both direct and indirect effects are quite important, an impact evaluation system should be considered, forming the basis for linking policy outcomes and the state of the environment.

The above outline is in general terms a coastal management information system which can be developed into a coastal management decision support system if additional information on lines of responsibility and rules of procedure is included.

Expressing coastal issues in terms of a set of pressure indicators is important because it can raise awareness and support for coastal management action by improving communication and understanding on coastal issues. It can help focus public policy on key aspects by eliminating the complexities involved. It can build support among decision-makers and lead to better interagency coordination by concentrating on linkages. In the context of shared responsibility it can help the public understand complex issues and provide a context for support and action.

At a European policy level, in particular, it can lead to the development of a common policy (guidelines, action programmes and so on) for coastal management by providing a common frame of reference (pressures). Thus a common set of pressure indicators can lead to an understanding that problems are common, beyond the particularities of each area or region, to the development of common policy frameworks for similar contexts and to facilitation of communication of experiences in successful coastal management practices.

NOTE

1. See terminology in Annex IV.

REFERENCES

Batisse, M. and M. Grenon (1989), *Futures of the Mediterranean Basin*, Blue Plan Scenarios (Oxford: Oxford University Press).

Carter, R.W.G. (1988), 'Coastal Environments: An Introduction to Physical, Ecological and Cultural Systems of Coastlines' (London: Academic Press).

CEC (Commission of the European Communities) (1993), *Towards Sustainability* Fifth Environmental Action Programme (Luxembourg: CEC).

Coccossis, H. (1984), 'Coastal Management as Public Policy', in D. Hall, N. Margaris and N. Myers (eds), *Proceedings of the International Symposium on Economics of Ecological Management* (The Hague: W. Junk).

Coccossis, H. (1985), 'Management of Coastal Regions: the European Experience', *Nature and Resources* (UNESCO journal on environmental affairs), **XXI** (1), 20–28.

OECD (Organization for Economic Cooperation and Development) (1993), *Coastal Zone Management Integrated Policies*, (Paris: OECD).

UNEP/MAP/PAP (United Nations Environment Programme/Mediterranean Action Plan/Priority Actions Programme) (1995), *Guidelines for Integrated Management*

of Coastal and Marine Areas (with special reference to the Mediterranean basin) (Split, Croatia: PAP).
WCED (World Commission on Environment and Development) (1987), *Our Common Future* (Oxford: Oxford University Press).

14. Pressure indicators in coastal zones

M. Cardoso da Silva

1. INTRODUCTION – COASTAL ZONE PROBLEMS

Coastal zones are known to be of a high ecological, social and economic value. As an interface between land and sea, the coastal zone is, by definition, a unique and fragile resource with a crucial role in the maintenance of a natural equilibrium based on sea–land exchanges. It also has a strategic role in the support of social and economic activities. In addition, the coastal zone has an irreplaceable recreation and leisure function for people living outside the area.

A large proportion of the world population lives in the coastal zone. This, together with the unique characteristics of the area and the unusually high diversity of natural resources, creates a potential for a great diversity of activities and for great associated pressures on this zone.

The urgency to create mechanisms that harmonize the need for economic development on the one hand and the need to preserve the natural resources of the coastal zone on the other, is generally recognized. These mechanisms should constitute a coastal zone management system based on the concepts of ecologically sustainable development and on the rational use of ecosystems, as defined by the third meeting of the contracting parties to the RAMSAR Convention on Wetlands of International Importance especially related to Waterfowl Habitat.

In the early 1980s, the Conference for the Peripheral Maritime Regions of Europe (1981) identified a set of problems and, at the same time, proposed methodologies for better use and, simultaneously, protection of the coastal zone – or the littoral. Those issues were assembled in the European Charter of the Littoral. A more recent study (OECD, 1992) identified more or less the same problems, showing that, although a decade separated the two occasions, there had not been movement towards solving these problems or towards a decrease in the existing pressures. Therefore there had been little progress towards a sustainable use of the coastal zone.

As a result of the human pressure both inland and in the coastal zone itself, coastal and marine ecosystems and resources are rapidly deteriorating in many parts of the world, not least in Europe. Urban, industrial, tourist and agricultural development projects are modifying the coastal ecosystems on a very large scale. Human pressure is increasing every year, with some regions supporting significant and continuing population increases, both permanent and seasonal.

In general terms, the problems identified can be categorized under the following headings:

- Urban encroachment into the coastal zone
- Pollution of estuarine and coastal waters
- Marine resources exploitation and nature conservation
- Coastal hazards
- Institutional problems.

Urban Encroachment into the Coastal Zone

Environmental problems from unmanaged urbanization are apparent in many coastal zones and there is growing awareness of the adverse environmental impact of intensified industrial development concentrated in coastal locations. Furthermore, the rapid growth of seasonal pressure in countries with major tourism industries has outstripped the capacity of infrastructure, resulting in serious local or regional environmental problems.

Pollution of Estuarine and Coastal Waters

Significant pollution problems in the coastal zone are faced in many countries. The most striking problems are those connected with the input of toxic substances and oil, eutrophication and bacteriological contamination.

Marine Resources Exploitation and Nature Conservation

Over-exploitation of traditional fishing grounds in such a way that stocks have been virtually eliminated, as well as the impact of the current fishing techniques (for example disturbance or destruction of benthos by bottom trawling) are frequently cited as serious problems. Furthermore, the ecological impacts of poorly integrated coastal zone management go beyond the direct effects on fish and shellfish. In several areas, there are increasing and irreversible losses of wildlife habitat, including mangrove swamps, dunes and wetlands.

Coastal Hazards

The hazards of flooding or erosion are cited by many countries as problems, especially in the context of the possible longer-term threat of expected sea-level rise resulting from climate change (IPCC, 1990, 1991 and 1992).

Institutional Problems

The difficulties faced by governments in coping with conflicting demands in the coastal zone are well known. It is recognized that coastal zone management includes not only science, but also the integration of political aspects and transformation of the institutional set-up, including legal and administrative arrangements. This means that a coastal zone management system, although based on rather general scientific and technical principles, cannot easily be generalized due to the fact that it depends to a large extent upon the social, economic and political circumstances in each country. Even cultural differences play a role in this.

2.   POLICY ISSUES

Political activity recognizing coastal zone problems, their severe consequences for both the aquatic and the terrestrial environment, and thus their possible effects on human activities and the specific ecological values of the coast, first started at European level. A synthesis of policy statements, decisions and issues pertaining to coastal zone protection and management is given in 'The Golden Fringe of Europe' (EUCC, 1991).

This chapter presents ideas on conservation and rational use of Europe's coastal zones, and suggests a strategy and action plan as a framework for the adequate conservation of the ecological and cultural resources of these zones.

EU Context

Coastal zone management is not restricted to national issues or national policy responses. There are several aspects of coastal management such as water quality and pollution management, monitoring of migratory and endangered species, and impacts of activities such as shipping, oil drilling, exploitation of living marine resources and international tourism that go beyond national perspectives and boundaries. It is therefore clear that no single programme or action of a national government or agency can resolve the wide range of issues that need to be addressed in the context of European coastal zones. Governments of the EU must work both individually and collaboratively to ensure the sustainable development of European coastal zones.

The reasons for defining a strategy for the conservation and sustainable management of coastal zones at European Union level are presented in the aforementioned paper (EUCC, 1991) as follows:

- The fact that European coastal zones form a coherent ecological system (e.g. for bird migration);
- The similarity in the problems facing the natural environment of the European coastline, while taking into consideration the specific character of problems of the various countries and regions;
- The European, sometimes even global, scale of many of these problems, and their clear cross-border character;
- The need to more explicitly take into account the vulnerabilities of the coastal environment in EC policies, especially in regional and agricultural policies;
- The opportunities to stimulate the Member States of the EU into coastline management, the exchange of information and experience, and co-operation on coastal conservation and management within an EU framework;
- The high potential of an EU environmental policy on coastal conservation and management;
- The need for a strong role for the EU in other relevant international fora dealing with coastal conservation and management.

Thus coastal zone management and conservation in the EU context may be perceived to operate at four different levels:

1. at the EU level itself
2. at regional level (for example, in the Mediterranean, the North Sea, the Wadden Sea and the Baltic Sea)
3. at national level, that is, in the national coastal zone management programmes in the Member States
4. at local level, that is, the sub-national programmes (for example, the Lagoon of Venice in Italy, the Hampshire coastal management programme in the United Kingdom, and the Eastern Scheldt estuary programme in The Netherlands).

In this structure experiences gained from local-level projects can serve to strengthen the national-level programmes and experiences from the national programmes can be used to build the regional programmes and the EU coastal zone management strategy.

A top-down approach must also be considered, whereby a coastal zone management strategy, defined at EU level, will provide the framework for coastal zone management strategies and plans to be implemented at the lower (country, regional, local) levels.

The definition of the tasks to be performed at each level should take into account the principle of subsidiarity. The following are examples of tasks that should be dealt with at EU level:

- definition of objectives, time schedules for implementation, establishment of the possible means and procedures for achieving objectives;
- definition of the tasks for the various agents involved, including the European Commission, Member States, regional authorities and non-governmental organizations;
- formulation of guidelines for Member States to draw up national conservation strategies and action plans for coastal zone management;
- assisting Member States in the preparation of national conservation strategies and action plans;
- establishment of additional funds for the support of the implementation of the national conservation strategies and action plans by Member States and the operation of awareness programmes.

At Member State level the tasks may include:

- formulation of national conservation strategies and action plans within a given period;
- designation of organizational structures in order to ensure the overall coordination and implementation of the necessary measures;
- implementation of conservation plans and related management activities within the framework of these strategies and action plans;
- application of environmental impact assessment procedures for economic projects which may significantly affect the ecological aspects of the coastal zone;
- reporting to the European Commission about the state of the implementation of the national strategies and action plans;
- monitoring the state of the environment by a set of ecological and economic parameters (indicators).

3.   ACTIONS TO REDUCE PRESSURE ON COASTAL ZONES

After identifying the main types of problem affecting coastal zones, it is necessary to define integrated management action plans and conservation policies. This requires the identification of concrete examples of actions that may contribute to the resolution of such problems and reduce the existing pressures on the coastal zone.

Examples of such actions have been proposed by several organizations. The Council of Europe (Albanese, 1991), in a resolution of the Council of Ministers of 1985, outlines some types of initiative for reducing pressures on the coastal zones and improving their environment. Some of these initiatives are as follows:

- Studies of the coastal environment
- Creation of special protection zones
- Collaboration in the case of natural or man-made accidents
- Raising public awareness and public participation
- Financing of some conservation actions.

These are very general types of action and the definition of the details of the most effective forms of intervention can only be done on a case-by-case basis. This is because the categories of problem identified above as those most commonly affecting the coastal area have a completely different relevance for each particular area. For example, urban encroachment and the human pressure associated with the seasonal tourism industry have a greater relevance in Southern Europe. Emission of toxic substances from industrial sources, as well as the occurrence of oil spills from maritime traffic accidents, are stronger pressures on the coasts of Northern European countries, where industrial development is more intense.

Examples of actions that may contribute to the alleviation of the problems of coastal zones are given below. They are presented under the general problem categories outlined in section 1 of this chapter.

Urban Encroachment into the Coastal Zone

Under this heading two different types of actions can be identified: first, the preservation of zones that are still undeveloped, and second, the improvement of zones already experiencing the problems of urban encroachment.

Land-use planning and the implementation of appropriate limitations to urbanization and building are the most common instruments available to regulate this kind of human pressure on the coastal zone. Recommended actions include the classification of zones with particularly sensitive habitats as natural reserves and the restriction of common access for motorized vehicles in these zones. However, in some tourist areas urban encroachment has reached such a level that it has caused the destruction of the natural beauty or other characteristics that first attracted the tourists.

Pollution of Estuarine and Coastal Waters

Most of the actions aimed at pollution abatement, in general, and with particular relevance to estuaries and coastal zones, are defined in the European legislation. The technical actions required, for example, by the directive on urban wastewater, the directive on dangerous substances and 'daughter' directives, have particular relevance in this context.

Research is still needed on the development of clean production methods and improved waste water treatment technologies. Study is also needed on the hydrodynamic and chemical processes of the coastal zones and estuaries in order better to assess their assimilation capacity and thus improve the design and location of pollution discharge systems. However, a great improvement in the ecological quality of coastal systems could simply be achieved by more stringent application of the existing EU regulation, and the recommendations and decisions of international conventions on the reduction of marine pollution (for example the Paris, Helsinki and Barcelona Conventions).

Marine Resources Exploitation and Nature Conservation

Among the most obvious measures to achieve a sustainable exploitation of biotic marine resources are the use of appropriate fishing techniques and the setting of quotas in conjunction with the establishment of restricted fishing zones and periods in order to give protection in the spawning season and nursery periods.

The exploitation of other natural resources may lead to other problems; for example, the extraction of sand in some estuarine and coastal areas may lead to the destruction of habitats. Morpho-dynamic loss of equilibrium may mean that there are also effects away from the location of the exploitation itself, such as an increase in erosion of sand beaches or the enhanced exposure to natural eroding agents of sensitive dune or sedimentary cliff systems.

Coastal Hazards

The measures to reduce the risk of coastal hazards such as flooding and erosion, either associated with episodic meteorological events or long-term sea-level rise, are strongly connected to areas of human occupation on the coast. Occupation of dune systems can lead to their destruction, by exposing them to the devastating effects of the sea from which they previously had a natural protection. The zoning and other land-use rules are among the most promising actions for effectively contributing to the decrease of the harmful effects of these problems.

Institutional Problems

It is recognized that there is a strong positive relationship between a well-organized, integrated, legal and institutional framework and efficient policy development and implementation.

4. ENVIRONMENTAL INDICATORS FOR THE ASSESSMENT OF COASTAL ZONES

Decision-makers at all levels are facing increasingly complex policy choices. Objective, systematic and quantitative information on the state, development and use of coastal zones is needed to support and evaluate policies. These needs often cannot be met from existing data collections and current analytical techniques.

Difficulties in assessing the effects of alternative policy measures or implemented programmes are not only due to a shortage of scientific information. They also arise from the need to present the results of research and monitoring in a practical context which can be used by policy-makers and the general public.

So-called environmental indicators (see, for example, Ten Brink et al., 1991; Environment Canada, 1991; Cardoso da Silva et al., 1993) provide a possible assessment system to aid decision-makers. These indicators should, on the one hand, give information on the condition of the system under study and, on the other, have a political value by providing a basis for setting policy objectives and a means of measuring the progress towards meeting these objectives. They should also be easily understood by the general public.

The construction of a system of indicators for sustainability based on the pressure–state–response model is becoming widely accepted and adopted (see, for example, OECD, 1993; WRI, 1994; UNEP, 1994). In the context of this model a proper assessment of the pressures exerted on a coastal zone, its state and changes in response to management activities, should be made on the basis of quantified objectives for the selected indicators. Essential elements in this respect are a set of reference values and target objectives for these indicators.

In practical terms this means setting as an overall goal that the status of the coastal and marine ecosystems best guarantees sustainable development. It is believed that a system which has not, or has only slightly, been influenced by human activities offers this guarantee. Such a system is called the reference. The setting of this reference level (in terms of quantitative values assigned to the selected indicators) is not, of course, an easy task. Nevertheless, it may be possible to define it for selected systems, with a reasonable degree of approximation, in a pragmatic way on the basis of literature and old inventories (Cardoso da Silva and Wetering, 1992).

It is then up to the political level to set objectives for the indicators which will, in essence, be a balance between the economic costs of the measures needed to reach the objectives and the loss of guaranteed sustainable development in the longer term. In general an objective will be set somewhere between the actual level of the indicators and the reference level. There will, of course, be a difference depending on the nature of the area. A nature reserve will get a higher level of protection than an industrial harbour.

By comparing the actual situation before policy implementation and its temporal evolution with the objectives set, the effectiveness of a policy can be judged and the need for changes in policy measures decided.

Table 14.1 Indicators for characterization of the coastal zone

Category	Type of indicator	Examples
Ecosystem quality	Chemical	Dissolved oxygen level
		Nutrient concentration in water
		Toxic substances in sediments and biota
	Biological	Productivity
		Populations diversity
		Population of selected species
		Area of shellfish beds
Physiographic	Morphology	Wetland and sand dunes area
		Bank morphology change
		Sedimentation/erosion rates
	Hydrography	Freshwater flows
		Salt intrusion
		Currents
Health		Fish diseases
		Reproductiveness of sea mammals
Economic and social	Recreational use	Number of bathers
		Number of recreational boats
		Sport fishing
	Urban use	Population/building density
		Industrial area
	Harbour activity	Commercial fisheries
		Loading/unloading
		Volume of dredging

Selection of Indicators

Table 14.1 includes broad categories, types and examples of indicators that can be used in the characterization of the coastal zone. The indicators given for ecosystem quality are examples of state indicators, whereas those given for economic and social factors are examples of pressure indicators.

The experience of the Oslo and Paris Commission shows that the process of getting agreement on the type and values of indicators can take some years, due to the different characteristics of coastal zones in Europe, lack of available information and the non-comparability of information.

The final list of indicators should be decided upon in a very systematic and careful way, in a process jointly undertaken by scientists and policy-makers. It should take into account the specific characteristics and problems to be addressed in the coastal zone of interest.

REFERENCES

Albanese, F. (1991), *Les Initiatives du Conseil de L'Europe en Faveur des Zones Cotières*. Proceedings of the European Coastal Conservation Conference, EUCC, Scheveningen, The Hague, The Netherlands, November 1991.

Cardoso da Silva, M. and B. van de Wetering (1992), 'Sustainable Management of Coastal Zones', International Conference on the Pearl River Estuary in the Surrounding Area of Macao, Macao, October 1992.

Cardoso da Silva, M., L. de Vrees and J.M. Medina Vilaverde (1993), 'Scoping Study on Integrated Environmental Assessment of Coastal Areas' (draft). Study for the European Environmental Agency in the framework of the European Topic Centre for Coastal and Marine Environment, LNEC (National Laboratory for Civil Engineering), Lisbon, 1995.

Conference for the Peripheral Maritime Regions of Europe (1981), *European Coastal Charter*, Rennes, France.

Environment Canada (1991), 'A Report on Canada's Progress Towards a National Set of Environmental Indicators', a State of the Environment Report; SOE Report no. 91–1.

EUCC (1991), 'The Golden Fringe of Europe. Ideas for a European Coastal Conservation Strategy and Action Plan', Working Document, European Coastal Conservation Conference, Scheveningen, The Hague, November 1991.

IPCC (1990), *Strategies for Adaptation to Sea Level Rise*, Report of the IPCC Coastal Zone Management Subgroup, Rijkswaterstaat, The Netherlands.

IPCC (1991), 'Assessment of the Vulnerability of Coastal Areas to Sea Level Rise: A Common Methodology', revision no. 1, IPCC, Coastal Zone Management Subgroup.

IPCC (1992), *Global Climate Change and the Rising Challenge of the Sea*, Report of the IPCC Coastal Zone Management Subgroup, Rijkswaterstaat, The Netherlands.

OECD (1992), *Coastal Zone Management: Integrated Policies* (Paris: OECD).

OECD (1993), Draft Synthesis report, Group on the State of the Environment, Workshops on Indicators for Use in Environmental Performance Reviews.

RIKZ (1994), *Aggregation of Data in the Water Dialogue – A Management Decision Support System for Water Quality*, RIKZ/AB-94.152x, The Hague, The Netherlands.

Ten Brink, B.J.E., S.H. Hosper and F. Colijn (1991), 'A Quantitative Method for Description and Assessment of Ecosystems: the Amoeba Approach', *Marine Pollution Bulletin*, **23**: 265–70.

UNEP (1994), 'Scanning the Global Environment – A Framework and Methodology for UNEP's Reporting Functions', UNEP/EATR.94-(advanced draft).

WRI (1994), *Environmental Indicators*, World Resources Institute, Washington, DC.

PART V

Ozone Layer Depletion

15. Introduction

P.E.M. Lammers[1]

1. THE OZONE LAYER DEPLETION POLICY FIELD

Ozone is a naturally occurring gas in the atmosphere, and protects the earth against ultraviolet radiation from the sun. Emissions of human-made compounds containing chlorine or bromine, such as CFCs and halons, have severe impacts on the stratospheric ozone layer. The destruction of the ozone layer was first discovered in the 1970s. Any damage to the ozone layer leads to increased ultraviolet (UV-B) solar radiation. It has been demonstrated that increased UV-B radiation is harmful to human health and terrestrial and aquatic ecosystems, and also affects the climate system (UNEP, 1993; WMO, 1995). The following three chapters provide a thorough overview of the ozone depletion problem, current scientific knowledge and possible adverse effects on human health and ecosystems. Each of the chapters in this part of the volume has been written by a recognized expert in the field of Ozone Layer Depletion (see Introduction to the contributors).

2. RELATION TO OTHER POLICY FIELDS

As outlined in the following three chapters, and as noted in the climate change chapters (Chapters 5–8), the policy field of Ozone Layer Depletion is closely related to the policy field of Climate Change. Since ozone is a naturally occurring greenhouse gas, stratospheric ozone depletion will result in radiative cooling. However, since CFCs and halons are effective greenhouse gases, overall effects on global warming are difficult to estimate. Several of the greenhouse gases also affect stratospheric ozone depletion by stratospheric reactions or indirect temperature effects. Currently, the adverse effect of ozone-depleting substances on the stratospheric ozone layer is partly counteracted by emissions of greenhouse gases. In the future, however, greenhouse gas emissions may increase the occurrence of polar stratospheric clouds. This could significantly increase the destruction of the stratospheric ozone layer.

Emissions of ozone-depleting substances and greenhouse gases are thus important indicators for both the Ozone Layer Depletion and the Climate Change policy fields. However, the indicators for climate change only take account of the (potential) effects on global warming, and the indicators for ozone layer depletion only take the effects on the ozone layer into account.

Further, the Ozone Layer Depletion policy field has links to the field of Air Pollution. Visconti (Chapter 16) points out that tropospheric pollution (ozone and particles) in industrial regions has partly masked the effects of ozone depletion in these regions. Pressure indicators for tropospheric ozone and particles have been accounted for in the Air Pollution policy field.

3.   INTERNATIONAL FRAMEWORK

International Treaties

To tackle the problem of ozone depletion, the Framework Convention for the Protection of the Ozone Layer was adopted in 1985 in Vienna. The main objective of the Vienna Convention is cooperation between nations for scientific research. Although it provides the legal basis for emission reduction measures, no consensus could be reached at that time for specific reduction measures due to the considerable economic consequences and a lack of scientific understanding of the ozone problem. Soon afterwards research findings proved that an urgent need for measures existed, and the Montreal Protocol on Substances that Deplete the Ozone Layer was signed in 1987. This contained obligations for all parties to phase out the use of ozone-depleting substances by 1996. Later amendments and adjustments (London 1990, Copenhagen 1992, Vienna 1995) call for stricter measures and include more substances.

Research Activities

Besides national programmes, research on ozone depletion includes international programmes such as the stratospheric research activities by NASA (the US National Aeronautics and Space Administration), and the research of the EU in its Environment and Climate programme. The World Meteorological Organization (WMO) carries out periodic scientific assessments on ozone depletion. In 1988, several large chemical manufacturers started the Alternative Fluorocarbons Environmental Acceptability Study (AFEAS), a panel established to help resolve uncertainties regarding potential environmental effects of HCFCs and HFCs. The Chemical Manufacturing Association (also funded by NASA) has set up a reliable monitoring network for the production/consumption of ozone-depleting substances and their substitutes.

Science versus Policy-making

Scientific consensus on the risks associated with depletion of the stratospheric ozone layer turned out to be one of the major factors in the success of the Montreal Protocol. Visconti argues that at the time of the international negotiations, the risks were actually exaggerated, forcing agreement on the reduction of the production and consumption of ozone-depleting substances. In particular, the discovery of the ozone hole had an immense impact on the political process.

Although general consensus exists on the risks associated with the ozone depletion problem, policy-makers do not accept all scientific results. In his chapter Isaksen provides an overview of ozone depletion potential (ODP), a measure for the relative breakdown of the stratospheric ozone layer by the various ozone-depleting substances. The ODPs provided by Isaksen are taken from the latest Scientific Assessment of Ozone Depletion (1994) by the World Meteorological Organization, in collaboration with the United Nations Environment Programme (UNEP). However, the Conference of Parties of the Montreal Protocol did not formally accept these ODPs and maintains the earlier figures. Only the figure for methyl bromide has been adjusted, from 0.6 to 0.7 (as agreed at the seventh Conference of Parties, Vienna, 5–7 December 1995).[2]

Policy Interventions

The time scale of the ozone depletion problem is several decades, due to the long lifetime of the ozone-depleting substances. According to Isaksen, there is a delay of emissions reaching the stratosphere of about five years. Accordingly, atmospheric concentrations respond very slowly to changes in emissions.

The Montreal Protocol has had a significant impact on the emissions of ozone-depleting substances. According to Isaksen, the emissions of most CFCs, for example, were reduced by 30–65 per cent during the period 1988–92. Due to the delay of emissions reaching the stratosphere, stratospheric concentrations of bromide and chlorine are expected to reach a maximum around the year 2000, with a gradual decline thereafter. Chanin (Chapter 18) is more concerned about a full implementation of the Montreal Protocol, especially with regard to methyl bromide, which is used in agriculture.

4. OVERVIEW OF PRESSURE INDICATORS FOR OZONE LAYER DEPLETION

Figure 15.1 provides an overview of the key indicators for the Ozone Layer Depletion policy field. The selection of the indicators and corresponding scores are the results of the second-round expert questionnaire conducted for the Eurostat Pressure Indicators Project. The figure provides the ranking for each indicator on its policy relevance (the importance of the indicator for policy-makers), analytical soundness (the correlation between changes in the indicator and changes in environmental pressure), and responsiveness (the response of the indicator to policy actions, in other words: how easy it is to take action to substantially reduce the pressure indicator). The core ranking of the indicators is also presented, expressed as a percentage of experts who included the indicator in their top five list of essential indicators.

It should be noted that the scores on policy relevance, analytical soundness and responsiveness are relatively uniform and quite high for all indicators,

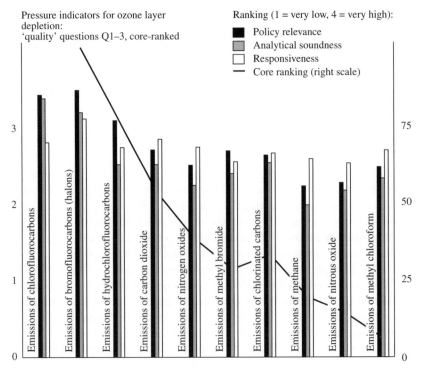

Figure 15.1   Results of second-round questionnaire for the Ozone Layer Depletion policy field

even for those indicators with a relatively low core ranking (meaning that they are not within the top five core indicators). Visconti argues that this may be explained by the fact that the scientific community is concerned about possible decreases in research funds. He suggests that by paying attention to all factors affecting the ozone layer, scientists aim to stress their importance and put pressure on governments for future research funding.

Visconti finds the inclusion of CFCs in the set of core indicators rather surprising, since the Montreal Protocol and its amendments call for a complete phase-out of these substances from 1 January 1996 onwards. This is also the case for carbon tetrachloride and methyl chloroform, as well as for halons (complete phase-out from 1 January 1994 onwards). Visconti states that he would have expected a core ranking based on an absolute level of chemical and radiative effects.

An indicator that will not change over time has no meaning as a core indicator to estimate the effects of current policy-making. On the other hand, the obligations of the Montreal Protocol allow for 'possible exemptions for essential uses', which still leads to substantial production and consumption figures. Moreover, a large black market exists for some ozone-depleting substances such as CFCs. According to Chanin, a large amount of CFCs are smuggled from the ex-USSR to Europe and the USA, coming second in a list of most-smuggled substances after drugs traffic. Visconti expects a black market for CFCs of about 10 000 tonnes, which is, however, still small if compared with the production figures of the 1990s (400 000 tonnes per year). Chanin feels that there is a great need for European integration, since all EU Member States have different control systems. Policy-makers take the problem of the black market seriously, and the Conference of Parties of the Montreal Protocol recently adopted resolutions aimed at a reduction of the black market.

Chanin is surprised by the relatively low score of methyl bromide, since this is currently a larger emission source than halons and HCFCs. To make such comparisons, the potential effects of the substances on the ozone layer, as expressed in their ODPs, also need to be taken into account.

The scores for policy relevance of the greenhouse gases are relatively high, even though any positive effects of greenhouse gases on the ozone layer are not long-term and are more than counteracted by the negative effects on climate change. The policy relevance of taking greenhouse gas emissions into account in an ozone layer depletion index is highly disputable. The effects of greenhouse gas emissions on the stratospheric ozone layer are currently positive because emissions of greenhouse gases counteract the breakdown of the ozone layer by ozone-depleting substances such as CFCs and halons. For a more detailed description of the effects of greenhouse gas emissions on the stratospheric ozone layer, see the chapter on ozone layer depletion in the

TEPI publication on *Indicator Definition*[3] and Velders (1997). Although green-house gases currently have positive effects on the ozone layer, emission reductions of greenhouse gases are needed to address the problem of climate change. It would be very confusing if reductions in emissions of greenhouse gases resulted in a lower climate change index and a higher ozone depletion index. Moreover, emissions of greenhouse gases are not beneficial to the ozone layer in the long run because they could contribute to a large break-down of the ozone layer, due to the formation of polar stratospheric clouds and other mechanisms (Velders, 1997).

Chanin states in her chapter that stratospheric cooling is only due to the decrease in stratospheric ozone concentrations, and that increased CO_2 concentrations do not play a role in the ozone depletion issue. However, CO_2 emissions are expected to be mainly responsible for a large decrease in stratospheric temperature in the twenty-first century, which can on the one hand reduce the effects of ozone-depleting substances, and on the other increase the formation of stratospheric clouds which might greatly increase the depletion of stratospheric ozone in the future (Velders, 1997).

Chanin adds a few important indicators; however, these are not included in Figure 15.1 since they are considered to be state indicators. They concern the total ozone change, the change of UV-B, and the time needed for recovery of the ozone layer. Further, she argues that for reasons of communication to the general public, the indicators should preferably be expressed in terms of change.

Emissions due to volcanic eruptions are not included as pressure indicators, since these are natural and not human-induced emissions.

5. DISCUSSION AND CONCLUSIONS

The indicators for ozone layer depletion are well defined and the consensus among scientists is relatively high. The following chapters discuss the best set of core indicators, and the relative importance of CFCs and methyl bromide.

The need for ozone depletion indicators is clearly described in all three chapters. One important argument for indicators is that they will enhance the feedback mechanisms between policy-makers and scientists.

An issue not yet addressed in the chapters is how to aggregate the indicators into one ozone layer depletion index. Partly, the concept of ozone depletion potentials can be used for this aggregation. However, the effects of greenhouse gas emissions on the ozone layer are not yet well understood, and these effects have not yet been fully quantified. The chapter on ozone depletion in the TEPI publication on *Indicator Definition* provides a more detailed discussion on the various aspects of aggregation.

NOTES

1. P.E.M. Lammers is senior researcher at the Institute for Environmental Studies (IVM), Vrije Universiteit, Amsterdam. The IVM has built up considerable experience in global environmental issues. It deals with a variety of complex environmental problems using multidisciplinary approaches. For more information, contact the IVM: De Boelelaan 1115, 1081 HV Amsterdam, The Netherlands, tel: 31-20-4449555, fax: 31-20-4449553, e-mail: secr@ivm.vu.nl, http://www.vu.nl/ivm.
2. The chapter on ozone layer depletion in the forthcoming publication on *Indicator Definition* (see Foreword) includes ODPs as agreed upon by the Conference of Parties of the Montreal Protocol.
3. See Foreword.

REFERENCES

UNEP (1993), *Action on Ozone* (Nairobi, Kenya: UNEP).

Velders (1997), *Effect of greenhouse gas emissions on stratospheric ozone depletion*, Report no. 722201 010. National Institute of Public Health and the Environment (RIVM), Bilthoven, Netherlands.

WMO (1995), *Scientific Assessment of Ozone Depletion: 1994*, Global Ozone Research and Monitoring Project Report no. 37 (Geneva: WMO).

16. Ozone depletion: the problem and the policy implications

G. Visconti

1. INTRODUCTION

The ozone depletion issue was first recognized in the early 1970s with the setting up of CIAP (Climatic Impact Assessment Program) promoted by the Department of Transportation of the US Government. The reason for establishing the programme was related to the assessment of the possible effects that a fleet of supersonic commercial planes could have on the ozone layer. During the development of the programme a discovery was made, which subsequently resulted in the award of the Nobel Prize in 1995,[1] that chlorine atoms produced in the photolysis of chlorofluorocarbons (CFCs) could destroy ozone.

Although this was prospectively an important declaration, it would have simply produced one more inconclusive assessment programme had it not been for the discovery in 1985 of the large ozone depletion occurring in the Antarctic stratosphere (popularly called the 'ozone hole'). In the same year the Vienna Convention was signed, followed two years later by the Montreal Protocol, which fixed for the first time a limit on the production of CFCs. These agreements reached a final form in 1992, with the Copenhagen amendments.

The international community for the first time reached an agreement to ban the industrial production at global level of a dangerous though useful product. This achievement is noteworthy because the ozone layer is something we cannot easily visualize or experience directly. The protocol, which included the possibility of producing alternative, less harmful products, was based on the assumption that a decrease in total ozone could have important consequences on the biosphere of the earth.

The relationship between ozone and the biosphere is through ultraviolet (UV) radiation. In a very limited range from 280 to 320 nanometres (nm), in what is called UV-B, solar radiation can be harmful to biological cells and therefore to plants and animals. The quantity of UV-B radiation reaching the surface of the earth depends critically on the amount of total ozone. Roughly a 1 per cent change in total ozone corresponds to a 1–2 per cent change in UV.

The international consensus on the measures to be taken to reduce the risks associated with ozone depletion was achieved with these consequences in mind. However, the way in which the ozone issue was largely solved may provide a clear example of how to proceed with other planetary emergencies. The danger related to a possible ozone reduction raised by the scientific community was somewhat exaggerated because the UV radiation has a large variability due to many factors which are still not fully understood. In fact, overstating the threat of ozone depletion was actually beneficial at the time because it has forced an early decision on the reduction of CFC production and its substitution. The effects of such measures are already visible, while the concentration of some of the chlorine-bearing gases is reaching a plateau and in the next few years will start decreasing. Present models show that global ozone will be at its minimum around the year 2000, with a roughly 4 per cent total decrease since 1980. As noted recently (Prather et al., 1996), without such an early decision ozone would have decreased by 10 per cent globally for the same period with a permanent ozone hole in the southern hemisphere. Such large changes would have seriously impacted not only the ultraviolet radiation reaching the surface of the earth, but possibly also the stratospheric circulation and the climate.

The present situation as far as ozone depletion is concerned seems to be largely solved. However, there still remain several aspects of the problem that are highly uncertain and some possible connections with the largely unpredictable global warming. A still more potentially serious threat is the surprise factor, in particular the possibility of unpredictable catastrophic volcanic eruptions. Therefore, while the chlorine levels remain relatively high there is always the possibility of large-scale ozone depletion.

2. HEALTH AND ENVIRONMENTAL EFFECTS

Ozone decrease is accompanied by an increase in the ultraviolet radiation at the surface of the Earth. UV radiation is harmful to the health of people and animals, and also to plants and aquatic life. We will distinguish between the human health impacts and all the other impacts, which we will call 'environmental'. The health impacts include different kinds of non-melanoma skin cancer and cutaneous malignant melanoma; cataracts; and changes in the immune system.

For skin cancer and malignant melanoma a mathematical formula is used to assess the fractional change in the incidence, given by (EPA, 1988):

$$F_i = (F_e + 1)^b - 1$$

where F_i is the fractional change in the incidence of the health effect, and
F_e is the fractional change in the UV flux reaching the surface.

The coefficient b is also referred to as the biological amplification factor or BAF. This coefficient depends on a number of parameters and is different for melanoma and non-melanoma.

Figure 16.1 shows superimposed the irradiance in UV and the erythemal action spectrum. The product of these two curves clearly shows that the action of the UV-B is concentrated around 308 and 310 nm. A change of 2 per cent in total ozone will affect very marginally the amount of radiation at the peak.

Figure 16.2 provides a rough idea of the variability of the incidence of skin diseases as a function of UV radiation. The figure shows that the incidence for a number of cases rises linearly with the increase in UV radiation. The changes in UV are within the range expected for the twenty-first century according to the results of accepted models for ozone depletion.

The basal and squamous skin cancers are the most curable, while melanoma can be lethal. In the USA about 800 000 cases of basal cell cancers are diagnosed every year, while the most serious melanoma is diagnosed in about 34 000 people. Melanomas are lethal in about 20 per cent of cases (Long et al., 1996). It is important to note that the incidence rate of melanoma has been increasing by 4 per cent per year for the last 25 years and simple calculations show that there will be millions of new cases of diagnosed diseases in the decades ahead due to ozone depletion. With the present models we can expect changes in the ozone column by the end of the century of between 4 and 8 per cent with respect to 1980 in the latitudinal zone between 40° and 60°N. This may roughly correspond to a change in UV radiation between 6 and 15 per cent, which is an average of less than 1 per cent per year until the year 2000. It is very hard to say whether the observed increase in melanoma and non-melanoma skin cancer observed in the USA is due to the ozone depletion of the last 25 years, but the expected changes in incidence are well within the variability. The observed increase in the incidence may be due to other changes in the environment, such as toxic chemicals or other teratogen substances. On the other hand, for the 15 years from 1979 to 1994 it is estimated that ozone has decreased by an average of 5 per cent per decade in the latitude band between 30° and 60°N. If the 4 per cent increase per year in skin diseases is due just to UV changes, the formula given above seriously underestimates the effects. Again we see that even if we limit ourselves to observed data and to the hypothesis that UV flux changes are linearly related to ozone changes, this particular

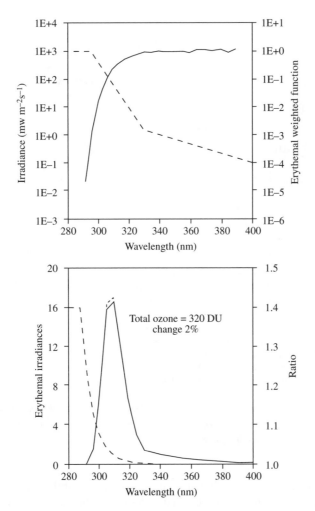

Note: In the first graph the solid line shows the power received from the sun in the UV at the surface of the earth. The dotted line shows the sensitivity curve for deoxyribonucleic acid (DNA) damage. The lower graph shows the product of these two curves for 320 DU (Dobson Unit) of ozone and overhead sun. Also shown is the ratio between two curves for a change of 2 per cent in total ozone.

Source: adapted from Long et al. (1996).

Figure 16.1   Product of irradiance and the erythemal action spectrum

Ozone layer depletion

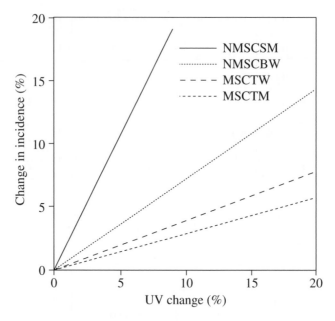

Notes:
NMSCSM Non-melanoma skin cancer squamous men
NMSCBW Non-melanoma skin cancer basal women
MSCTM Melanoma skin cancer trunk men
MSCTW Melanoma skin cancer trunk women

Figure 16.2   *Percentage change in incidence of different kinds of skin cancer as a function of percentage change in UV radiation at the earth's surface*

health effect can still be hidden in the statistical variability. Changes in the erythemal exposure can be evaluated based on the total ozone mapping spectrometer (TOMS) data on total ozone. In the 1980–90 decade a maximum increase of around 12 per cent was calculated in the polar regions in spring, with values between 4 and 8 per cent in the middle latitudes going down to zero or negative values in the tropical regions. Calculated changes in the UV radiation at 310 nm between 1978 and 1993 show a possible positive trend in the latitude band 45–55 (north and south), with large positive and negative fluctuations which in some cases reach even 40 per cent with respect to the average.

The damaging process on DNA should have a stochastic character and although it may be sensitive to the absolute level, large fluctuations could be important as well. This means that until the origin of such fluctuations (for example UV flux from the sun and cloudiness) is understood, it is very difficult to assess the importance of small yearly changes in the amount of UV.

As for cataracts, it is again the case that the changes in UV flux will produce a linear response in the increase in incidence. Although a slight dependence on age exists, a 10 per cent increase in UV will roughly correspond to a 5 per cent increase in the response. It is estimated in the USA, where the latest data available are for 1993, that 1.35 million cataract operations are performed each year, but it is not clear how many of these are attributable to UV exposure. Also in this case the weight of the UV irradiance in determining the present number of cases is very uncertain and consequently large uncertainties exist in the future estimate.

The effects on the immune system cannot be quantified at the moment.

We now consider the possible effects of increased UV-B radiation on plants. Studies have shown that an enhanced exposure to UV may reduce photosynthesis in many C3 and C4[2] plants. The production of dry matter and yield also decreases in most plants with increased UV, and the same happens with leaf area. On the other hand, mixed data or no effects are shown for drought tolerance, crop maturation and flowers.

Specific studies have been carried out with respect to harvest and have shown that the effect will be noticeable only for very large changes (around 100 per cent) in UV radiation while small changes in the order of 2–3 per cent will be observed as a consequence of the CFC policies mentioned above and expected in the near future (around 15 per cent). It is quite clear that larger variability in the crop yields and harvest is related to short-term climatic fluctuations (drought and floods).

Another possible environmental effect includes that on marine life. UV radiation is readily absorbed by seawater in the first two metres, so that changes may affect only those plants and animals living in the surface waters. Phytoplankton are usually abundant in these regions and constitute the base of the long food chain. However, not all the phytoplankton species are affected in the same way by UV-B and a change in the radiation could lead to some selection in the species, favouring those resistant to UV-B. This in turn could affect zooplankton, the next step up the food chain, but again because of the small depth of water involved the variability in the mixing processes could introduce a rather difficult parameter to evaluate. Higher marine organisms may also be affected by increases in the UV radiation (for example eggs) and fish are sensitive to the point of developing cancers and skin lesions. Other possible effects due to increased UV radiation include the degradation of polymers, but again in this case a quantitative evaluation remains difficult.

3. CLIMATIC EFFECTS

Ozone is a radiatively active gas, that is it can absorb UV radiation, heat the atmosphere, and emit and absorb infrared radiation. Changes in ozone may affect the thermal structure of the atmosphere and it is known to be a greenhouse gas. On the other hand, gases which are sources for depleting chlorine absorb long-wave radiation and may affect the radiative balance as well. Ozone has a rather variable mixing ratio with latitude and altitude, and while stratospheric ozone determines the thermal structure of the stratosphere and may also affect the radiative balance of the surface, tropospheric ozone mainly contributes to the greenhouse effect.

Calculations carried out with radiative models (WMO, 1990, 1992, 1995) show that the observed decrease in stratospheric ozone may have contributed to cooling the surface of the earth in the decade 1980–90. In the same period the increase in concentration of the main greenhouse gases such as carbon dioxide, nitrous oxide and methane caused a warming of about 0.14°C, while stratospheric ozone has caused a cooling of 0.03°C (on a global basis). A reduction in stratospheric ozone can produce an increase in tropospheric ozone, but the main reason for the latter is the observed increase in pollution in the lower atmosphere. The increase in tropospheric ozone since pre-industrial times may have contributed by around 0.15°C to global warming, with 0.7°C due to all other gases.

Ozone may be related to the issue of global warming directly through changes in the total column and indirectly through the warming caused by CFCs. The indicator comparing the effects of CFCs with those of CO_2, known as the global warming potential (GWP), is defined as the radiative forcing (expressed in W/m^2) of 1 kg of gas with respect to the forcing of 1 kg of carbon dioxide. Although this indicator has to be handled carefully, it can be used to give a comparison between CFCs rather than with CO_2. For example, GWP for CF-11 ranges between 4500 and 1400, while that for CF-114 is between 6000 and 7000. However, in absolute terms, in the decade 1979–90 the contribution of CFCs was in the order of 0.1 W/m^2 while all other gases have contributed five times as much. The Copenhagen Agreements have given careful attention to GWP and in absolute terms it is not expected that ozone, CFC or HCFC will make a significant contribution to global warming.

It remains to be seen what effect large changes in stratospheric ozone may have on stratospheric circulation. The thermal structure of the stratosphere affects the propagation of planetary waves from the lower atmosphere so that large changes in ozone may be expected to have a considerable effect on stratospheric circulation, mixing and surface temperature. These effects have been only marginally explored with general circulation models of the stratosphere, and a more thorough investigation of these problems is required. However, radiative effects in the stratosphere and global warming may have much more subtle effects on stratospheric ozone. The increase in the concentration of greenhouse gases warms the troposphere and cools the stratosphere. This may increase the geographical area in the high-latitude regions for the formation of polar stratospheric clouds (PSC), the surface of which enhances the ozone losses through heterogeneous chemistry. The timetable of ozone depletion recovery could then be delayed in the twenty-first century by this process.

4. THE MEASURES TAKEN

Each successive agreement after the 1987 Montreal Protocol (London 1990 and Copenhagen 1992) has requested a much larger and earlier reduction than envisaged at Montreal. The following figures show the major reductions requested from the industrial countries. The agreements are based on a parameter similar to the one introduced for radiative forcing known as ozone-depleting potential (ODP). This is defined as the total ozone destroyed by 1 kg of substance with respect to a similar amount for CF-11, the most diffuse of the CFCs. CFCs are the oldest and most used ozone-depleting substances (ODS). The best known are CF-11 and C-12. Halons are chemically similar to CFCs but with bromine substituting for chlorine. Although they have a much larger ODP (between 4 and 16), their production is much lower. HCFCs (hydrochlorofluorocarbons) are substances developed as substitutes for CFCs. Their molecules contain hydrogen, which makes them vulnerable to reaction in the lower atmosphere, and their lifetime is very short. Their ODP is between 0.01 and 0.11. Hydrofluorocarbons (HFC) are more advanced than HCFCs because they do not contain chlorine or bromine, and their ODP is zero. Of particular interest is methyl bromide because it is produced both naturally and from industry, and its ODP is around 0.6.

The first agreement addressed only CFCs and halons and asked for a freeze of the production of CFCs at the 1989 levels followed by a cut of 20 per cent and a further cut of 50 per cent from 1998. For halons it required a freeze at the 1992 level. Under the Copenhagen amendments CFCs had to be eliminated completely by 1996 and all halons have been banned since 1994. The same drastic cuts apply to carbon tetrachloride, methyl chloroform and hydrobromofluorocarbons (HBFCs).

If the Copenhagen amendments are observed, the situation for total chlorine in the atmosphere should be very similar to the situation illustrated in Figure 16.3. The maximum is reached around the year 2000 with a slow but significant decrease by the end of the twenty-first century below 1.5 ppb (parts per billion).

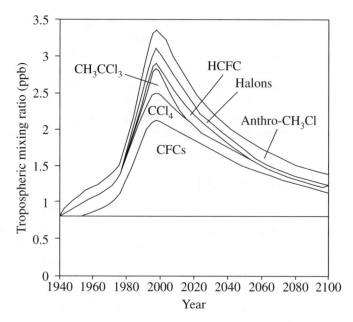

Source: adapted from WMO report no.37 (1995).

Figure 16.3   *Concentration of total chlorine in the atmosphere to be*
expected with basic compliance with the Copenhagen
amendments, showing the contribution of each substance

A major improvement of the substitutes for the old ODSs is that they have
a shorter lifetime because they can react in the lower atmosphere. This
property, however, raises new environmental concerns. To assess these problems the chemical manufacturers set up the Alternative Fluorocarbons
Environmental Acceptability Study (AFEAS) in 1988, and this panel has
reached some important conclusions. The most serious of these concerns the
possibility that HCFCs and HFCs may form trifluoroacetyl halides in the
atmosphere which, when dissolved in water, will form salts of trifluoro-
acetate (TFA). In several decades concentration levels of these salts, especially
in wetlands, could be harmful to some forms of aquatic life. Some environmental parameters are still poorly known, so a large effort is required to
clarify the possible impact of the new products.

5. OZONE IN THE TWENTY-FIRST CENTURY

Based on projections for chlorine loading expected in the twenty-first century, models can evaluate ozone depletion. Figure 16.4 shows for comparison two

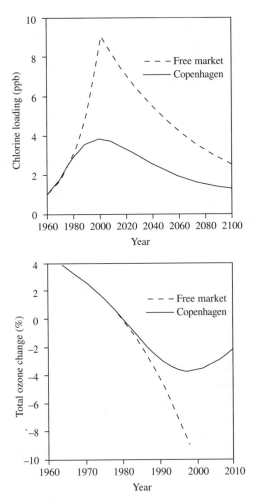

Note: The graph above shows the chlorine levels for the Copenhagen scenario (solid line) and the free market (dashed). The graph below shows the calculated ozone depletion between 65°N and 65°S for the same scenarios. Note the different time scale.

Source: adapted from Prather et al. (1996).

Figure 16.4 Two scenarios for chlorine loading and ozone change

such scenarios, one in which the Copenhagen agreements are implemented and the other under free-market conditions. In this latter case the total concentration of chlorine would reach about 9 ppb around the year 2000 but after that the growing concern about global ozone depletion and the permanence of the ozone hole would force a reduction of CFC production. In the case of compliance with the Copenhagen agreements, depletion since 1980 would reach about 4 per cent by the year 2000 and then recover slowly. It is assumed that the ozone hole would persist if the chlorine level remained above 2 ppb.

These figures give a dramatic idea of what would have happened without the international agreements. The situation would be even worse than just the 10 per cent reduction in global ozone seen in the lower graph of Figure 16.4. In some sense these large changes could even be unpredictable. The high chlorine levels would persist throughout the twenty-first century, accompanied by severe ozone depletion. Therefore, not only would the impacts on flux be very large, but also the climatic consequences are totally unexplored.

Such large ozone losses in the twenty-first century can be prevented because of the agreement. However, there are still a few potential dangers to be considered. The most-studied one has been the possible effect of a fleet of supersonic civil aircraft. Both in Europe and the USA assessment programmes have shown that this could very well be a limited problem. Models estimate that total losses are of the order of 1 per cent, which is within the possible errors of the model and is a marginal effect. Another danger is that while the chlorine levels remain high, large ozone losses, even for a brief period, could be expected in the case of volcanic eruptions. Hydrolysis of both chlorine nitrate and dinitrogen pentoxide may enhance the concentration of active chlorine and thus contribute significantly to ozone losses. Volcanic aerosols are a solution of sulphuric acid and water, and may be the major contributors to hydrolysis processes. It has been suggested that large eruptions like Pinatubo in 1991 could induce ozone losses as large as those observed in the Antarctic region during springtime. Although these losses have not been observed in the tropics, recent simulations show that both in the polar region and at mid-latitude the ozone decline was substantially controlled by volcanic aerosols after the El Chichon eruption in 1982. At that time chlorine concentration was about 2.5 ppb. The factors controlling ozone losses are both aerosol surface area and chlorine level, and so while generally we should expect an ozone recovery, this could be delayed by unpredictable volcanic eruptions.

Other uncertainties relating to the expected scenario arise from a partial compliance with the international agreements.

Compliance with the Montreal Protocol and subsequent agreements has been generally acceptable. However, there are still unresolved questions related mainly to the particular laws of the different countries. The most serious questions refer to the shortage in refills that will be felt with the cessation of

CFC production after 1996. A black market for CFCs is expected to amount to about 10 000 tonnes per year (Parson and Greene, 1995). These figures are, however, small considering that production even in the 1990s was about 400 000 tonnes per year. The production in developing countries has been increasing since 1986 but remains small. Although it is reasonable to expect some delay in phase-outs and general implementation of the agreements, we should observe (see Figure 16.4) that the chlorine load may reach a maximum around the year 2000 and then start a slow decline, with the threshold of 3 ppb reached towards 2020 and the 2 ppb threshold reached around 2040.

6. THE OZONE ISSUE AND THE PRESSURE INDICATORS

Eurostat has developed indicators to guide political and economic actions in relation to the solution of environmental problems at EU level. The history of the solution of the ozone problem shows, however, that political actions are strongly constrained by the economic conflicts between different countries. Because the environmental issues involve several countries, sometimes progress can only be made if an agreement is reached at the highest political level.

International scientific consensus on the issue is an important condition for agreement. For this reason governments need to have their national representatives at the international committees (for example IPCC, the Intergovernmental Panel on Climate Change). Their capacity to participate actively in discussions on the relevant issues depends on an adequate amount of original research carried out in their countries. Funding of the research activity by the governments can then be seen also as a political decision. Another important role that government may have is that any regulations agreed by them may accelerate industrial research into finding valid substitutes.

The indicators chosen by Eurostat all refer to the ozone-depleting substances and major greenhouse gases. The results of the survey show that the right choice has been made, at least in isolating the possible causes of ozone depletion. However, the results do show a rather surprising absence of large differences in the importance given to different indicators. The presence of CFCs among the top indicators is not really justified because all international agreements have required their complete phase-out well before the end of the century. One would also expect a rating based on the absolute value of chemical and radiative effect.

The uniformity of the ranking may have a more subtle explanation. The scientific community (that is, the scientists involved in these issues) may fear that the solution of the ozone problem will result in a decrease in research funds. A possible way to avoid this is to give factors about which there is uncertainty a high ranking. This view seems to be supported at least by two results. In the 'responsiveness' and 'core indicators' criteria, the emissions of NO_x and CO_2 have a very high ranking. Emission of nitric oxides is related to high-speed aircraft transport which is presently the most actively pursued research subject in the ozone field. However, we have seen that this effect is still quite marginal and, within the undetermined errors of the models, ozone depletion at the steady state is substantially absent. The increase in the carbon dioxide burden interacts with the ozone problem through the cooling of the stratosphere. A lower temperature in the stratosphere may favour the extension of some of the heterogeneous chemistry effects to other geographical regions besides the high latitudes. Again, this is a speculative problem with great uncertainties.

As stated several times, international scientific consensus is one of the conditions to be met for an agreement. This in turn gives the scientific community considerable influence on any decision. Possible feedbacks between scientific issues, government research funding and assessment studies need to be addressed properly. The parable narrated by Dotto and Schiff (1978) about 'birds' that 'could also lay golden eggs' is even more illuminating today.

7. CONCLUSION

The response to ozone depletion is an example of the way in which the international community could deal with other global environmental problems. At the present time, more than 20 years after the first warning from scientists, the cause of the problem is being dealt with but it will take several decades before it is cured completely. The recovery may be complicated through interaction with global warming and by unpredictable events such as volcanic eruptions.

When the Montreal Protocol was signed in 1987, the ozone hole had been discovered only two years earlier and neither the issue of polar ozone nor mid-latitude ozone was really understood. The work by Solomon et al., giving an early suggestion that heterogeneous chemistry could be important in producing the ozone hole, was published in 1986, and the work by Hofmann and Solomon on heterogeneous processes at mid-latitudes on sulphate aerosols was only published in 1989. The Scientific Assessment of Stratospheric Ozone in 1989 could only include these new suggestions marginally, and predicted a decrease in ozone in the polar region by 2060 of up to 20 per cent. The very mild decisions contained in the Montreal Protocol were the results of such scientific uncertainties; however, the London amendments agreed in 1992 reflected some more sound scientific results. The point is that although the detail of the proof had not been worked out, the immense impact of the ozone hole on the political process forced the agreement. It was not just the fear of some increase in UV radiation at high latitude that really worried people, but rather the almost visible proof that man had changed the natural sequence of events.

Another important point that has to be considered in evaluating the agreement reached on limiting the production of ozone-depleting substances is the way in which the chemical industry provided alternatives to CFCs (Benedick, 1995; Rowlands, 1995). This was quite evident in the USA where the campaign 'ban the can' forced industry to look for new and less harmful products, but at the same time the initial legislation banned only those products for which substitutes were more likely to be found in the short term. The industry was able to provide a short-term temporary solution with HCFC and a long-term one with HFC.

As we have seen, there are still many problems related mainly to substitution in less developed countries and although, according to industry, the present substitutes are not producing any financial benefit, the substitution will be beneficial in the long term.

Monitoring techniques have helped in the implementation of measures to limit ODS production. The chemical producers of CFCs and their substitutes are a few very large companies, so their output can be monitored easily. The early measuring network developed by the Chemical Manufacturing Association and then funded also by NASA is extremely reliable and gives such precise results that a major deviation from the international agreements can easily be spotted.

The ozone issue is a very good example of how to deal with global environmental problems. However, it may have been dealt with simply because of a number of favourable circumstances (for example scientific consensus, political will, cost-effectiveness). The conclusions drawn by James Lovelock about fifteen years ago on a debate on the ozone problem are appropriate to this point (Lovelock, 1982):

> Maybe it also represents a part of a learning process. For we need to know a great deal more before the much more difficult problems consequent upon it such as the carbon dioxide increase can be tackled. The ozone depletion affair has been discussed almost exclusively among Western middle class professionals with their common cultural background. With the well known competitiveness of their society and the conflicting interests involved, it was remarkable that so much agreement took place. But can we conceive a similar consensus reached among the other numerous political, tribal, and religious communities of the World who need so much more urgently to agree on what should be done about depletion of the forests and the living creatures within them. Indeed the depletion of the Biosphere itself.

It would be wrong at this point to propose that the path followed to solve the ozone problem be used as a paradigm for other global environmental issues.

NOTES

1. 1995 Nobel Prize for Chemistry to Paul Crutzen (The Netherlands), Mario Molina (USA) and F. Sherwood Rowland (USA).
2. This refers to the categorization of plant species according to mechanisms of photosynthesis.

REFERENCES

Benedick, R.E. (1995), 'Ozone diplomacy', in K. Conca, M. Alberty and G. Dabelko (eds), *Green Planet Blues*, (Boulder, CO: Westview Press).

Dotto, L. and H. Schiff (1978), *The Ozone War* (New York: Doubleday).

EPA (1988), *Regulatory Impact Analysis: Protection of Stratospheric Ozone. Vol. 1: Regulatory Impact Analysis Document* (Washington, DC: US Environmental Protection Agency).

Long, C.S., A.J. Miller, H.T. Lee, J.D. Wild, R.C. Przywarty and D. Huffurd (1996), 'Ultraviolet Index Forecast issued by the National Weather Service', *Bulletin of the American Meteorological Society*, **77**: 729.

Lovelock, J. (1982), 'Epilogue', in F.A. Bower and R.B. Ward (eds), *Stratospheric Ozone and Man*, Vol. 1 (Florida: CRC Press).

Parson, E.A. and O. Greene (1995), 'The complex chemistry of the international ozone agreements', *Environment*, **37**: 16.

Prather, M., P. Midgley, S.F. Rowland and R. Stolarski (1996), 'The ozone layer: the road not taken', *Nature*, **381**: 551.

Rowlands, J.H. (1995), 'Ozone layer depletion and global warming: new sources for environmental issues', in K. Conca, M.Alberty and G. Dabelko (eds), *Green Planet Blues* (Boulder, CO: Westview Press).

WMO (1990), *Scientific Assessment of Stratospheric Ozone: 1989*, Global Ozone Research and Monitoring Project Report no. 20 (Geneva: WMO).

WMO (1992), *Scientific Assessment of Ozone Depletion: 1991*, Global Ozone Research and Monitoring Project Report no. 25 (Geneva: WMO).

WMO (1995), *Scientific Assessment of Ozone Depletion: 1994*, Global Ozone Research and Monitoring Project Report no. 37 (Geneva: WMO).

17. The ozone depletion problem

I.S.A. Isaksen

1. THE SCIENTIFIC ISSUE

The ozone depletion issue has been on the scientific agenda almost continuously since Paul Crutzen (1971) and Harold Johnston (1971) pointed out that a projected fleet of supersonic aircraft could harm the protecting ozone shield around the earth. At that time it had been shown through measurements that ozone was present in the stratosphere in amounts sufficient to filter out harmful solar radiation. It was also known that ozone was generated in the stratosphere through the photodissociation of molecular oxygen by short-wave solar radiation (Chapman, 1930), and that redistribution by transport processes taking place in the lower stratosphere, at heights between approximately 15 and 30 km, played a significant role in ozone distribution. There is a large variation in ozone distribution and in the column amount of ozone, with latitude and longitude, and with season. This temporal and spatial variation in ozone was well known before the ozone depletion issue was raised. It was well recognized by the beginning of the 1970s that the key point in the ozone depletion issue is how the chemical loss process controls the overall ozone distribution in the stratosphere through different catalytic chemical reactions.

Our present state of knowledge of the ozone depletion problem is a result of a large and concentrated research effort over more than 25 years, where the focus has been on understanding man's impact on stratospheric ozone through the emission of certain chemical compounds (for example nitrogen, chlorine and bromine-containing compounds). This research consists of laboratory studies, atmospheric measurements and model simulations of atmospheric processes; it has been performed through national research programmes or through international programmes organized through, for instance, NASA's stratospheric research activities and the EU's research on environment and climate. Of particular importance for improving our understanding of atmospheric processes in general, and of the impact of man's activities in particular, are the international ozone assessments which have been performed regularly since the early 1980s (WMO, 1982, 1985, 1990, 1992, 1995).

Issues raised regarding the ozone problem have been strongly linked to the development of our understanding of the atmospheric science behind ozone formation and distribution in the stratosphere. There have been three major advances in this process which are strongly linked to scientific discoveries:

1. The importance of ozone depletion by NO_x emitted from high-flying aircraft became an issue shortly after Paul Crutzen (1971) showed that stratospheric NO_x played a key role in the loss of stratospheric ozone. This started a concentrated international research effort that continued after the chlorine issue was raised.
2. The catalytic destruction of stratospheric ozone by chlorine compounds originating from the release of CFCs was originally suggested by Molina and Rowland (1974). Their findings were published shortly after Stolarski and Cicerone (1974) had demonstrated the potential of catalytic chlorine reactions in reducing stratospheric ozone. Lovelock (1974) had shown through measurements that CFCs were distributed throughout the troposphere.
3. The significance of man-made emissions for the development of the 'ozone hole' became apparent after the discoveries of large springtime (October) ozone reductions over Antarctica. This was first shown by Joe Farman and his collaborators (1985). The discovery of the Antarctic 'ozone hole' has led to highly focused research over the last ten years on ozone depletion processes in the lower stratosphere, and the causes of reduced ozone.

2. CURRENT STATUS OF STRATOSPHERIC OZONE LOSS

The most recent analysis of the decrease in total ozone column densities based on satellite observations shows a global average decrease of 4 to 6 per cent over the last two decades. The significant winter/springtime decreases in the two polar regions are positively shown to be a result of human activities (WMO, 1995).

The springtime (October) decrease of 50 per cent or more in the total ozone column over the Antarctic continent known as 'the ozone hole' is as large as ever, covering an area of approximately 20 million km^2 (European Commission, 1997).

Observations made by European scientists in the northern polar region during the last three or four winter seasons show a significant ozone loss in the lower stratosphere at heights around 20 km that can be traced back to enhanced chlorine levels. The ozone loss was particularly large during the

1995 and 1996 winter seasons. In some cases chemically induced local ozone losses of over 30 per cent have been observed.

The man-induced ozone losses at northern latitudes are of particular interest since these losses occur close to or in some cases above populated areas.

3. PROBLEMS RELATED TO OZONE LAYER DEPLETION

Penetration of Ultraviolet Solar Radiation at the Earth's Surface

The main consequence of ozone layer depletion which has been recognized as important for several decades is that the reduction in stratospheric ozone will lead to a reduction in the total ozone column, thereby allowing more ultraviolet (UV-B) solar radiation to penetrate at the earth's surface.

The solar UV-B radiation at wavelengths shorter than approximately 310 nanometres is harmful in several respects. It has been demonstrated that UV-B radiation is harmful for human health. Increased UV-B radiation will lead to suppression of the immune system, resulting in possible increases in the severity of infectious diseases; adverse ocular effects (increases in cases of cataracts per year); and increases in cases of non-melanoma skin cancer. In the latter case, for instance, a 4 per cent reduction in the total ozone column worldwide has been estimated to lead to an increase in cases of non-melanoma skin cancer of approximately 100 000 by the international WMO panel for assessing the effects of ozone depletion (WMO, 1992).

UV-B radiation will have an impact on terrestrial plants. Growth and photosynthesis can be inhibited; however, UV-B radiation interacts with other environmental factors (for instance pollution, acid deposition), making it difficult to predict the effect.

The aquatic ecosystem is also affected. It is already under UV-B stress, and increased UV-B radiation will cause further detrimental effects, and could have an impact on the uptake of CO_2, thereby affecting climate and leading to reduced biomass production.

Problems with enhanced UV-B radiation as a result of decreased ozone column densities have been recognized for several decades. Whether this depletion occurs in the stratosphere (at a height above approximately 15 km and below 55 km) or in the troposphere (at a height below approximately 15 km), it is the total integrated amount of ozone above the surface that filters out the harmful solar radiation that is of importance. However, since 90 per cent of the ozone in a column above the surface is located in the stratosphere, changes in stratospheric ozone are of primary importance for the UV-B fluxes.

Apart from industrial regions, where low-level pollution (ozone and particles) has partly masked the effect of ozone depletion, there is now clear evidence that ozone depletion leads to enhanced UV-B radiation. For instance, solar flux observations over Antarctica show that the intensity of short-wave solar radiation is more pronounced during the period of the 'ozone hole' in the spring months (October) than at mid-summer (end of December), when the ozone distribution is back to normal for that time of year. These particular observations are a clear result of the observed behaviour of the ozone layer. There are also studies that indicate that the enhanced UV-B radiation has led to enhanced levels of organism mortality at the surface level of the oceans along the ice sheets. This is probably a first indication of a link between reduced stratospheric ozone from man-made chemicals and environmental effects caused by the enhanced intensity of harmful solar radiation.

The relation between ozone depletion and enhanced UV-B radiation has not been as clearly demonstrated at northern latitudes as we have seen in the southern hemisphere, although there is evidence of ozone depletion in the northern polar latitudes. However, it has been shown that the significant ozone reductions which have been observed over Europe during the last five years have led to enhanced UV-B fluxes. This has been, for instance, very evident in solar flux observations over Thessaloniki in Greece since 1991 (Zerefos et al., 1995).

The current situation is, therefore, that there are available data which link the observed ozone decreases during recent years to increased harmful solar radiation.

Climate Change

There are also links between ozone depletion and climate change. Changes in the height profile of ozone, particularly in the lower stratosphere and in the upper troposphere, are of relevance to the earth's climate.

Ozone is an efficient greenhouse gas that contributes to the heating of the earth's surface (IPCC, 1996). The observed stratospheric ozone depletion is largest in the lower stratosphere (15 to 25 km), and changes in this region have the largest effect on surface temperatures. According to model studies, the result of the observed ozone decreases is that there will be a cooling effect, particularely at high latitudes in the two hemispheres where the largest ozone reductions have been observed. Since it has now been clearly demonstrated that the ozone loss is to a large extent a result of enhanced CFC levels, the secondary effect of ozone cooling should be taken into account when the radiative heating from the very potent CFC greenhouse gases is considered. The result of this is that CFCs are becoming less important climate change gases than previously assumed, when the chemical effect on gases like ozone was not considered.

Increases in the Oxidation Capacity of the Troposphere

Another area of research on the impact of ozone layer changes which has drawn considerable attention is the increases in the oxidation capacity of the troposphere. Recent model studies of the tropospheric chemistry have shown that enhanced UV-B radiation that has followed the reduction in stratospheric ozone experienced during the last few years is likely to have the effect of significantly enhancing the oxidation process (oxidation capacity) in the troposphere. This in turn will affect environmental processes such as surface ozone generation, acid rain and the oxidation of greenhouse gases such as methane (Fuglestvedt et al., 1994).

The last two issues above represent new areas of research where the environmental impact of changes in the ozone layer is only partly understood.

4.   THE NEED FOR A COORDINATED POLICY RESPONSE

The ozone depletion problem is a global problem which acts on a time scale of several decades rather than years or less. This is due to the very long lifetime of CFCs, the primary sources, and the time it takes for surface-emitted source gases to reach the stratosphere. This delay is estimated to be approximately five years. Gases emitted at different locations at the earth's surface will be completely mixed before they reach the stratosphere. The CFC gases emitted in one country will have the same global impact as the CFC gases emitted in other countries. There is one other consideration which is of importance. Due to the very long lifetimes of CFCs, the atmospheric concentrations respond very slowly to changes in emissions, and it takes decades to reduce their atmospheric concentrations to acceptable levels once the emissions have taken place. The long lifetime and the history of previous emissions also mean that reductions in CFCs need to be significant before we have significant chlorine reductions in the stratosphere. As an example, in order to stabilize the CFC concentrations at the 1990 levels it has been shown that emissions of the major compounds needed to be reduced by 70 to 80 per cent compared with the 1986 emissions. This stabilization is still to be achieved in spite of reductions taking place.

Significant chlorine reductions over the coming decades as a result of the agreement obtained in the Montreal Protocol and in later amendments are now being discussed. Such reductions can only be achieved with nearly full compliance with the Montreal Protocol. It is therefore important that there is full international agreement about the phase-out of ozone-depleting substances, and that this agreement is followed up by all countries.

5. ACTION TAKEN TO REDUCE OZONE-DEPLETING SUBSTANCES

A large number of chemical compounds emitted due to human activities have been identified as ozone-depleting substances (ODS), and their ozone depletion potential (ODP) has been estimated based on global atmospheric model studies. These are primarily organic chlorine and bromine compounds. The ODP of a gas is given as the global reduction of ozone for a certain emission (1 kg) of the gas, compared with the reduction of ozone for a similar emission of a reference gas over an indefinite time horizon. CFC-11 ($CFCl_3$) has been adopted as the reference gas. Table 17.1 shows ODP for different man-made chlorine and bromine compounds presented in the 1994 ozone assessment (WMO, 1995).

The large variation in ozone depletion caused by the chlorine and bromine source gases reflects the difference in the efficiency of the gases in depleting stratospheric ozone. The CFC compounds are the original chlorinated source gases which in general have high ODPs. HCFCs consist of CFC substitutes which, for most gases, have substantially smaller ODPs than CFCs. The last group in the table represents the main bromine source gases. The presence of bromine compounds in the stratosphere will in general lead to a much more efficient ozone depletion than chlorine compounds. The bromine source gases will therefore have a higher ODP than the chlorine source gases.

The difference in ODPs between the compounds is mainly a result of the difference in atmospheric lifetimes of the gases. Long-lived compounds (for example CFCs) will build up larger concentrations than the short-lived compounds before they are removed from the atmosphere, thereby making them more efficient ODSs.

The emissions and the time horizons for the phase-out of the ODSs are determined by the agreements obtained through the Montreal Protocol in 1987 and the later amendments in London (1990) and Copenhagen (1992), and the Vienna adjustment in 1995. Under these agreements the restriction in the use of the major chlorine sources in the stratosphere, CFCs (such as CFC-11 and CFC-12), methyl chloroform, carbon tetrachloride and halons, have been gradually strengthened. The current situation is that the major emissions of these man-made sources are being phased out. For the less efficient HCFCs there is an agreement for phase-out over the next two to three decades.

*Table 17.1   Main ozone-depleting substances regulated through the
Montreal Protocol, their atmospheric lifetime and ozone
depletion potential*

Trace gas	Lifetime (years)	ODP
CFC-11	50.0	1.00
CFC-12	102.0	0.82
CFC-113	85.0	0.90
CFC-114	300.0	0.84
CFC-115	1700.0	0.40
CCl_4	42.0	1.20
CH_3CCl_3	5.4	0.12
HCFC-22	13.3	0.04
HCFC-123	1.4	0.014
HCFC-124	5.9	0.03
HCFC-141b	9.4	0.10
HCFC-142b	19.5	0.05
CH_3Br	1.3	0.64
H-1301	65.0	12.00
H-1211	20.0	5.10

Note: CFCs refer to fully halogenated compounds (e.g. CFC-11 is $CFCl_3$), HCFCs to hydro-
gen-containing compounds (e.g. HCFC-22 is $CHClF_2$), and H refers to halon compounds (e.g.
H-1211 is CF_2Br_2).

It seems clear that the Montreal Protocol has had a significant impact on
the emissions of ODSs over the last eight to ten years. Reported changes in
the emissions of key ODSs after 1988, when these changes started to become
significant, for most of the gases affected by the Montreal Protocol, are
shown in Table17.2.

The reported emissions of CFCs (except CFC-115) and the halons have
been reduced significantly, and this trend has continued after 1992. For
HCFCs the situation is different, partly because they are substitutes for CFCs.
The increase has been particularly large for the less abundant HCFCs, for
which the emissions were very low before the CFC ban. These compounds
are here represented by HCFC-142b which had a mixing ratio in 1992 of 3.5
pptv (parts per trillion by volume) compared with the mixing ratio of CFC-12
of 500 pptv. The observed rapid increase in the HCFCs will therefore have a
moderate impact on the stratospheric chlorine burden. It is clear that the total

Table 17.2   Estimated changes in the emissions of some of the ODSs regulated by the Montreal Protocol, 1988–92

Trace gas	Estimated percentage change in emissions: 1988–92
CFC-11	−45
CFC-12	−30
CFC-113	−30
CFC-114	−65
CFC-115	+10
CH_3CCl_3	−15
HCFC-22	+30
HCFC-142b	+450
H-1301	−25*
H-1211	−25*

Note: * Change is between 1988 and 1990.

Source: WMO (1995).

emission of chlorine-containing compounds contributing to the stratospheric burden of ODSs has decreased significantly since the late 1980s.

Observations of the atmospheric concentrations of the major human-emitted chlorine compounds have shown a reduced growth rate during the last few years, undoubtedly as a result of reduced emissions. All major CFCs, methyl chloroform, carbon tetrachloride and halons were reported in the recent WMO report (1995) to show significant slower growth in the atmosphere for the period 1990 to 1992 than that reported before 1990.

One of the gases which has shown the clearest reduction in growth rate is CFC-11. During the last couple of years its growth has levelled off. In fact, recent observations of the tropospheric burden of total man-emitted chlorine compounds indicate that the chlorine peak has been reached in the troposphere. It is therefore likely that we can expect a gradual decline in the tropospheric burden in the future. There is a delay of approximately five years for the chlorine peak to reach the stratosphere due to the slow transport processes. It is therefore likely that maximum chlorine levels in the stratosphere will be reached around the year 2000, and levels will decline in the twenty-first century.

The conclusions of these studies must be that there is a distinct effect on the ODSs in the stratosphere as a result of the agreement reached under the Montreal Protocol. This agreement has already resulted in reduced chlorine levels compared with those expected without the Montreal Protocol. This effect will be more apparent on chlorine levels and on ozone reduction in the coming decades as the total chlorine burden in the stratosphere starts to decrease as a result of the reduced emissions.

6.   FUTURE ACTIONS

A future reduction in the levels of chlorine as outlined above will require nearly full compliance with the Montreal Protocol. It has been shown that only moderate deviations in certain sectors of ODS use could, particularly in the long run, result in marked deviations from the expected decline in the total ODS loading. Further research will determine future requirements for ODS regulations. Since the Montreal Protocol was agreed in 1987, we have seen a more or less continuous strengthening of the agreement, primarily as a result of development in our scientific understanding of the problem over the last ten years. Even if we are able to control future chlorine increases, as seems to be the case at present, we are above all interested in the impact on ozone, where there are still uncertainties to be solved. The bromine chemistry is less well known, and the importance of the interaction with stratospheric particles needs to be better understood. In particular, changes in ozone levels which are connected to temperature changes could be significant. For instance, the enhanced ozone loss in the lower stratosphere of the northern hemisphere during recent winters seems to be linked to a colder winter stratosphere. There is a possibility that this is linked to climatic changes (there has been a general decrease in lower stratospheric temperatures over the last two decades), and that there will be enhanced ozone loss in the future due to a colder stratosphere. In that case it is possible that ozone recovery would not only be determined by the change in chlorine levels, but also by other atmospheric factors.

It will therefore be important to follow closely the developments in the ozone layer and in the chemical composition of ozone-depleting gases over the next decades to better understand the interaction between ozone-depleting gases and the ozone layer. It will also be of importance to follow the development in the global distribution of HCFCs through observations and global modelling. These compounds, which are substitutes for the CFCs, and which according to the Montreal Protocol will be phased out over an extended time period, have shown a rapid increase in their global distribution over the last few years. Such studies will give valuable information on the global emissions of ODSs.

REFERENCES

Chapman, S. (1930), 'A theory of upper atmospheric ozone', *Mem. Royal Meteorological Society*, **3**: 103–25.

Crutzen, P.J. (1971), 'Ozone production in an oxygen, hydrogen, nitrogen-oxide atmosphere', *Journal of Geophysical Research*, **76**: 7311–27.

European Commission (1997), *European Research in the stratosphere: The contribution of EASOE and SESAME to our current understanding of the ozone layer* (Luxembourg: European Commission).

Farman, J.C., B.G. Gardiner and J.D. Shanklin (1985), 'Large losses of ozone in Antarctica reveal seasonal ClOx/NO$_x$ interaction', *Nature*, **315**: 207–10.

Fuglestvedt, J.S., J.E. Jonson and I.S.A. Isaksen (1994), 'Effects of reductions of stratospheric ozone on tropospheric chemistry through changes in UV and photolysis rates', *Tellus, 46B*, 172–92.

IPCC (1996), *Climate Change 1995 – The Science of Climate Change: Contribution of Working Group I to the Second Assessment Report of the Intergovernmental Panel on Climate Change*, edited by J. Houghton, L.G. Meira Filho, B.A. Callander, N. Harris, A. Kattenberg, and K. Maskell (Cambridge: Cambridge University Press).

Johnston, H.S. (1971), 'Reduction of stratospheric ozone by nitrogen oxide catalysts from supersonic transport exhaust', *Science*, **173**: 517–22.

Lovelock, J.E. (1974), 'Atmospheric halocarbons and stratospheric ozone', *Nature*, **252**: 292–4.

Molina, M.J. and F.S. Rowland (1974), 'Stratospheric sink for chlorofluoromethanes: Chlorine atom-catalyzed destruction of ozone', *Nature*, **249**: 810–12.

Stolarski, R.S. and R.J. Cicerone (1974), 'Stratospheric chlorine, A possible sink for ozone', *Canadian Journal of Chem.*, **52**: 1610–15.

WMO (1982), *The Stratosphere 1981. Theory and measurements*, Global Ozone Research and Monitoring Project Report no. 11 (Geneva: WMO).

WMO (1985), *Atmospheric Ozone 1985, Assessment of our understanding of the processes controlling its present distribution and change*, Global Ozone Research and Monitoring Project Report no. 16 (Geneva: WMO).

WMO (1990), *Scientific Assessment of Stratospheric Ozone: 1989*, Global Ozone Research and Monitoring Project Report no. 20 (Geneva: WMO).

WMO (1992), *Scientific Assessment of Stratospheric Ozone: 1991*, Global Ozone Research and Monitoring Project Report no. 25 (Geneva: WMO).

WMO (1995), *Scientific Assessment of Ozone Depletion: 1994*, Global Ozone Research and Monitoring Project Report no. 37 (Geneva: WMO).

Zerefos, C.S., A.F. Bais, C. Meleti and I.C. Ziomas (1995), 'A note on the recent increase of solar UV-B radiation over northern middle latitudes', *Geophysical Research Letters*, **22** (10): 1245–7.

18. Ozone layer depletion

M.-L. Chanin

1. POTENTIAL IMPACTS OF OZONE DEPLETION

Three sets of recent observations can explain the concern of all European countries about the issue of ozone depletion, and their support for fundamental scientific research aimed at obtaining a better understanding and forecasting of the problem.

First, the decrease in total ozone is confirmed to be about 5 per cent per decade at mid-latitudes in the northern hemisphere, with a maximum of 6 per cent to 8 per cent in winter and spring, increasing with latitude. Current models including our understanding of chemical, dynamic and radiative processes can reproduce the observed depletion qualitatively; however, to date the simulated depletion is smaller than that observed.

Second, the Antarctic 'ozone hole' continues to be observed each austral spring, with a decrease of up to 60 per cent in total ozone. During the winters 1994–95, 1995–96 and 1996–97 in the northern hemisphere, total ozone decreased by as much as 30 per cent over large areas in February–March. This situation was due to the particularly low temperature of the lower stratosphere.

Third, recent reliable results from continuous measurements at a number of stations show an increase in UV-B radiation, mostly in the southern hemisphere, but also locally at mid- and high latitudes in the northern hemisphere.

Traditionally the main concern of the population and policy-makers regarding ozone depletion has been its potential impact on human health, and more precisely on the occurrence of skin cancer and cataracts, due to the increase in UV-B. Even though this widely held perception of the issue is justified, other consequences of ozone depletion, such as the effects on the whole immune system, and the impact on ecosystems, on biodiversity and on climate in general have added to the concern of scientists about the consequences of ozone depletion.

The state of knowledge on these different issues can be summarized as follows.

Influence of UV-B Increase

An important potential impact of increases in UV-B is related to the fact that deoxyribonucleic acid (DNA) is known to be UV-B-sensitive, and ozone changes could therefore modify all biological processes. One critical notion in this matter is the spectral weighting function or biological 'action spectrum', as it determines whether a change in ozone (which disturbs the UV-B spectrum between 280 and 320 nanometres (nm)), is significant for the biological processes involved. Insufficient knowledge of the action spectrum often limits the ability to draw conclusions on the probable impact of UV-B-induced change on different processes.

UV-B radiation and health

The accumulation of UV radiation exposure has proved without doubt to be a cause of non-melanoma skin cancer; however, recent work indicates that UV-A radiation (that is, the 320–40 nm range, which is not affected by ozone depletion) could also play an important role, because it penetrates deeper into the skin and can initiate damage of DNA. Therefore the increase in skin cancer may be related more to changes in the population's habits than to ozone depletion. The awareness of the public to the danger of exposure to UV should be encouraged, whether or not it is uniquely related to the ozone issue.

The action spectrum of cataracts has been shown to peak in the UV-B radiation range, and should therefore be affected by ozone depletion. However, more data are still needed to measure the impact on humans and animals.

UV-B radiation has unequivocally been shown to suppress specific immune functions on mice, and the study of the impact on humans is now actively pursued, as UV-B-induced immunosuppression could be at the origin of a much larger number of infections, diseases, tumours than the two examples mentioned above.

UV-B radiation and global ecosystems

This issue has not yet been examined to the same extent as the impact on human health, even though changes in terrestrial and aquatic ecosystems would eventually have an impact on the human population. Since the concern about protecting biodiversity is now at a high level of perception, this issue should be given more attention. It has already been demonstrated in aquatic ecosystems in the highly disturbed coastal seas around Antarctica that UV-B exposure alters primary productivity. On terrestrial ecosystems, the issue is usually downplayed compared with that of CO_2 increase, even though the respective impacts of UV and CO_2 changes need to be studied simultaneously to draw conclusions about their respective roles. For both aquatic and terrestrial ecosystems, the adaptive mechanism to increases in UV-B radiation is unknown.

Influence of the Change in Stratospheric Ozone on the Climate

This aspect of ozone depletion was downplayed until the beginning of the 1990s. The climatic scientific community was primarily concerned with the consequences of the increase in greenhouse gases; and the stratospheric scientific community with ozone depletion and its consequences for UV penetration. But many of the greenhouse gases that are responsible for greenhouse warming of the troposphere are important for ozone photochemistry. Also, since ozone is itself a greenhouse gas, changes in stratospheric ozone must be considered when predicting changes in future climate due to greenhouse gases. The importance of the role of the stratosphere in the climatic issue was only recognized after evidence was found of a cooling of the lower stratosphere during the 1980s due to ozone depletion. In 1992, the World Climate Research Programme (WCRP) implemented a new component devoted to understanding the influence of 'Stratospheric Processes and their Role in Climate', the SPARC Project.

The main arguments can be summarized as follows. The role of the stratospheric ozone layer in determining the amount of biologically harmful solar radiation reaching the surface is well known and has been briefly described above. Less familiar is the fact that the downward flux of stratospheric ozone into the troposphere is largely responsible for oxidation and consequent removal of many of the gases emitted from the surface, from either biogenic or anthropogenic sources. Some of these gases may in turn affect the concentrations of stratospheric ozone, that is, those which are relatively inert to oxidation in the troposphere and, therefore, have sufficiently long lifetimes to be transported into the stratosphere. They include the biogenic gases, N_2O and CH_4, and the industrial halocarbons. The photochemical breakdown of these gases by ultraviolet radiation in the stratosphere leads to chemical fragments which catalytically destroy ozone. There is thus a potential feedback process because changes in natural or anthropogenic surface emissions may affect stratospheric composition and hence penetration of UV-B radiation, and this in turn can modify surface emissions.

Stratospheric composition also plays an important role in the attenuation of solar radiation, which affects both tropospheric climate and biological activity at the surface. Again, we should note a potential feedback process. For instance, sulphur gases of biogenic origin, for example dimethyl sulphide (DMS) and carbonyl sulphide (COS), once transported into the stratosphere, form layered aerosols. These aerosols reflect incoming solar radiation and thereby influence the climate of both the stratosphere and the troposphere.

Direct emission of sulphur gases and particles into the stratosphere by volcanoes also contributes to the increase in the aerosol layer in the stratosphere. These particles have a long residence time in the stratosphere and may thus correspondingly influence the global radiation balance. In addition, variations of solar intensity on several time scales may have a modulating effect.

Another issue to consider is the possible effects of large fleets of supersonic aircraft in the stratosphere in the near future. At present subsonic aircraft spend more than half of their cruise time in the low stratosphere, in a sensitive region with potentially serious effects on climate and on ozone concentrations. Furthermore, this region is undergoing a change under anthropogenic influences (mostly a cooling under the influence of both greenhouse gases increase and ozone depletion), and the emission of water vapour by aircraft over polar regions may lead to a large increase in polar stratospheric clouds, which could generate more ozone depletion. Major studies are needed to provide a basis for assessing these effects and for warning governments of the possible dangers.

2. THE NEED FOR CENTRALIZED POLITICAL INTERVENTION

The ozone issue is the first and one of the few issues to have given rise to an international agreement which is already in operation. The Montreal Protocol, signed in 1987 and amended in London in 1990, in Copenhagen in 1992 and more recently in Vienna in 1995, has already shown its first results: the rates of increase in CFC-11, CFC-12, halon-1301 and halon-1211 are slowing down, and consequently the rates of increase in tropospheric chlorine and bromide have slowed down since 1990. The stratospheric concentration trend of chlorine/bromide lags the tropospheric trend by a few years and the peak concentration was reached by the year 2000. However, there are still several reasons to be concerned about the future.

First, the chlorine/bromide concentration is decreasing, but aerosols and water vapour are increasing in the upper troposphere/lower stratosphere, and this may lead to a different and new equilibrium. Second, the application of the Protocol is uncertain, mainly with respect to the use of methyl bromide for agricultural activities, and this, together with a widespread lack of compliance with the Protocol, may delay the recovery process by several years. Third, the verification of the recovery of the stratospheric ozone layer itself will not be possible with complete certainty for another 10 to 15 years, due to the large variability of ozone resulting from many natural causes (solar, volcanic, internal forcing and so on). Finally, many of the substitute products for CFCs are powerful greenhouse gases, and their emissions into the atmosphere in large quantities may contribute significantly to the budget of green-house gases.

Therefore central political intervention is required to ensure the control of the situation. Its five principal aims should be:

- to check on the compliance with the amended Montreal Protocol from the agreed and measured rates of emissions of CFCs, halons and methyl bromide;
- to study the need for recycling of CFCs and control the incidence of major leaks in installations (whenever CFCs are still in use);
- to survey and prevent the traffic of illegal CFCs. The smuggling of CFCs is presently the second most common form of smuggling after the traffic of drugs, and affects mostly the USA and Europe. The origin is known, for example, the former USSR countries. The USA seems to have taken severe measures, but European nations all have different control systems. *The need for European coordination on this issue is urgent*;
- to check the quality of substitute products for both ODP (ozone depletion potential) and GWP (global warming potential);
- to control the compliance with regulations to reduce the impact of aircraft, specifically relating to the reduction of NO_x, sulphur, aerosols and soot emissions, the maintenance of the energy efficiency of the engines, and the optimal choice of cruise altitude.

3. REDUCING THE PROBLEM PRESSURE

The issue of ozone depletion is already sufficiently well understood and 'under control', so that concrete actions can be envisaged immediately, even if some of them will not have an immediate effect (for example education) or will need to be pursued for a long time (for example monitoring).

Concrete actions include the following components.

Research Organizations (national and international)

The action mostly concerns the long-term monitoring of critical parameters such as CFCs, halons, HCFCs and the total content of chlorine and bromide products in the atmosphere. There should also be long-term monitoring by ground network and satellites of total ozone, ozone vertical profiles and temperature profiles as well as minor species involved in the ozone destruction processes such as Cl, Br, NO_x, aerosols, and H_2O. Finally, long-term monitoring of UV-B should be implemented and maintained in a large number of sites both in populated areas and away from local pollution, in order to identify the cause of the UV variation (whether ozone, clouds or pollution).

Public Education

The public should be encouraged to save energy in all its uses. This is necessary not only for reducing the production of greenhouse gases, but also to reduce the use of air conditioners, in particular those in cars in the USA. Furthermore, the public should be trained to recycle those products affecting ozone depletion which are still in use to produce a win–win policy.

Public awareness of the danger of UV exposure should be enhanced. A more thorough explanation of the accumulation process, the time lag between exposure and manifestation of the effects, and the statistics on cancer and immunological disease occurrence should be given in order to have a real impact on the behaviour of society. Information through the media on the daily UV levels, as already available in the summer in France, should be extended to other countries. Installations for UV artificial sunbeds should be controlled with the prospect of an outright ban within a relatively short term, if it is confirmed that UV-A is as damaging as UV-B.

Industry

The industry concerned by CFCs, HCFCs and halons, and regrouped into the Alternative Fluorocarbons Environmental Acceptability Study (AFEAS) has been highly involved and is working very effectively on substitute products. Due to the economic pressure which was applied, the industry is taking its share of the problem very seriously. One aspect which has not been stressed enough, possibly for economic reasons, is recycling (for example the recovery of CFCs from household fridges). A study should be made to assess the need (or otherwise) for recycling the products of first generation (CFCs and halons) and to stimulate the replacement of old machines, hence avoiding their second-hand sale elsewhere. The perception of the problem is obviously very different in highly developed countries such as Europe than in developing countries.

Government

All governments in Europe should cooperate to define and enforce severe regulations to prevent the traffic of CFCs and halons, and identify the origin of the traffic in order to eradicate the problem.

Governments should provide enough funds through the appropriate funding organizations such as the Global Environment Facility (GEF) to help developing countries to equip themselves immediately with modern equipment and, as early as possible in the process of development, train the population to reduce energy consumption.

4. THE NEED FOR AN OZONE LAYER DEPLETION PRESSURE INDEX[1]

Pressure indices are needed by different communities for different purposes. Policy-makers need them to ensure that ongoing actions are justified, to monitor their results and to ensure sensitivity to the need for new actions or policies. The public, as well as industry, when asked to restrain their use of ODSs, should be informed of the state of the problem through easily accessible indices. Scientists usually have their own access to data and derived indices, giving them a complete picture of the situation, generally through assessment studies, but they obviously require long-term data sets of a larger number of parameters.

Pressure indices, in order to be easily perceived by the public and the policy-makers, should be composed of a very small number of parameters, and should be given as rates of change (in per cent per year or per cent per decade depending on the rate of change). It is well known that most people do not memorize absolute values but are only sensitive to their change (for example a doubling of CO_2, an ozone depletion of 50 per cent); even climate change is perceived in terms of change of temperature or sea-level rise and not in absolute value. Thus the changes occurring in the ozone issue should not be given in concentrations of pollutants or gases, but in terms of rate of change of emissions. I suggest the most relevant indicators are:

- Total ozone change (per cent per decade)
- UV-B change at a specific place (per cent per decade)
- CFCs' rate of change in the troposphere (per cent per decade)
- Halons' and HCFCs' rate of change in the troposphere (per cent per decade)
- Methyl bromide rate of change in the troposphere (per cent per decade)
- Rate of change of NO_x production (per cent per decade).

More elaborate indices could also be easily perceived by the public, even though they need sophisticated models to be evaluated. An example of this is the contribution of the substitutes for CFCs and halons to the global greenhouse gases budget, and its evolution with time. This time evolution index is an important issue at a time when the relative contribution of CO_2 should be decreasing. This index will be common to both this policy field and the Climate Change policy field.

A second example is the time needed to return to a situation similar to that existing before the Antarctic ozone hole appeared, if the amended Montreal Protocol is implemented. Such a figure can be updated regularly from the observed application of the Protocol, and it gives the public an important notion of the duration of a disturbance. This would be of benefit to other issues such as the control of greenhouse gas emissions, when discussing the impact of delaying a decision to reduce emissions.

5. CONCLUSION

There are a number of surprising results from this survey. First, the absence of methyl bromide CH_3Br from the top five in the list is surprising because methyl bromide will be a larger contributor than halons and HCFCs to the load of chlorine in the atmosphere until 2100. Second, CO_2 should not be mentioned in the ozone depletion context because it plays no role. It has been proved that the cooling of the stratosphere results more from ozone depletion and water vapour increase than from CO_2 increase, and there is no other scientific reason to mention it. It would be justifiably highly placed in the Climate Change indicator list.

The main parameters to use for monitoring ozone depletion, after the source gases responsible for the depletion, are total ozone and the UV penetration to the surface. However, these indicators are not even present on the survey list. They are essential since, although there is a good initial understanding of the causes of ozone depletion, the observed depletion is larger than predicted, and one should always be aware that surprises may occur in a non-linear system (as in the case of the Antarctic ozone hole). Also, the consequences of UV radiation on terrestrial and aquatic ecosystems is crucial for policy-making in the coming years.

NOTE

1. The condensation of the indicators into a set of indices has now moved further down the political agenda, although such a development is not excluded at a later stage. See Fore-word.

REFERENCES

WMO (1990), *Scientific Assessment of Stratospheric Ozone: 1989*, Global Ozone Research and Monitoring Project Report no. 20, vols 1 and 2 (Geneva: WMO).

WMO (1992), *Scientific Assessment of Ozone Depletion: 1991*, Global Ozone Research and Monitoring Project Report no. 25. vol. 1 (Geneva: WMO).

WMO (1995) *Scientific Assessment of Ozone Depletion: 1994*, Global Ozone Research and Monitoring Project Report no. 37, vol. 1 (Geneva: WMO).

WMO (1999) *Scientific Assessment of Ozone Depletion: 1998*, Global Ozone Research and Monitoring Project, Report no. 44 (Geneva: WMO).

PART VI

Resource Depletion

19. Introduction

A. Viergever[1] and W. Sauer

1. BACKGROUND

Eurostat, the Statistical Office of the European Communities, has embarked on a project to define pressure indicators for ten of the major policy fields within the EU's environmental policy, as laid down in the Fifth Environmental Action Programme (5EAP).[2] One of these ten policy fields is Resource Depletion, which is the subject of this part of the volume. Elements of the Eurostat project comprise the operationalization of the ten policy fields in terms of delimitation with respect to other policy fields. Three essays, drafted by noted experts within each policy field, contributed to this aim and also provided a starting-point for the development of a limited set of about thirty indicators per policy field. Based on these essays, the suggestions made by the 'Scientific Advisory Groups' (SAGs – some 200–300 experts per policy field throughout the EU) and the expertise from earlier projects, INFOPLAN Environmental Consultants, contractors of Eurostat, have created a framework allowing the delimitation, aggregation and positioning of indicators for Resource Depletion on a European scale.

The potential indicators were obtained by sending a questionnaire to the SAG for Resource Depletion, asking for suggestions. This produced a huge and heterogeneous set of indicators, which had to be reduced to a 'manageable' set of specific pressure indicators for Resource Depletion, to be used as the basis for the second round of the survey – the ranking of the indicators. Similar suggestions were grouped into pressure indicators which are compatible, as far as possible, with those already identified or in use by the OECD, the EC and/or the appropriate Member State organizations and agencies, producing 27 indicators for Resource Depletion. The SAGs were asked to rank these indicators according to the three quality criteria of policy relevance, analytical soundness and responsiveness. The SAGs were also asked to rank their top five 'core indicators'. Figure 19.1 shows the results of the 'quality' questions with indicators ranked from 1 (very low) to 4 (very high) and core rankings expressed as a percentage of experts who included the indicator in their top five list of essential indicators.

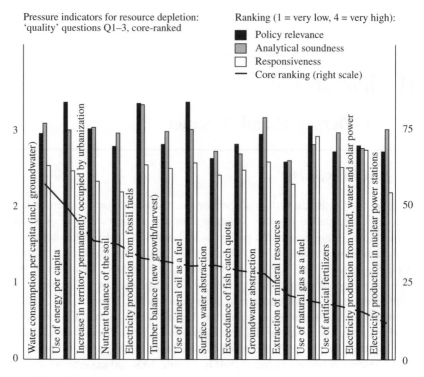

*Figure 19.1   Results of second-round questionnaire for the Resource
Depletion policy field*

2.   POLICY FIELD DELIMITATION

Environmental pressure can, in principle, be exerted on natural resources in
two ways: resources may be subject to depletion (diminishing the quantity
of the resource) and to degradation (deteriorating the quality of the resource). Degradation of the quality of the resource in most cases reduces
the availability for human use. The geographical scale is important for
natural resources: they may be used in Europe, but the stocks may be
depleted elsewhere. In these cases the depletion should be depicted in terms
of consumption in the Member States versus global reserves. Where the
resources are strictly European, the depletion within the Member States can
be depicted.

As to the exact definition of natural resources, there is none. Natural
resources are perceived to be many things, depending on the eye of the
beholder. The Pressure Indicators Project (PIP) has brought more clarity to

the question of what natural resources are and, more particularly, what they are meant to be within the PIP.

The PIP is seeking to develop pressure indicators for ten policy fields, more or less derived from the issues within the Fifth Environmental Action Programme (5EAP). The ten policy fields more or less artificially split up various phenomena into several categories. This division is responsible for the placement of biodiversity, water resources, marine resources and waste (all of which may be perceived to be natural resources) into separate policy fields. Also natural resources may be depleted, and degraded by several types of pollution, covered by the remaining policy fields, although these policy fields are mostly defined from the perspective of human toxicity or ecotoxicity and not from the perspective of natural resources degradation. An indication of the relationship between natural resources and other policy issues and economic sectors within the 5EAP is given in Figure 19.2.

The figure shows that there are various relations between the policy fields. It also shows that certain elements are only covered by the policy field of Resource Depletion. The elements on the left: biodiversity, marine resources and water resources (and even waste) may be perceived to be subsets of natural resources. The pollution-oriented policy issues below (water pollu-

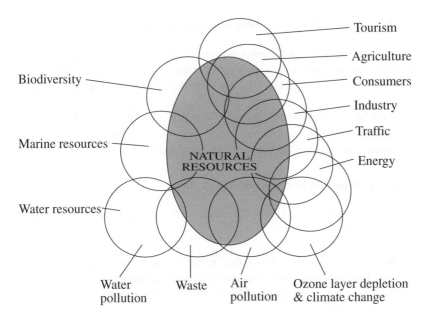

Figure 19.2   Relationship between Natural Resources and other policy issues and economic sectors within the 5EAP

tion, waste, air pollution, ozone layer depletion and climate change) all have to do with resource degradation. The economic sectors either deplete resources (materials and energy input) or degrade resources (pollution and interventions).

3. APPROACHES USED IN THE CONTRIBUTIONS

The contribution were prepared following Eurostat guidelines and a general description of the project. The contributors were asked to describe the following aspects of resource depletion:

1. Resource depletion as a (European) problem
2. The need for national or EU political intervention
3. Short-term and long-term priority actions/measures
4. Expected benefits of a pressure index for natural resources.

Additionally INFOPLAN requested comments on which resources are valuable for European policy development, and whether only resources *within* Europe should be taken into account, or all resources relevant *to* Europe.

Similarities and Differences between the Contributions

The chapters each cover different aspects of resource depletion. Lone covers all resources and comes up with a categorization, classification and selection of resources. Pearce considers the methodological aspects of indicator development and proposes that pressure indicators can feed into measures of sustainability. Weber focuses more on the character of the problems caused by resource depletion and comes up with a selection based on the relative significance of these problems on a European scale.

Resource Depletion as a (European) Problem

Lone suggests that, in essence, three categories of natural resources may be distinguished:

1. Renewable resources, which may either be inflowing or cyclic
2. Conditionally renewable resources (environmental media or biota)
3. Non-renewable resources, either recyclable or transient.

Although this categorization has its shortcomings, it serves very well to distinguish renewability and depletability. Lone argues that in the context of the PIP only conditionally renewable resources are of importance. The condition of renewability is that a certain level of depletion is not superseded. By definition this level would be a sustainability level. Human actions may also degrade renewable resources through disruption of cycles or through pollution. The latter is the subject of other policy fields, as explained above.

Pearce argues that potentials for renewal are an important issue from an economic point of view, using national 'genuine savings' as an example. He states that depletion on the whole is not an issue in the EU as there is no scarcity, but argues that degradation of resources through pollution is an issue.

Weber pleads for the maintenance of, or improvement in, the availability of resources for present and future use, and for the conservation of the potential for renewal of resources. It should be noted, however, that the conditions for renewal are not fixed. They depend on the actual state of depletion or degradation and on the demands for the services to be rendered (and the choice therein). Weber agrees with Lone on the choice of resources, but specifically adds land and ecosystems, by which he means intensified land use by several economic sectors such as agriculture and infrastructure.

The Need for National or EU Political Intervention

Lone emphasizes the need for management of soils, inland water, wood and fish resources. All of these resources are already the subject of national and international policies, but for these resources he gives arguments for specific European concern.

Pearce argues that the EU should aim towards the creation of a consistent system of sustainable development indicators that goes beyond the pressure–state–response system and that includes the savings and assets of the Member States. His chapter is particularly useful in showing the feasibility of political measures to be taken in the field of resource depletion. People seem to be more than willing to pay for the improvement of the quality of environmental resources. The chapter also demonstrates the necessity for the EU to take political responsibility for natural resources even beyond the EU territory, even though Pearce mostly uses examples within the policy fields of Biodiversity and Water Resources.

Weber argues that a link between environmental and other policies such as economic and social policies is needed. He elaborates this using land and ecosystems as main examples.

Short-term and Long-term Priority Actions/Measures

Table 19.1   Recommended actions for the Resource Depletion policy field

Lone	Weber	Pearce
Reduced grazing and cultivation intensity (soil)	Improved energy/ materials efficiency	Economic accounting procedures
Reduced ground- and surface-water withdrawals (water)	Improved land use planning	Reduced pollution for agents prioritized by epidemiology and economy
Reduced deposition of airborne pollutants, forest fires, grazing intensity and removals (wood)	Enhanced environmental responsibilities for the agriculture sector and transport infrastructure	Continued reform of the Common Agricultural Policy
Reduced catches of stocks and species (fish)	Support to developing countries to reduce ecological pressures	Programme on soil conservation and decontamination

Expected Benefits of a Pressure Index for Natural Resources

Lone sees the benefits in an increase in consciousness and the operational-ization of sustainability levels.

Pearce advocates sound and transparent indicators, such as his 'genuine savings', as they best influence both policy-makers and the general public. The benefits lie in public awareness and political embarrassment (for not being 'high up the ladder'). The weighting procedure within the Pressure Indicators Project may also contribute to priority setting, but he would like to see a weighting by more than one societal group (the SAG).

Weber talks of anticipation of problems, understanding of responsibilities and adjustment of behaviour, and would like to see an integral array of pressure–state–response indicators.

The Framework

The chapters have contributed to the construction of a framework for Resource Depletion indicators. The SAG suggestions resulted in the construction of a framework with a third category besides depletion and degradation introduced – namely self-sufficiency: the degree to which countries provide for their own demand for natural resources. If this indicator is negative, the country leaves an ecological footprint elsewhere. The SAG suggestions for indicators for Resource Depletion have been clustered into this framework, which is presented in Table 19.2.

The framework produced a list of indicators which was not directly suitable for the second questionnaire to the SAG, as these indicators used percentages and exceedance of sustainable levels as metrics. As explained in the questionnaire, sustainable levels are not yet available and some of these indicators would also not allow the depiction of pressures in relation to economic sectors. Therefore other indicators had to be defined in terms of physical units of measurement and linkages to economic sectors. This produced the list of 27 indicators included in the second-round questionnaire for core ranking and for ranking according to the three quality criteria.

4. CONCLUSIONS

The full list of core ranked pressure indicators for the Resource Depletion Policy Field is given in Annex I(B).

- The framework is a helpful instrument in making the policy field of Resource Depletion operational in terms of pressure indicator development.
- The indicators which are directly derived from the framework cover all aspects of the policy field of Resource Depletion.
- The SAG suggestions are not evenly distributed throughout the indicators. This could either be due to a non-random distribution of the expertise within the SAGs, or due to the possibility that the various subjects are not evenly well known among the SAGs. In any case it should not automatically be interpreted as giving insight into the relative importance of the subjects.
- The framework and the derived indicators constitute the infrastructure needed to define sustainability levels for Resource Depletion.
- The ranked indicators enable a prioritization of policy goals.

Table 19.2   SAG suggestions for Resource Depletion indicators

Non-renewable resources	Depletion	Self-sufficiency[a]
Metals	Consumption vs global proven reserves	Production vs consumption
Minerals	Production vs reserves	Production vs consumption
Fossil fuels	Consumption vs global proven reserves	Production vs consumption

Renewable resource	Depletion	Self-sufficiency
Non-fossil fuels	Energy production from wind, water, solar and nuclear energy sources	Production vs total energy consumption

Conditionally renewable resources	Degradation	Depletion	Self-sufficiency
Fresh surface-water	Acidification above sustainable level Salinization above sustainable level Eutrophication (index) above sustainable level Human toxicity index above sustainable level	Abstraction plus discharge vs inflow	Production vs consumption
Fresh groundwater	Acidification above sustainable level Salinization above sustainable level Eutrophication (index) above sustainable level Human toxicity index above sustainable level	Abstraction vs inflow	Production vs consumption
Air	Human toxicity index above sustainable level	X	X
Soil	Fertility (nutrient balance) Human toxicity index above sustainable level	Soil loss (run-off)	X

Table 19.2   continued

Conditionally renewable resources	Degradation	Depletion	Self-sufficiency
Territory	X	Permanent occupation by urbanization, infrastructure, waste-tipping and quarrying	X
Fish	Percentage of catch unfit for human or animal consumption	Fish catch above sustainable level	Fish production vs consumption
Wood	Vitality index (tree-health)	Timber balance (new growth vs harvest)	Wood production vs consumption
Biodiversity	Number of hectares of natural reserves (possibly divided in classes of quality or ecotopes)		X

Note: [a] It should be noted that self-sufficiency is not necessarily a reliable measure of sustainability when taken alone. A country's production may provide for total national consumption but this does not take into account the exploitation of resources for export.

NOTES

1.   Director of E*M*A*I*L, Leiden (NL), see list of Specialized institutes in Annex II.
2.   See terminology in Annex IV.

20. Resource depletion

Ø. Lone

1. PROBLEMS OF NATURAL RESOURCE DEPLETION

Considered from the perspective of depletion, exhaustion or over-exploitation, natural resources may be classified as *renewable* or *non-renewable*. It is essential, however, to develop this classification further, by introducing a third category, intermediate to natural resources that are absolutely renewable or non-renewable. This important category concerns resources which are *conditionally renewable*: they may be used and managed as renewable within certain limits, but may also be over-exploited. Each of these three main categories may further be divided as follows:

- *Renewable* resources are either inflowing, such as solar and cosmic radiation, or cyclic, such as wind, waves, tides and the hydrologic cycle, and cycles of the ocean and atmosphere.
- *Conditionally renewable* resources are either environmental media, such as land, including soil, water and air, or biological, such as plant and animal species, and populations.
- *Non-renewable* resources are either recyclable, such as minerals, or transient, such as fossil and nuclear fuels.

To a large extent, of course, this classification cuts across fundamental environmental and ecological relationships, as all the categories are closely linked. 'Cyclic' and 'environmental media' resources are here just two separate aspects (energy, materials) of the same physical resources. Soil is, similarly, an environmental medium as well as a biological resource. At a deeper level, all life is ultimately dependent on the inflowing resources of the sun, which drives the cycles, maintains the environmental media, produces the biological resources, and produced the fossil fuels through geological time. The purpose of this classification is simply to focus on renewability and depletability, not to exhaust every aspect of natural resource characteristics.

Renewable resources will not be considered further here, though human intervention may of course interfere with and even disrupt oceanic and atmospheric cycles (for example climate change through anthropogenic greenhouse gas emissions). Such considerations are here assumed to be dealt with under one or more of the other nine policy fields in the Pressure Indicators Project (PIP).

The last two main categories (four, including sub-categories) are depletable or exhaustible resources, the use of which may be irreversible (they are always irreversible in the case of transient/energy resources). In addition to these categories, another critical distinction is the one between material (and energy) resources that provide humanity with goods that are mostly traded and largely substitutable, and environmental resources that more frequently provide services that are mostly non-traded (public goods or common property resources) and non-substitutable.

Material (and energy) resources that are traded and substitutable are not considered further here. This means that non-renewable natural resources are not regarded as critical issues in a national or EU context. Such resources can, when depleted, be substituted by other resources or imported. From an analysis limited to environmental aspects, as laid down in the guidelines for these contributions, this seems a logical conclusion. Concern over non-renewable resource scarcity was very much a focus of attention in the 1970s, for example in the discussion about 'limits to growth'. However, concern has now shifted to issues related to the outputs (discharges, emissions) from the use and throughput of natural resources more than their availability, and to the issue of technological and economic development of substitutes, for example of optical fibres for copper, or of solar energy for fossil fuels. National or EU policies for such resources may of course be formulated for political, economic or strategic reasons (trade, national/regional security and so on).

The type of resources relevant here for national or EU policy is therefore *conditionally renewable resources*. These may be irreversibly over-exploited or degraded, but may, under responsible management, continue to provide goods and services for a long time into the future.

The general problem of depletion of conditionally renewable resources is that this may cause reduced production of environmental services and/or material goods, a reduction that, in contrast to that from non-renewable resources, is avoidable. This may cause physical scarcities, but, more seriously, increased prices, reduced employment and reduced quality of environmental services.

At this point, it is necessary to examine the relation between Resource Depletion and the other nine policy fields in this project. The division of issues in Eurostat's project is along two separate lines, partly according to environmental challenges or threats (climate change, ozone layer depletion, loss of biodiversity, resource depletion, dispersion of toxic substances), but also partly according to environmental media (air, water, marine, urban), and, additionally, a management category (waste). This could, unfortunately, cause problems of double treatment and, in index construction, double-counting. It may be helpful to illustrate this comment. 'Air Pollution' would seem to cover 'other air pollution than greenhouse gases, ozone-depleting substances and local/urban air pollution' and might perhaps more precisely be called 'acidification and oxidation' (this seems, from the illustrative example indicators, to be what is covered by this policy field). Another example is the double treatment given to toxic substances under the various environmental media (Marine/Coastal, Water, and Waste) in addition to the main treatment under 'Dispersion of Toxic Substances'.

From the perspective of natural resource depletion, the other nine policy fields as presently set up are interpreted so that environmental quality aspects of conditionally renewable environmental media resources are not considered under the Resource Depletion heading; nor are species/sub-species and eco-system protection, concerning conditionally renewable biological resources. These aspects are assumed to be dealt with under the appropriate media and biodiversity policy fields. There is one modification to this rule, when the physical volume and yield (production) of biological resources are affected by environmental quality changes. These cases are considered just as much, or even more, a natural resource concern than an environmental quality concern. An obvious example of this is the effect of acidification on forest and freshwater fish stocks.

2. NEED FOR NATIONAL OR EU POLITICAL INTERVENTION

Because of well-known market failures (concerning common property resources with open access, externalities and provision of public goods) and sometimes government failures (market barriers, subsidies and so on), there is a need for national intervention and in many cases EU intervention in the management of conditionally renewable natural resources.

Stressed here as cases of particular concern are soils, water resources, wood resources and fish resources. Soil resources are, in many European countries, over-exploited, degraded and eroded. Because of climatic conditions, such problems are perhaps particularly severe in southern and Mediterranean Member States. Most countries have, in their agricultural and/ or environmental policies, provisions to deal with soil erosion and degradation, though the effectiveness of such policies may still be increased. The issue is also of EU concern, if not for other reasons, because of the Common Agricultural Policy (CAP), including its quotas and price supports, and its provisions for environmental policy measures following the 1992 reforms.

Water Resources

Water resources are in short supply in a number of countries, and to the extent that water quantity problems can be distinguished from water quality problems, are an obvious candidate for an indicator of pressure on resources. Though some quantity issues may be dealt with by the private sector or by local government, national intervention is necessary, *inter alia* because of the national importance of many major river networks. In some cases (archetypically the Rhine) several European countries need to cooperate in water management. (Special attention to coordination with the Water Pollution and Water Resources policy field is necessary here for developing indices.)

Wood Resources

Wood resources are under pressure in European countries in different ways, although the classic problem of over-exploitation is not, except in a few cases, really pressing. However, the serious effects of airborne pollutants on forest health and long-term production (yield), particularly in northern countries, and the incidence of forest fires and to some degree overgrazing, particularly in southern countries, are both examples of pressures on natural resources necessitating national and, in the case of transboundary air pollutants, international action.

Fish Resources

Finally, as is evident from the highly politicized debate on fisheries policies within the EU and in negotiations with neighbouring countries, the state of oceanic fish resources in European and adjacent ocean areas is perhaps the most critical natural resource depletion issue in Europe. The EU is already strongly involved in this field which, by its nature as a common property resource with open access, requires national and international action. Aquatic fish resources also require policy action, partly in relation to water management policy (quality and quantity), and partly in relation to airborne pollutants (acidification), as discussed above in connection with wood resources.

Even though renewable resources (energy, minerals) have not been considered here to constitute a European resource management issue, because of import and substitution possibilities, global considerations should still be taken into account. The import of *conditionally* renewable resources, for example tropical wood and wood products, or cassava (manioc) as animal feed, is an issue to the extent that resource stocks in exporting countries are not managed sustainably. The EU is such a large trading bloc that such impacts on the rest of the world need to be taken into account.

With regard to the actual pressure indicators, the following comments may be offered. *Pressure* is probably most usefully expressed in relation to stocks and/or yield, rather than as gross figures of extraction, harvests, removals or catches. The quality and volume and/or yield of the resource stocks themselves would seem the most appropriate measures for the *state* of the resources in each environmental policy field, while actions and measures would indicate the societal *responses*. To illustrate this approach for the Loss of Biodiversity field, 'protected areas' would most usefully serve as a response indicator (at most as an indicator of the state of the resource), not as a pressure indicator/index, while 'fragmentation' would be an indicator of the state of the resource. Appropriate indicators of pressure could be (new) road construction, *increased* fragmentation, or (new) drainage of wetlands in agriculture and forestry.

3. SHORT-TERM AND LONG-TERM ACTION/ MEASURES

Action and measures to reduce pressures on soils include reduced grazing and cultivation intensity, implemented as changes and reforms to national and EU agricultural policies. This can be part of a move towards a reduced proportion of price supports and other production-linked financial measures, and an increased proportion of land and land-use-linked measures, including active conservation management practices, with regulations concerning, for example, stocking densities, cultivation intensities and fertilizer application, all of which might be linked to financial incentives.

For water resources action should be taken to reduce withdrawals, both from surface water and groundwater. This could be implemented using administrative quotas and/or proper, full-cost pricing, including resource and environmental costs. EU policies or guidelines on implementing the user pays and polluter pays principles may be important in this context.

For wood resources, action should include lower removals in some cases, but mainly reduced deposition of air pollutants, especially in northern Europe, and reduced intensity of grazing and incidence of forest fires, especially in southern Europe. Air pollution and agricultural/forestry policies at both EU and national level are of importance here.

Action for fisheries should include reduction in catches for a number of stocks and species, to be carried out as part of a much-needed reform of national and EU fisheries policies. This is probably the most critical issue faced by the EU in the field of natural resource depletion, as present policies do not seem to be adequate or implemented with sufficient force.

4. EXPECTED BENEFITS

The benefits of a pressure index for communication to the general public and policy-makers would consist of raised consciousness concerning natural resource depletion and increased attention to these policy issues.

Specifically, these benefits would result from clear and understandable indices for the pressure on conditionally renewable natural resources with a definite, if changing and not always easily determined, critical limit ('carrying capacity'). Both indices or indicators may be of considerable use for various issues and at different levels of analysis, by making it apparent how far the existing resource exploitation situation is away from policy objectives, and in which direction and how quickly trends are moving. They could therefore play an important role in evaluating and assessing policy effectiveness. The general public, business sectors actively involved in managing such natural resources, and civil servants and policy-makers at national and EU levels would be given appropriate and relevant information to improve policies and the economic management of soils, water, forests and fish resources.

5. COMMENTS ON INDICATORS SELECTED IN THE PRESSURE INDICATORS PROJECT

Of the 27 indicators resulting from the PIP questionnaires (see Annex I), RD-1 to RD-12 relate to energy and minerals, where the concern, in my opinion, is more about the environmental resources affected by such resource use than the stock or quality of these resources. RD-13 to RD-27 deal with conditionally renewable resources, and are more directly relevant to the issue of resource depletion. With the exception of RD-21 and RD-22, which are relevant mainly to the issue of biodiversity, these are all relevant and useful indicators.

The most relevant ones are those that combine 'gross' pressures with some measure of carrying capacity or balance, such as RD-20 Nutrient balance of the soil, RD-23 Exceedance of fish catch (but only in relation to quotas, not to stocks, yields or annual increment), and particularly RD-26 Timber balance (new growth/harvest). Concerning timber, the impact of air pollution and of forest fires/overgrazing might also be considered, since commercial overharvesting of wood is probably not the major resource depletion problem in Europe.

For the issue of water abstraction, it would be highly desirable to have some measure of abstraction or withdrawals in relation to available resources (such as run-off). This measure may be most meaningful at local or regional (river-basin) level, although it does have some relevance at national level since Northern European countries withdraw only 0.5–2 per cent of run-off, whereas Southern European countries withdraw on average 30–40 per cent of overall run-off.

Finding data for the selected indicators may be a very difficult task; however, the crucial point is that relative indicators are much more useful and relevant than those measuring gross pressures, even if these may be useful in showing trends and the speed of changes in trends. To evaluate pressures in relation to critical levels, however, pressure/capacity indicators are strongly preferred.

21. Natural resources

D. Pearce

1. NATURAL RESOURCES AS A EUROPEAN PROBLEM

Article 130r(1) of the Treaty on European Union calls for Community action to contribute to the 'prudent and rational utilization of natural resources', but nowhere defines what is meant by 'natural resources'. In this chapter we take natural resources to refer to non-renewable resources (minerals and fossil energy), to renewable resources (forests, fisheries, wildlife, habitat), and to mixed renewable and non-renewable resources (soils, groundwater).

Is there a Natural Resource Problem in the European Union?

Minerals
As far as minerals are concerned, it can be argued that there is no major issue to be addressed. This is because the available economic indicators of mineral scarcity suggest that there is no problem. Scarcity is measured by assessing whether or not there is a significant 'scarcity premium' in the price of the mineral resources. This scarcity premium is more usually known as the 'rental'. It can be found by calculating the costs of replacing any given mineral at the time the supply of the mineral is expected to be exhausted. Table 21A1.1 of the Annex to this chapter reports scarcity premia for crude oil, natural gas, metals and minerals. In both absolute terms and relative to the figures for pollution damage, it can be seen that the figures are very small, indicating no serious scarcity issue.

Fossil energy
As far as fossil energy is concerned, the problems do not lie in the availability of energy but in two aspects of their use: (a) the environmental pollution from energy conversion and use, and (b) significant energy reserves to reinvest proceeds from the exploitation of those reserves.

Issue (a) is not within the scope of this chapter, but some comment is required. Tables 21A1.1 and 21A1.2 in Annex 1 show some preliminary estimates of the value of resource depletion and air pollution damage in EU countries, plus Norway. Air pollution damage is seen to produce a substantial level of damages as measured by monetary values of willingness to pay. Pearce and Crowards (1996) suggest that damages from particulate matter may be seriously understated in these measures: health damage in the UK from particulates alone may be as high as 2 per cent of GNP.

Issue (b) is also potentially important. We can define a nation's 'genuine savings' as its gross savings less the depreciation on its capital assets, where capital includes environmental capital (Atkinson et al., 1997). Failure to achieve a positive genuine savings level over a reasonable period of time amounts to 'mining' natural resources, that is, to potentially unsustainable behaviour. Commentary on measures of genuine savings for the EU countries plus Norway is given in Annex 2 to this chapter. There it is suggested that energy-rich countries in the EU may not have reinvested rentals at an adequate rate to ensure overall sustainability. In one other case, Greece, genuine savings are also at a level that gives rise to sustainability concerns.

Biological diversity

Biodiversity is a natural resource that is seriously undervalued in the world, and in the EU. Biodiversity refers to the number, variety and variability of living organisms and covers genetic, species and ecosystem diversity. Its importance is indicated by the fact that it provides the following functions for humankind: current food resources, insurance for future food resources, pharmaceuticals, amenity, scientific information and maintenance of basic ecological processes ('life support').

Within the EU, biological diversity is most important with respect to the basic maintenance of ecological processes and for amenity. Available evidence suggests that Europeans value their natural amenity very highly. One way of measuring individuals' concern for the environment is to assess how much they are willing to pay to conserve it. Thus it is known that people are willing to pay a premium in the housing market for quieter property and for areas with less pollution. This premium measures their willingness to pay (WTP). Similarly, people express a willingness to pay for a recreational area by spending money on travel to reach the site, and this can also be interpreted as a willingness to pay. Various techniques are available for inferring willingness to pay.

Allowing for income variations in the EU, and a population of some 370 million, such valuations would suggest that basic habitat is worth at least 2 billion p.a. in the EU (taking the modest 6 ECUs p.a. for amenity with substitutes), and very much more once heritage sites are accounted for.

Taking the world's threatened species, wider Europe (including Eastern Europe) has about 12 per cent of the plant species, 4 per cent of mammals, 15 per cent of the birds, 4 per cent of the reptiles, 22 per cent of amphibians and 9 per cent of fish. Some individual EU countries figure prominently in the

Table 21.1   Percentage of pan-European threatened species in one country

	Plants	Mammals	Birds	Amphibians	Fish
Spain	35	9	6	20	4
Italy	8	4	5	12	6
Greece	20	6	5	–	13
Portugal	9	9	5	7	–
France	5	9	5	7	6

Note: all data computed from WCMC (1992).

lists of threatened species, as shown in Table 21.1. The prevalence of countries of large area in these lists is not surprising since the number of threatened species generally varies positively with land area (WCMC, 1992).

Obviously, the EU's role in biodiversity conservation does not end with conservation efforts within its own borders. It extends immediately to the potential new entrants to the Union and more broadly to the rest of the world through the various international conventions, including the Convention on Biodiversity.

Fisheries
EU countries took around 7 per cent of the world's marine fishery catch in 1990, a similar percentage of the diadromous catch and a minor 0.4 per cent of the world's freshwater catch. None the less, as is widely known, the state of EU fisheries is poor despite the existence of the Common Fisheries Policy. The state of cod and herring fisheries in the North Sea is repeatedly threatened by overfishing.

Groundwater
Press (1995) reports the findings of a groundwater quality study for Milan, Italy. Average WTP for improved water quality was in the range of 0.4–1.0 million Italian lire per household per annum, that is, some 190–475 ECUs per annum. Press remarks that these values are suspiciously high, but it is noteworthy that they are in the range of the US studies. On the other hand, Hanley (1989) reports a study for an eastern region of England in which householders were asked their WTP to improve water quality in their area so as to achieve the EC standard for nitrate. The mean WTP was some £13 (15.6 ECUs) per household per annum, a long way below the Milan study and perhaps supporting that study's author in doubting the validity of the Milan responses. On the other hand, £13 p.a. is sufficient when aggregated to suggest that the benefits of nitrate control exceed their costs comfortably.

Soils

Soil quality is a neglected issue in the EU. There is a temptation to think that it is a problem confined to tropical countries, but several problems occur in the EU. The first is soil erosion. Community data suggest that perhaps 65 per cent of land in the South of France is at high risk of erosion, 55 per cent in Italy, 30 per cent in Greece, 23 per cent in Spain and 14 per cent in Portugal (CEC, 1992). The second problem is soil contamination by acidic depositions, organic compounds and heavy metals. The importance of erosion relates mainly to the effects on crops, but it also has an impact on biological resources. Contamination has the potential for toxic effects on human health but it is more importantly related to loss of biological diversity (see above).

Conclusion on Natural Resources as an Issue in the EU

There is no direct 'natural resource scarcity' problem in the EU, but there are problems arising from the depletion of biological diversity, soil quality and fisheries. In all these cases over-use of the resource is the proximate problem: habitat is not so much directly converted to other uses, but is eroded by competing uses. Agricultural practice has done much to reduce biological diversity, but pollution generally is also a major concern.

2.   THE NEED FOR COLLECTIVE ACTION

Action is required at both national and Community level in several respects. First, with respect to reinvestment of exhaustible resource proceeds, national policy is relevant since it is up to individual nations to choose potentially sustainable or unsustainable paths. But a consistent set of indicators on sustainability is required across nations to enable them to determine the early warning signals if sustainability is threatened. In the context of the pressure–state–response paradigm, the pressures here are not normally ones that would be wholly detected by conventional indicators. This is because PSR indicators do not rest on any theory of what constitutes sustainable development. The approach taken here is to adopt a theory of sustainable development that stresses the relationship between a nation's savings and the wearing out or damaging of its assets (depreciation), including its environmental assets. This depreciation is measured in monetary terms. What this means is that, effectively, the 'weights' that combine conventional physical indicators are (marginal) WTP estimates ('shadow prices'). Accounts must be consistent across nations and hence the Commission would itself have a role to play in this process, building on initiatives it has already undertaken (for example this project, ExternE, Commission DG XII's sustainability indicators projects and so on).

Second, air pollution damage is particularly associated with the transport sector, especially the role played by small particulates, nitrogen dioxides and VOCs (volatile organic compounds) as low-level ozone precursors, and perhaps air toxins such as benzene. Any policy intervention in transport raises problems of competitiveness, and hence policy measures should be integrated across countries as far as possible. More generally, there is a need for a coordinated European transport policy and a strong focus on the health of EU citizens as the main issue at stake.

Third, biodiversity conservation will not be tackled adequately by piece-meal policies of habitat protection. This is because biodiversity is being lost through the pervasive influence of economic policies generally. Tourism, urban development, roads, pollution and forestry all have impacts on biodiversity. Moreover, biological resources are not respecters of national boundaries, necessitating integrated policies. Hence biodiversity protection becomes a matter of integrated economic and environmental planning at both the national and community level.

Fourth, it is well known that fisheries loss can only be resolved in a cooperative fashion between governments. This is because the Community waters are effectively an 'open access' resource that is over-exploited because of the failure to regulate entry and use.

3. PRIORITY ACTIONS

A number of actions are required to deal with these natural resource issues. There is a need rapidly to develop economic accounting procedures that reflect the overall macroeconomic pressures that threaten sustainability. The suggestion above was that the 'genuine savings' approach goes a long way towards this. It is important to understand why it is more useful than other approaches. Conventional indicators, however weighted and aggregated, must reflect the general macroeconomic pressures giving rise to non-sustainability. But most indicators do not do this. Trends in pollution, for example, tell us that things are getting worse or better but they have no 'natural origin', so we cannot say that this level of pollution threatens sustainability while another level does not.

The savings approach, on the other hand, does have a natural origin. If genuine savings are negative it is a sign of unsustainability in an absolute sense. If they are positive they do not guarantee sustainability but give a reasonable indication that the right macroeconomic policies are being pursued. In the same vein, green GNP measures, while useful, do not tell us about sustainability. Green GNP (or, rather, net national product) may be rising or falling without any clear indication of whether sustainability is threatened.

Immediate attention is required to reduce the levels of those pollutants which both epidemiology and economics suggest are priorities. Within the EU, air pollutants of priority must be small particulate matter (PM_{10} or less), nitrogen dioxides and VOCs. This is because all these pollutants are associated with significant human health impacts. EU-wide indicators of trends in these pollutants should be established on a more comprehensive basis than is currently the case, especially with respect to the measurement of small particle matter and ozone levels.

Early attention to the continued reform of the Common Agricultural Policy (CAP) is required. The evidence is that the technology induced by the CAP has been responsible for major losses of biodiversity in the EU and for contamination of water supplies, including groundwater. Reversing this trend is not a short-term policy. It will take decades, but the work should start now. Indicators of biodiversity loss and measures of priority areas for conservation intervention are needed. Such indicators must encompass not just species measurement and endemism, but also the degree of threat to those resources and the chance of a successful policy intervention (Moran et al., 1996). The aim must be to reverse the decline in biodiversity within the EU.

A programme needs to be initiated on soil conservation and decontamination. Again, this is a long-term policy but with an urgent need for action now.

4.   THE BENEFITS OF ACTION

If the above concerns can be entered into a 'pressure' indicator, what benefits are likely to ensue?

A preliminary remark is in order because advocates and creators of environmental indicators are guilty of having exaggerated the benefits likely to ensue from their development. The result has been a rush to generate indicators of doubtful value. It is important to understand the audience for such indicators. The general public is unlikely to be influenced by any indicator that is not transparent. To this end, simple state indicators such as the decline in bird numbers are the best. Cleverly weighted and aggregated physical indicators are unlikely to have an influence because they are not transparent. Where they do have an influence, it is often of the wrong kind. An example is the widely disseminated Index of Sustainable Economic Welfare (ISEW) produced for the USA by Daly and Cobb (1989) and by Jackson and Marks (1994) for the UK. Atkinson (1995) has shown that this index is fundamentally flawed and contains a multiplicity of errors.

As far as policy-makers are concerned, the same considerations apply to some extent, except that experience shows they are most influenced by 'league table' indicators. The success of the Human Development Index produced by UNDP, for example, arises from the fact that countries can identify where they are in some league table ranking of 'standard of living' or 'human development'. This suggests that indicators need to be fairly transparent, fairly simple, and capable of being ranked. Simple indicators such as trends in bird numbers have these general characteristics, but so does the less obvious indicator of genuine savings. This is because everyone is familiar with the idea that one cannot 'mine' assets for very long before becoming bankrupt, and because the savings indicator has a natural origin.

The benefits of providing soundly based and persuasive indicators therefore arise from raising environmental awareness among the general public, and from instilling a sense of urgency and even shame among policy-makers if their country is not highly ranked in a league table of indicators.

In terms of influencing priority setting, great care needs to be taken in deriving indicators, or rather an index based on a set of indicators. This is because indicators themselves tell us nothing about priorities, but the weighting procedure used to aggregate them does tell us about priorities, or should. The weights must therefore be based on some rational assessment of importance. This could be public or expert opinion about environmental risks, but we know that these do not coincide. It could be a set of monetary weights that reflect opinion via willingness to pay plus expert assessments of the epidemiology or general dose response function. What is dangerous is to have a set of weights based on public opinion alone or on expert opinion alone, or even on decision-maker opinion alone. Nor is 'consensus' on weights necessarily a good thing, as this may reflect compromise rather than the truth.

How do the considerations addressed in this chapter link to the core indicator list? As noted, one major problem with the literature on environmental indicators is that the chosen measures are generally unsupported by any coherent model of what an indicator is for. Indicators of resource consumption, for example, do not contain adequate information about whether or not there is a problem for the environment or for sustainable development. What is required first is a theory of sustainability. This then generates hypotheses about the factors causing non-sustainability, and those hypotheses can be tested against the indicators. For this reason this chapter has focused on measures of sustainability, such as 'genuine savings'. At best, the core indicators feed into such measures but of themselves do not provide information which could be used by policy-makers to determine whether or not the EU is on a sustainable development path.

192   *Resource depletion*

REFERENCES

Atkinson, G. (1995), 'Measuring Sustainable Economic Welfare: a Critique of the UK ISEW', Centre for Social and Economic Research on the Global Environment, University College London and University of East Anglia, Paper 95-08.

Atkinson, G., M. Munasinghe, K. Hamilton, D.W. Pearce, R. Dubourg and C. Young (1997), *Measuring Sustainable Development: Environment and Macroeconomy in the Developing World* (Cheltenham, UK and Northampton, USA: Edward Elgar).

Commission of the European Communities (1992), *The State of the Environment in the European Community*, Vol. III (Brussels: CEC).

Daly, H. and J. Cobb (1989), *For the Common Good: Redirecting the Economy Toward Community, the Environment and a Sustainable Future* (Boston, MA: Beacon Press).

Hamilton, K. (1995), 'Genuine Savings in the European Union', Centre for Social and Economic Research on the Global Environment, University College London and University of East Anglia, mimeo.

Hanley, N. (1989), 'Problems in valuing environmental improvements resulting from agricultural policy changes: the case of nitrate pollution', in A. Dubgaard and A. Nielsen (eds), *Economic Aspects of Environmental Regulations in Agriculture* (Kiel: Wissenschaftsverlag Vauk Kiel).

International Council for Bird Preservation (ICBP) (1992), *Putting Biodiversity on the Map: Priority Areas for Global Conservation* (Cambridge: ICBP).

Jackson, T. and N. Marks (1994), *Measuring Sustainable Economic Welfare – a Pilot Index 1950–1990*, Stockholm Environment Institute, Stockholm.

Moran, D., D.W. Pearce and A. Wendelaar (1996), 'Global biodiversity priorities: a cost effectiveness index for investments', *Global Environmental Change*, **6** (2), 103–19.

Pearce, D.W., E. Ozdemiroglu, E. Calthrop, K. Hamilton and G. Atkinson (1997), *The Future of Environmental Policy in Europe: Assessing the Priorities* (Cheltenham, UK and Northampton, USA: Edward Elgar).

Pearce, D.W. and T. Crowards (1996), 'Particulate matter and human health in the United Kingdom', *Energy Policy*, **24** (7), July, 609–20.

Press, J. (1995), 'Establishing Priorities for Groundwater Quality: a Contingent Valuation Study in Milan', *Fondazione Eni Enrico Mattei Newsletter*, No. 1, pp. 7–10.

World Conservation and Monitoring Centre (1992), *Global Biodiversity: Status of the Earth's Living Resources* (London: Chapman and Hall).

ANNEX 1

Table 21A1.1 *Cost of resource depletion and air pollution damage in the EU (million ECU, 1990)*

Country	Resource depletion				Air pollution damage						
	Crude oil	Nat. gas	Metals & minerals	Total	SO_2	NO_x	PM_{10}	Total (conventional air pollutants)	CO_2	CH_4	Total (greenhouse gases)
Austria	60	64.0	33.0	157.0	738	1 278	888	2 904	370	84	454
Belgium	0	0.6	0	0.6	3 212	1 612	n.d.	4 824	747	n.d.	747
Denmark	312	0	0	312.0	1 724	1 893	n.d.	3 617	421	49	470
Finland	0	0	80.0	80.0	2 092	1 639	n.d.	3 732	328	25	353
France	157	146.0	64.0	367.0	9 784	8 517	6 252	24 553	2 541	n.d.	2 541
Germany	190	783.0	32.0	1 000.0	7 920	15 436	10 545	33 901	5 487	625	6 112
Greece	40	8.0	195.0	243.0	1 335	281	n.d.	1 616	452	n.d.	452
Ireland	0	110.0	0	1 104.0	836	402	1 305	2 543	189	73	262
Italy	242	811.0	108.0	1 161.0	18 030	10 508	10 431	38 968	2 859	256	3 115
Luxembourg	0	0	0	0	90	95	n.d.	185	61	n.d.	61
The Netherlands	184	3 159.0	0.5	3 344.0	1 530	2 909	1 500	5 939	1 118	84	1 202
Portugal	0	0	226.0	226.0	576	272	n.d.	848	247	n.d.	247
Spain	41.0	0	514.0	555.0	11 206	3 415	n.d.	14 621	1 467	93	1 560
Sweden	0.2	0	780.0	780.0	1 266	2 752	n.d.	4 018	335	46	381
UK	4 582.0	2 367.0	12.0	6 961.0	24 642	12 721	8 563	45 925	3 407	441	3 848
Total EU	5 808.0	7 448.0	2 045.0	15 301.0	84 981	63 730	39 484	188 195	20 030	1 777	21 807
Norway	4 150.0	1 397.0	73.0	5 620.0	499	1 494	540	2 534	212	28	240

Notes: 0 denotes no data and/or non-existent resource; n.d.: no data available.

Source: Pearce et al. (1997).

193

Table 21A1.2 Cost of resource depletion and air pollution damage expressed as percentage of GNP (%)

Country	Resource depletion				Air pollution damage						
	Crude oil	Nat. gas	Metals & minerals	Total	SO$_2$	NO$_x$	PM$_{10}$	Total (conventional air pollutants)	CO$_2$	CH$_4$	Total (greenhouse gases)
Austria	0.05	0.05	0.03	0.13	0.6	1.04	0.73	2.37	0.3	0.07	0.4
Belgium	0	neg.	0	0	2.16	1.08	n.d.	3.24	0.5	n.d.	0.5
Denmark	0.3	0	0	0.3	1.74	1.91	n.d.	3.64	0.4	0.05	0.5
Finland	0	0	0.08	0.08	2.08	1.59	n.d.	3.62	0.3	0.08	0.3
France	0.02	0.02	0.01	0.05	1.04	0.91	0.67	2.62	0.3	n.d.	0.3
Germany	0.02	0.06	neg.	0.08	0.69	1.34	0.91	2.93	0.4	0.05	0.5
Greece	0.08	0.02	0.4	0.5	2.93	0.62	n.d.	3.55	0.9	n.d.	0.9
Ireland	0	0.4	0	0.4	2.53	1.21	3.94	7.68	0.6	0.2	0.8
Italy	0.03	0.09	0.01	0.13	2.15	1.25	1.24	4.64	0.3	0.08	0.3
Luxembourg	0	0	0	0	1.3	1.37	n.d.	2.66	n.d.	n.d.	n.d.
The Netherlands	0.08	1.4	neg.	1.5	0.7	1.33	0.69	2.71	0.5	0.04	0.5
Portugal	0	0	0.5	0.5	1.29	0.61	n.d.	1.91	0.5	n.d.	0.5
Spain	0.01	0	0.1	0.1	2.93	0.89	n.d.	3.82	0.4	0.02	0.4
Sweden	neg.	0	0.4	0.4	0.72	1.55	neg.	2.27	0.2	0.03	0.2
UK	0.6	0.3	neg.	0.9	3.21	1.66	1.11	5.98	0.4	0.06	0.5
Norway	5	1.7	0.09	6.8	0.62	1.85	0.67	3.13	0.3	0.03	0.3

Notes: as for Table 29A1.1; neg.: negligible.

Source: Pearce et al. (1997).

194

ANNEX 2   GENUINE SAVINGS IN EU COUNTRIES

Genuine savings are defined as gross savings less depreciation on conventional capital assets less depreciation in natural resources (as measured by rental rates) less pollution damage. Full details are reported in Hamilton (1995). Brief comments on the savings curves for individual countries are as follows:

Austria	Savings rates are above average, with relatively little variation over time.
Belgium	Savings rates begin below the mean, but converge to the overall average by 1990.
Denmark	Savings rates were on a generally upward trend, starting below the mean and converging to the mean by 1990.
Finland	Savings rates were everywhere above average, with a very slight downward trend.
France	Savings rates were near the mean, with low levels of variation over the decade.
Germany	Rates were above average and on a steady upward trend from 1981.
Greece	Savings rates dropped sharply in 1982, with gross rates remaining level at roughly half of the EU average for the remainder of the decade. Genuine savings rates were nearly zero from 1990 onwards.
Ireland	Savings rates climbed sharply in 1982 and remained on an upward trend thereafter, exceeding the EU average by 1984.
Italy	Savings rates started off above the EU average in 1980, then declined gently but steadily towards the average in 1990.
Luxembourg	Savings rates were highly variable, above the EU average and with an upward trend.
Netherlands	Gross savings rates were above the EU average over the decade, falling in 1987 with the decline in petroleum prices, then rising steadily thereafter. Genuine savings rates increased steadily, from below the EU average in 1980 to substantially above it in 1990.
Norway	Gross savings rates were substantially above those of other EU countries until 1984, followed by a sharp fall in 1985 and 1986. Genuine savings rates were variable and generally below the EU average, becoming negative in 1986.
Portugal	Initially lower than the EU average, gross savings in Portugal increased to near the average by 1986. This situation was mirrored by the genuine savings rate.

Spain   Spanish savings rates, both gross and genuine, were nearly
               constant over the decade, at a level approximating the EU
               average.

Sweden   From a level below the EU average in 1980, Swedish savings
               rates increased to near EU averages by 1986.

UK   UK gross savings were notable for starting below the EU
               average and actually declining moderately over the decade.
               Genuine savings rates were roughly zero up until 1987 and
               were considerably below the EU average thereafter.

Of the individual country results, the striking examples are Greece, the UK
and Norway. Genuine savings rates in Greece were effectively zero from
1982 onwards, and effectively zero in the UK up to 1987. Norwegian genuine
savings rates were erratic and below the EU average.

For the petroleum producers, genuine savings rates were zero or negative
at times over the decade. The oil price drop in 1986 shows up clearly in the
apparent boost in genuine saving that resulted from the halving of unit
resource rents, causing the value of depletion to decline by the same proportion. However, this apparent jump in genuine saving is counterbalanced by
lower income from the petroleum sector and a corresponding decrease in the
value of petroleum in the national balance sheet.

22. Resource depletion

J.-L. Weber

1. WHY IS RESOURCE DEPLETION A PROBLEM?

The issue of resource depletion is, of course, a major concern of environment and sustainable development policies. However, this chapter is limited to environmental aspects in the context of the elaboration of a pressure index. This leads us to consider a restricted interpretation of resources.

To what extent is the depletion of resources such as fossil fuels, ores and minerals an environment problem? The excessive use of these resources generates problems such as toxic pollution, waste generation, force feeding of the ecosystems, and changes in the composition of the atmosphere. But these problems derive from the use of the resource, not from the depletion itself. For this reason, and because it is covered by other policy fields, the pollution aspect is outside the scope of this chapter. In addition, the depletion of the economic assets caused by these pollution aspects, which is a basic parameter in sustainable development policies, is not included here.

Resource depletion is only an environmental problem if we consider the relationship between resource use in the production/consumption process and the ecosphere. We can identify three types of natural resource: material and energy, the ecosystems and land. These can be economic assets or non-marketed resources.

Water resources and biodiversity, as one dimension of the biosphere re-source, could be included as essential issues in the resource cluster. As they constitute separate items in this book, they are less developed in the present chapter.

From the point of view of pressure on the environment, resource depletion (in a narrow sense) of material and energy is limited to renewable resources. Such depletion leads to degradation; in other words, it threatens the renewing capacities of the environmental assets.[1]

The depletion of resources which are renewable (or potentially renewable) is a question of availability of the various uses (present and future) and of the potential for renewal. It means that we have not only to consider the changes in volume of a resource but also their characteristics, including their capacity for renewal. This leads us to define ecosystems as resources, as well as the land that supports them. It also means that degradation which upsets the balance of the ecosystem, leading to losses in terms of uses or to irreversible changes, has to be considered as a depletion of an available resource of a determined quality, or of a potential for reproducing the resource.

Thus the political objectives should be to maintain (or improve) the availability of the resource for the various uses and to conserve its potential for renewal. Due to the changes in both natural systems and human demand, an overall approach seems necessary. Due to the competition which may result from multiple uses of the same resources, related to a possible contradiction between short-term and long-term perspectives as well between individual and collective interest, the definition of optimal policies requires debate and consideration of the trade-offs.

2. THE IMPACTS OF CONCERN

In Europe, the main resources to encompass in a pressure index[2] from an environmental point of view are: land and ecosystems, water, soils, forests and fish stocks.

As long as, first, Europe relies heavily on imported resources in many areas and, second, global concerns are covered by the Pressure Indicators Project, the imports of such resources have to be considered on the same level as the European ones, due to the problems that they generate in the country of origin.

Keeping the Potential of Land and Ecosystems

From the development of agriculture on deforested land in the Middle Ages to the agricultural revolution in the middle of the twentieth century, the countryside in most countries in Europe has been an outstanding example of a sustainable system. Moreover, the symbiosis between nature and traditional agriculture led in many areas to improvements in biodiversity. The combination of cattle breeding and cultivation produced rich soils, and hedgerows and small walls along country lanes produced habitats for a rich fauna and flora. The situation changed in many countries with the need to increase food production after the Second World War and the subsequent development of intensive agriculture. The use of chemical fertilizers and pesticides, the amalgamation of land (required by the mechanization process) together with industrial development, the ongoing development of modern transport networks and the extension of urbanization generated high pressure on land. This has led to an impoverishment and erosion of soils in many areas, the destruction of habitats and species, a partitioning of land and the sealing of soils, and the degradation of landscapes, including those considered as amenities and the basic resource for tourism. The results are an increase in the artificiality and the intensity of land use in terms of structure, anthropic input and withdrawals of resource.

Topical Issues

The overall approach, which concentrates on the potential of land use, is able to take into account complex issues. In particular, it is the correct analytical basis for identifying thresholds and addressing the trade-offs between uses with respect to the availability and vulnerability of the resources (including ecosystems). Such trade-offs refer to specific periods of time and areas, from the local to the global, with the regional level, in terms of administrative regions, natural areas or watersheds, being essential for many policy issues. Of course, the general situation results from a variety of specific problems related to specific issues. Some of these can be identified as follows.

Probably the most important global concern related to environmental resources is water. Certain regions are presently in a crisis situation, due to natural scarcity or/and uncontrolled pollution. Due to the climatic conditions, the situation is, on average, less critical in Europe. However, scarcity problems leading to desertification do exist in Spain. In other regions, the excessive consumption generated by huge irrigation networks or by tourism generates seasonal shortages. The problem of unsafe drinking water may result, at local level, from the pollution of underground water. Eutrophication of water bodies is an increasing concern. From an ecological point of view, as adopted by the new European framework directive on water, the hydraulic conditions of the rivers should be considered. In particular, this concerns the increase in the level of artificiality of river systems resulting from *in situ* uses of water, for example large as well as small dams and other equipment which hamper the circulation of fish and the periodic renewal of wetlands associated to river courses.

A second major issue relates to biological resources, in terms of quantities (surface area of natural habitats, populations of various species) and of biodiversity. In the medium term, the ability of land to produce habitats for fauna and flora[3] is not only a question of nature conservation but also relates to the functions of natural systems such as purification and regulation. Although they are free, these services delivered by nature are important. Other services, linked to the amenity dimension of natural landscapes, have an even more direct economic impact, in particular on tourism. At European level, the dramatic decline of biological resources which started in the middle of the twentieth century is the consequence of pressures from agriculture (extension of intensive cultivation practices, the destruction of hedgerows and small features in rural landscape, and excessive use of pesticides), urbanization and the development of transport networks (which generate partitioning of the ecosystems, hindering the circulation of species).

Other important issues which should be considered from the point of view of the depletion and degradation of natural resources are soils, forests and fish stocks.

Although European soils are generally rich, serious problems occur in some regions. First, erosion processes can be seen in southern Europe and in other regions resulting from the mechanization of agriculture. Another major issue is the contamination of industrialized areas. While abandoned industrial sites are being progressively decontaminated, severe problems of industrial contamination of soils are faced in central Europe, the 'Black triangle' region symbolizing such degradation.

The pressure on European forests is generally low to moderate. The ratio between felling of timber and natural growth at country level is generally below one, and in many areas the resource could be harvested to a greater extent without creating sustainability problems. However, problems of artificialization related to the excessive planting of conifers occur in some areas. Acid rain damage is severe but limited to central Europe. In the Mediterranean region, fires are a serious pressure on forests, their multiplication hampering the reconstitution of the forest ecosystem. Beyond these problems, a major concern is the high level of tropical wood imports into Europe. Decisions have recently been taken at EU level to create a label for timber from 'sustainable forests' in order to alleviate the pressure on tropical rainforests.

Sea fish stocks are presently threatened due to high investment levels by fishing companies in recent decades. The level of catch becomes an environmental problem when it hinders the reproduction of fish populations.

3. WHY CENTRAL POLITICAL INTERVENTION AND/OR SOCIETAL DISCUSSION IS NECESSARY

As stated earlier, there may be many uses for each natural resource and therefore trade-offs between competing uses are necessary. In particular, an optimal policy in many cases needs to link environmental and economic policies. At European level, a major issue is the impact of environmental protection on production costs: fair economic competition requires harmonized legislation. Other problems such as the transport of goods have to be analysed at national or European level. As long as there are many functions of natural resources (for example raw material, natural asset and amenity), their use has to be discussed at various policy levels.

For land and ecosystems, which are the central issues of this chapter, policy intervention and societal discussion may relate to four issues: land planning, transport, agriculture and quality of life.

It is probable that the assessment of the environmental impact of the European Structural Funds will conclude that insufficient attention has been paid to the pressure on land by regional and local development.

In the case of transport, consideration of these issues is being made in the context of the so-called Trans European Network (TEN) programme. Impacts of major existing and planned transport routes are presently being assessed. Overall impacts are being considered as well as the more direct pressure generated in the corridors affected by road and rail routes. The question of transport should be seen as part of a more general issue, that of the rapid development of transnational trade in Europe, which has probably been stimulated by transport prices that are below the real social cost.

The importance of the pressure by intensive agricultural practices has previously been mentioned. It is likely that the assessment of the Common Agricultural Policy and the need to define a new European strategy in this area will push forward the debate on environmental concerns. It will cover water and soils issues, a wide problem area relating to European or national agricultural policies which foster the development of large irrigation projects (with subsequent evapotranspiration), the excessive use of fertilizers and pesticides, and the industrial breeding of cattle.

Natural and cultural landscapes, as amenities and quality of life providers, may increasingly become a European concern. Seasonal migrations and tourism are the causes of this interest. A more fundamental long-term demographic move, from Northern Europe to the Mediterranean coast, has also to be considered.

European forests require the continuation of sustainable management strategies and improvements when necessary, but also an optimal use of European woods. Forests should also be considered as ecosystems and the resource must be protected in order to maintain biodiversity. Finally, the EU must continue and deepen its action to protect rainforests, which means, in the medium term, some decrease in the imports of wood from developing countries.

Fish stocks should also be considered because of the consequences for marine life of tough competition between countries. Financial incentives have led to investment in large boats which in turn prompts an over-exploitation of fish stocks. Current policies aim to reduce fish catches; however, this creates periodic social crises. In the fishing industry a strong contradiction typically exists between short-term and medium-term interests, and it is necessary that common rules be applied.

Finally, there is the issue of EU imports. This mainly relates to low-cost raw materials imported from developing countries and introduces new responsibilities for importing countries. Consumption patterns are particularly important to this area; however, the issue is complex and also covers EU cooperation policies.

4. CONCRETE ACTIONS TO REDUCE THE PRESSURE ON NATURAL RESOURCES

The identification of the main pressures on natural resources suggests ways to reduce them. For material and energy, technological research should be directed towards products with low material/energy input, and generally material and energy savings. The benefits can be found both in terms of sustainable management of the resource and the reduction of a major source of pollutants.

Regarding land use and ecosystems, land planning is a key issue. This should be seen in a broad sense, encompassing regional development as well as transport and agriculture policies.

The high productivity of modern agriculture, as well as the burden of the subsidies to agriculture on the European budget, are now leading to a shift in policies. Farmers are no longer considered as mere producers of low-price food, but also as landscape managers.

Better planning of future transport networks from an environmental point of view should be considered in the context of both managing the transport of goods through real price calculations and consequent taxes or tariffs, and through risk legislation, and support to local development.

Support to developing countries in order to alleviate the pressure on their resources due to international trade is essential.

5. EXPECTED BENEFITS OF COMMUNICATING THE SUCCESS OR FAILURE OF SUCH ACTIONS VIA PRESSURE INDICATORS

An indicator is basically a tool for communication. It provides a warning, and helps in educating and clarifying the public debate. It is like a hazard light that flashes to inform people that there is a potential problem. Additional investigation is then necessary in order to identify the exact nature of the problem.

A pressure indicator, or a small set of such indicators, could therefore help policy-makers, the public and business to anticipate the problems, to understand their responsibilities more fully, and to adjust their demands and behaviour towards the environment.

Concentrating on pressure on the environment is particularly relevant for providing policy-makers and the public with operational information: first, because it is in general much more efficient to prevent impacts than to repair them, and second, because the responsibilities for the pressures seem easier to determine. For the policy-maker, the demand for action to reduce the pressure can be closely targeted on the source, the sector from which the pressure arises. The individual or the enterprise can also consider immediately modifying their own behaviour, according to their understanding of the problem. However, several conditions have to be met for the correct operational use of a pressure indicator.

The first is that the make-up of the composite has to be clear enough to the user. Only then can practical and relevant decisions be induced by the pressure indicator. Since there should also be as few indicators as possible, this is not easy to achieve.

Action can only be taken to reduce a pressure when a causal relationship can be clearly established, not only between activity (driving forces) and pressure, but also between pressure and state and impacts. Then policies as well as individual actions can arise from the indicator. This happens in the case of relatively high pressure, such as that found in industrialized regions. When the pressure is moderate, its effect on the environment is the result of synergy, which can be positive or negative. For example, the use of fertilizers is not a sufficient indication that anti-eutrophication policies should be adopted. What is important is the quantity that filters into the water bodies. This quantity is the leakage from the application of fertilizers (and not the application itself) to which one should add, *inter alia*, the consumption of household detergents with phosphates and household waste water from sanitation. Individual responsibilities may, in such cases, be more difficult to establish; however, this does not mean that indicators are useless.

What the difficulties mentioned above suggest is that pressure indicators should be supplemented by state and impact indicators. The latter may be necessary for communicating the relevant indicators of the nature and magnitude of the environmental problem, and for assessing the efficiency of the policies to reduce the pressure. Since these policies have a cost (for example the expenditures for environmental protection), indicators of the response may also be essential.

6. CONCLUSION

Since natural resources are under stress in many regions of Europe, pressure indicators are of major importance. A further development could be an index which could be a synthetic expression of a coordinated set of pressure indicators targeted at major environmental issues. Due to the difficulty of producing such a synthesis, several ways to achieve this should be explored. The production of an indicator of the state of environmental systems, identified by means of landscape analysis (homogeneous regions), could be a useful supplement.

NOTES

1. From a short-term economic point of view, depletion and degradation have to be clearly distinguished. As long as the value of the depleted resource is part of the value of the products resulting from its extraction, it can be substracted from the value added to the production. Conversely, degradation is not in the value of the products, so no substraction is possible. In the context of a pressure indicator on resources, which aims at covering more than short-term economic issues, degradation and depletion can be considered together.
2. The condensation of the indicators into a set of indices has now moved further down the political agenda, although such a development is not excluded at a later stage. See Foreword.
3. This expression is borrowed from the Canadian biologist, Paul-Emile Lafleur.

PART VII

Dispersion of Toxic Substances

23. Introduction

P. Ostlund

A very large number of human activities related to the production and use of toxic substances were identified and suggested as pressure indicators by members of the European scientific community. From these, 31 were chosen for a list of proposed indicators to be ranked by respondents of the second-round questionnaire.[1]

1. RESULTS OF THE SECOND-ROUND QUESTIONNAIRE

The 15 highest-ranked indicators in the second questionnaire are presented in Figure 23.1. The figure provides the ranking of each indicator for policy relevance, analytical soundness and responsiveness. Also, the core ranking of the indicators is presented expressed as a percentage of experts who included the indicator in their top five list of essential indicators.

The ranked list of essential core indicators is in general comparable to the ranking of the three quality criteria. The one clear exception to this is TX-18 'Emissions of dioxins by economic activity', which is ranked lower as an essential core indicator than for the quality criteria. The reason for this is not clear but may be related to the fact that even though dioxins are known by society as a component of high toxicity, the amounts in use are low due to reduction measures that have already been undertaken.

The indicators on the proposed list can be divided into two groups: those focusing on specific elements or substances, for example, emissions of lead, mercury, polychlorinated biphenyls (PCBs) or dioxins; and those focusing on general groups of elements or substances, for example, heavy metals, radioactive materials, pesticides or chlorinated compounds. In the short-list of 15 most favoured indicators given above, all the specific indicators are missing except dioxins, which suggests a need for general indicators. However, general indicators are likely to be less feasible than specific indicators and may be limited if elements or substances treated as a group have inherently different properties. Ways of overcoming these difficulties may be to introduce

Pressure indicators for dispersion of toxic substances:
'quality' questions Q1–3, core-ranked

Ranking (1 = very low, 4 = very high):
■ Policy relevance
▨ Analytical soundness
☐ Responsiveness
— Core ranking (right scale)

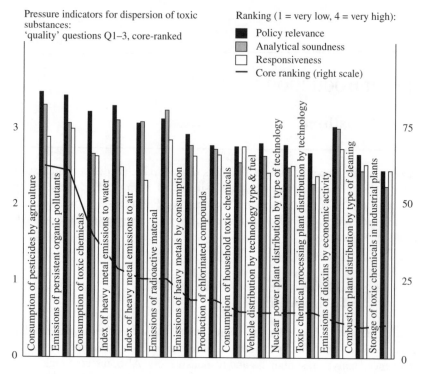

Figure 23.1   Results of second-round questionnaire for the Dispersion of Toxic Substances policy field

effect-related weighting such as those used for the estimation of the contribution of a substance to global warming (expressed as global warming potential, GWP), or depletion of stratospheric ozone (ozone formation factor, ozone depletion factor).

There are three basic clusters of the ranked indictors (Figure 23.1). Thirteen of the 15 indictors focus on organics, metals and/or radioactive substances. Four deal only with organics, three only with heavy metals, two with radioactive materials and the remaining four with both organics and metals.

2.   DELIMITATION OF THE POLICY FIELD AGAINST OTHER POLICY FIELDS

It is important to note that some of the other policy fields also deal with issues closely related to the Dispersion of Toxic Substances policy field.

These related policy fields, such as Waste, Air Pollution and Water Pollution, Marine Environment and Coastal Zones, and Urban Environmental Problems, concentrate on substance flows in society, or on societal activities where the substances are used. In this context society comprises both its physical dimensions and its activities. Societal activities are, for example, industrial production, farming, forestry, power production, combustion processes, pesticide use and diffusive spreading of substances.

Toxic Substances

Toxic substances are chemical substances that are harmful to biological systems. The term 'toxicity' can be defined in several ways, such as the ability for a given substance to cause damage to living tissue, impairment of the central nervous system, reproductional malfunctions, genotoxic effects or, in extreme cases, death, when ingested, inhaled or adsorbed. However, it has often been stated that it is the dose which makes a chemical substance toxic. That is, any chemical substance *per se* can be toxic to an organism above a critical concentration. The critical dose or potential of exposure varies widely from one substance to another, and also from one type of organism to another. Those substances or elements for which the critical dose is generally small, and thus the potential of exposure large, are referred to as 'toxic'.

The way chemicals cause damage to biological systems varies. Some substances and elements that an organism is unfamiliar with, and does not possess mechanisms to deal with, are toxic because they interact with functional processes like protein synthesis or the transfer of signals in the central nervous system. Other substances are toxic due to their interaction with the organism at a molecular level, for instance breakage of chemical bonds in bio-molecules by radicals or ionizing radiation.

Toxicity is only one of the properties that governs the ability of a given substance to be harmful. Other properties that must be considered are persistence of the substance as well as its ability to be accumulated in an organism. One factor which is related to persistence is the fate of the substance in an environment. The chemical and (micro)biological interaction with a substance or element affects the properties of the substance in a way that is often difficult to foresee. These processes include the formation of new species, for example methylated mercury or arsenic species, and organic metabolites. Many of these new species and substances often have toxicity properties totally different from their mother substances. The number of chemical elements, limited to just over one hundred, may appear in an unknown number of different species. The number of organic and inorganic substances that may be transformed to new substances in the environment is huge, and only a part of these are known or chemically described. The toxic potential of all these species and substances is extremely difficult to assess.

Sources of Toxic Substances

Some toxic substances are produced and used by society due to their toxic properties, for example, biocides, pesticides, fungicides, herbicides, disinfectants and antifouling substances. Others are related to industrial production processes, waste incineration and energy production, or to use in building and construction materials. The dispersion of toxic substances from the latter group is more complex since the emissions are often diffuse and take place over a long time period, during the whole life-cycle of the products. For example, emissions of metals from a car start during the mining of component materials and continue during production and use, and end when the car is deconstructed or handled as waste after use. This perspective is often referred to as 'a life-cycle perspective'. To some extent, toxic substances are also produced by organisms (for example botulinus toxin produced by bacteria) or emitted by natural processes like volcanic eruptions or forest fires.

Indices of Toxic Substances

To be able to measure the pressure of toxic substances on society from a certain area, the ideal would be to know the emissions, fate and the toxic effects of every substance. Preferably, the combined effects of several substances should also be known. Unfortunately, this knowledge is far from what is known today, and will probably never be fully available due to the speed at which new chemicals are invented and used. Instead, the index for toxic substances, as indeed the environmental activities to reduce the spreading of toxic substances, will always be limited to current knowledge. This means that if a certain list of substances is chosen for an index, new substances are likely to be added over time. If all the substances are weighted together, this will make comparisons from year to year, and between different countries, rather difficult. However, this situation may have to be accepted, for lack of better alternatives.

In the framework of international conventions, slightly different approaches are used for metals and organic substances. With regards to metals, a small and fixed number of high-priority metals (Cd, Hg and Pb) has been selected. By focusing on these most relevant metals the improvement of the heavy metal pressure on the environment is most cost-effective. At the same time, they can be used as indices of the progress of emission reductions for heavy metals in general since they represent various source types. Organic substances are treated differently and as a larger group since new substances frequently appear, and older ones are phased out. Effect-related assessment systems are also used to rank substances, for example chlorinated organic compounds (UNEP) or different types of radioactive materials.

3. APPROACHES USED IN THE CONTRIBUTIONS

In the chapter by Renzoni (Chapter 24), a straightforward description of the current global environmental situation is given. Environmental pressure due to unevenly distributed population growth with an uncontrolled need for energy and materials is seen as the cause of adverse effects such as acidification, climate changes and worldwide contamination.

Renzoni suggests that 'to evaluate environmental pressure in a selected site, one of the key requirements is to quantify the dispersal of toxic substances, their environmental fate and toxic potential' and that quantitative data can be classified in different groups, each corresponding to a numerical index to be combined into a general 'Dispersion of Toxic Substances Index'.

The message of this chapter is that changes in human pressure on environmental systems are needed. The necessary measures and technologies for these changes are known. The general approach to reducing human pressure is to relocate man into nature. To achieve this needs international coordination in changing social, economic and conservation strategies. Global changes may be achieved only by adopting global policies for sustainable development. These will ultimately cause a drastic reduction in environmental pressure and a recovery in quality of life.

The chapter by Dr Feidler and Professor Hutzinger concentrates mainly on the question of how to arrive at analytically sound pressure indicators for the dispersion of toxic substances. It explains that the 'risk' from toxic substances is not simply defined by the toxicity of emitted chemicals, but also by such factors as dose, exposure and human acceptability. Two approaches to categorizing environmental pressures are outlined, the substance-based approach and the activity-based approach. The authors then explain the process of assessing pressure on the environment using a substance-based approach by reference to their own research into the assessment of harm to the aquatic environment by chlorinated organic compounds and by the example of risk assessment for chlorinated pesticides.

The authors stress that, in the case of persistent compounds, recent actions to stop their release can prevent further environmental damage, but possibilities for reducing the impact of past emissions are limited. The recovery from contamination will often depend on the environmental media that are degraded, for example, the atmosphere and vegetation will have faster recovery times than soil, sediment or the human body. The chapter concludes that harmonized international action for reductions in pressures is necessary because the transport of pollutants is not contained within national boundaries.

4. INTERNATIONAL FRAMEWORK OF THE POLICY FIELD[2]

International cooperation to address global and regional environmental problems, including the degradation of natural resources, has grown dramatically in the past 25 years. This is reflected in the adoption of a large number of international conventions (approximately 180). Before 1970, most of the signed treaties were directed towards the protection of flora and fauna in different regions. These agreements related to the dispersion of toxic substances such as oil spills at sea, the use of nuclear power and protection of transboundary watercourses, including the Convention on the High Seas (United Nations, 1958), the Convention on Third Party Liability in the Field of Nuclear Energy (Paris Convention, 1960), the Nordic Mutual Emergency Assistance Agreement in Connection with Radiation Accidents (1963) and the Vienna Convention on Civil Liability for Nuclear Damage (1963).

There was a major breakthrough for international cooperation on environmental issues at the 1972 United Nations conference in Stockholm, which led to the establishment of the United Nations Environment Programme (UNEP). This has resulted in a large number of conventions, protocols and treaties mostly covering regions or sub-regions, such as a number of regional sea conventions, negotiated under UNEP and outside UNEP, aimed at protecting the marine environment from toxic substances. Among these, the Convention for the Prevention of Marine Pollution by Dumping from Ships and Aircraft (The Oslo Convention, 1972) and the Convention for the Prevention of Marine Pollution from Land-based Sources (The Paris Convention, 1974) have had the largest impact.

Some other conventions function as frames within which the parties concerned accept principles and methods for cooperation. An example of such a convention is the Convention on Long-Range Transboundary Air Pollution (1979). Five protocols were later added to this convention, of which at least two are related to emissions of toxic substances. These two are the Protocol to the 1979 Convention on Long-Range Transboundary Air Pollution on Long-Term Financing of the Co-operative Programme for Monitoring and Evaluation of the Long-Range Transmission of Air Pollutants in Europe (EMEP) (Geneva, 1984), and Protocol to the 1979 Convention on Long-Range Transboundary Air Pollution concerning the control of Emission of Volatile Organic Compounds or their Transboundary Fluxes (Geneva, 1991).

Other conventions of importance for the regulation of toxic substances are:

- Basel Convention on the Control of Transboundary Movements of Hazardous Wastes and their Disposal (Basel, 1989), and the amendment to this (Geneva, 1995)
- Convention on the Protection and use of Transboundary Watercourses and International Lakes (HELCOM) (Helsinki, 1992)
- Convention on the Transboundary Effects of Industrial Accidents (Helsinki, 1992)
- Convention for the Protection of the Marine Environment of the North-East Atlantic (OSPAR Convention, 1992)
- A protocol on atmospheric transboundary transport of persistent organic pollutants was negotiated in 06/1998 under the UN-ECE LRTAP convention
- A protocol on atmospheric transboundary transport of the heavy metals Hg, Cd and Pb was negotiated in 06/1998 under the UN-ECE LRTAP convention.

Also, reductions of emissions of radioactive materials to waters are agreed upon in the OSPAR and HELCOM conventions. Nuclear safety, which is under the control of IAEA (International Atomic Energy Agency), is regulated in a large number of guidelines but also in a number of signed conventions, for example the Convention on the Physical Protection of Nuclear Material (1979) and the Convention on Nuclear Safety (came into force in 1996).

NOTES

1. First questionnaire: December 1995; second questionnaire: October 1996. See Editors' introduction and section 1 of this chapter. See indicator lists in Annex I A and I B.
2. See also information on targets on TEPI Web site (http://e-m-a-i-l.nu/tepi/what's new/the documents/download example).

24. Human pressure on environmental systems: the need for change

A. Renzoni

1. NATURAL SYSTEMS AND HUMAN PRESSURE

Human population density has, for the first time, reached an average density of around ten inhabitants/km^2 for the total surface of the earth, or 100 inhabitants/km^2 for total usable land. Wastes and over-exploitation of natural resources are now generating dramatic new problems for present and future generations. The use of large quantities of fossil fuels is, at present, one of the main causes of environmental degradation at both local and global level. Atmospheric chemistry is changing with consequences for the earth's temperature. The deposition of nitrogen and sulphur oxides originating from combustion processes has caused acidification of soils and vulnerable freshwater systems (Scorer, 1994). Even non-toxic substances derived from concentrated human activities can have harmful environmental impacts. For example, the excess of nutrients and non-toxic organic matter discharged into the sea modifies biological (especially microbiological) community composition, reducing species abundance and diversity, and transforming coastal waters into a malodorous gelatinous soup. The Northern Adriatic Sea has increasingly frequent and intense proliferations of mucilages. Past use of recalcitrant chemicals in agriculture and in vector control operations is generating worldwide contamination (without damage to biological systems) and inadvertent, and still little known, pollution (with damage to biological systems).

When toxic substances are released into natural systems, they move from release points, in the case of the so-called point-sources such as chimneys and sewage outfalls, or areas, in the case of pesticide spraying in agriculture or in vector control operations, and migrate from one inorganic environmental phase (that is, water, air, soil) to another, reaching biological targets with varying efficiency. In the environment, the chemical may undergo varying rates of complete or partial degradation, producing other substances, which may be safer or more toxic than the mother compound. In some cases, relatively non-toxic substances may be transformed, in nature, into extremely toxic compounds, for example when inorganic mercury is transformed into methyl mercury in aquatic environments. Mixtures of chemicals in the environment may enhance each other's toxicity (known as 'toxic synergism').

Human activities imply the production, use and dispersal of great quantities of pollutants, which exert increasing pressure on natural systems, in which ecological disasters are continuously occurring (Odum, 1989). To evaluate total environmental pressure in a selected site, one of the key requirements is to quantify the dispersal of toxic substances, their environmental impact and toxic potential. Quantitative data can be classified in different groups, each corresponding to a numerical index to be combined in a general 'Dispersion of Toxic Substances Index'. The main problem is the normalization of indices for different substances. Although the evaluation of input (how much is discharged into the system) may be easy, problems arise from the evaluation of environmental impact in different conditions and in measuring effects, particularly at ecosystem level (Bacci, 1994). Substances can be grouped on the basis of their partition and reaction properties, and for chemicals having the same mechanism of action it is possible to determine, on a toxicological basis, normalization factors to calculate how much of a given substance is equitoxic to one unit of another. For instance, dioxins can be converted into equivalents of the most famous congener (the 2,3,7,8-tetrachlorodibenzo-p-dioxin). The problem of normalizing different groups can be solved by a similar approach, but this requires more knowledge and can be regarded as our present frontier in environmental toxicology research.

Another aspect of primary significance is the need to shift from anthropocentric safety criteria, directed at preserving human health, to more ecocentric approaches directed at preserving the integrity of natural systems. To evaluate anthropic pressure in a selected area due to the dispersion of toxic substances, first the size and density of population should be known, and then data are required for the input–output mass balance of toxicants in the area and the local production of toxic substances (if any). Transfrontier contaminants should also be included. Sometimes the import (and export) of a toxic substance may occur via the atmosphere or water. A detailed list is only possible in a real case study. In general, as human lifestyle is becoming increasingly homogeneous, the following strategic indications can be considered.

Unwanted Compounds from Energy Production

The significance of an environmental problem is only rarely proportional to the number of publications, and it may happen that new ideas need several decades to be understood by the scientific community. The case of the 'greenhouse effect' produced by the increase in tropospheric CO_2 concentration due to the combustion of fossil fuels is typical. Svante Arrhenius, a Swedish scientist with an unusually broad view of the functioning of natural systems, ranging in scale from molecules to the whole universe, published the first paper on the influence of changes in CO_2 level in the atmosphere on global warming in 1896. Only in the second half of the 1950s were systematic measurements initiated, and more recently the existence of a man-made warming has begun to be recognized (Rodhe et al., 1997).

At present, only 8 per cent of the world's population own cars, but this corresponds to about 550 million vehicles (Miller, 1994) and the growth of car numbers is expected to be more rapid than population growth. In urban areas car densities may be high enough to cause very substantial contamination (and pollution) and constitute one of the main causes of the degradation of urban environments, due to the various chemicals originating or deriving from motor vehicles (carbon oxides, ozone, polycyclic aromatic hydrocarbons, dioxins, asbestos fibres). The incidence of lung cancer in humans seems to be related to air quality.

The present rate of combustion of fossil fuels (non-renewable resources) in the production of energy for various uses (transportation, space and water warming, electrothermal power plants) is producing a significant modification in the carbon cycle, with increasing levels of atmospheric CO_2, coupled with a decrease in O_2 (Helmann, 1997). This will produce global climatic changes the intensity and effects of which are unknown. Sulphur and nitrogen cycles are also modified, with increasing acidification of precipitation causing deleterious effects on freshwater organisms living in lakes or running water in acidic soil areas, where departure from the natural acid-base equilibrium is easier. Fish mortality due to freshwater acidification has been well known since at least the beginning of this century, and in the 1950s liming was found to increase fish production in lightly polluted Swedish lakes. However, only during the 1960s was acidification recognized as a large-scale phenomenon in Sweden and Canada, where pH decreased in acid sensitive lakes to below 5, causing changes in the water chemistry (mobilization of toxic elements, such as aluminium), and to organisms and the ecosystem, including the decline or disappearance of fish populations (Fleischer et al., 1993). Since the 1970s, more than 6000 lakes in Sweden have been limed to detoxify waters and restore living conditions for aquatic organisms. In terrestrial systems, acid deposition can mobilize aluminium which is toxic to plants, causing forest decline in the acidic soils. Recently it was observed that the atmospheric wet deposition of airborne nitrates can enhance primary productivity in oligotrophic areas of the oceans, where nitrogen limitation is prevalent (Zhang, 1994).

The combustion of fossil fuels can pollute the air, water and soil. Solid wastes from mining, and oil and gas drilling are significant, with about 30 billion metric tons (tonnes) of non-fuel minerals extracted from the earth's crust every year. Together with the extraction of fossil fuels, this activity accounts for 75 per cent of all solid wastes (Miller, 1994).

Hyper-urbanization

In recent decades an extraordinary concentration of people in 'megacity urban areas' (MUAs) has been observed in several developing and technologically advanced countries, for example Tokyo–Yokohama (26 million inhabitants), São Paulo do Brasil (19 million), New York–north-eastern New Jersey (16 million) and Mexico City (15 million; Miller, 1994). Parts of these MUAs are heavily degraded by violence, poverty, homelessness, and hygienic and sanitary problems, but even if they are 'perfectly functioning' from an anthropocentric point of view, they are not self-sustaining. There is a continuous input of food, water, energy, minerals and other resources from local and distant sources corresponding to an output of gaseous, solid and liquid wastes which pollute air, soil, water and organisms inside and outside the megacity boundaries. In these conditions, fossil fuel combustion may produce very high levels of local pollution, causing an increase in the incidence of respiratory impairments in mammals.

More attention should be paid to the domestic chemical arsenal, which has a significant capacity to modify water bodies. Cleaning products, including soap and detergents, contain surfactants and associated impurities (such as the linear alkylbenzenes), bleaching agents, phosphates and new 'builders' (materials that serve to condition water-increasing surfactant efficiency). Each house uses cleaning products in great quantities, which, when expelled in urban sewage, cause severe modifications to the receiving water bodies. The consumption rate of household detergents in the USA and Canada is in the order of 3 000 000 metric tons/year, representing half of the global total (Thayer, 1993). Strong acids and bases, solvents, glues, paints and pesticides are used in much lower quantities, but their effects may become significant when the human population density is high. The use of oxidants (such as sodium hypochlorite, $NaClO$) in the treatment of water for human consumption makes the water toxic to aquatic life. Solid wastes should be reduced and material recycled, as happens in natural systems.

Agricultural Chemicals and Biocides

Fertilizers (especially nitrates) infiltrate groundwater and may reach levels exceeding the standards for drinking water. This process may be quite slow, sometimes taking decades depending on the frequency and intensity of rainfall, soil permeability and water table depth. Pesticides are applied at different rates (from a few grams to several kilograms per hectare per year), but particular attention should be paid to the more recalcitrant compounds, which can continue to contaminate soil, water, air and organisms over a long period. Knowledge of the physico-chemical properties of the various active ingredients is necessary for evaluating and predicting their environmental impact. Relatively new chemicals, such as the sulphonylurea herbicides (Beyer et al., 1988), are applied at very low annual rates (5–25 g/ha), but should be evaluated carefully because they are toxic to several species of plants at very low concentration levels. Compounds which can migrate from treated soils by vapour drift should not be used in order to avoid inadvertent residues in crops (Ross et al., 1990).

Antifouling products, such as the organotin compounds tributyltin (TBT) and triphenyltin (TPT), are applied to limit the growth of fouling organisms on submerged parts of boats and ships, and on the cooling pipes of coastal power stations and industrial plants. TBT and TPT, which are well tolerated by mammals, are extremely toxic to many target and non-target aquatic species, even at trace concentrations (Alzieu et al., 1991), and may modify biological communities, producing declines in sensitive populations (Gibbs and Bryan, 1986).

2. THE NEED FOR NEW APPROACHES: THE ROLE OF GOVERNMENTS

To minimize the problems discussed above, there is a need for international coordination in changing social, economic and conservation strategies. Global changes may only be achieved by changing global politics. These should be directed toward sustainable development, seeing man as part of nature. There is a need to control and gradually to reduce the growth of the world's human population, and to change the world's distribution of people. Megacities should be avoided by changes in urban planning at least at national level. The use of perpetual and renewable energy resources should be encouraged, as already happens in some countries, both in Europe and North America. Natural systems take energy from solar radiation and recycle materials. This is now technologically possible for humans, but requires political and governmental actions. Action is needed to engender the recycling of solid and liquid waste production, which considers the life-cycle of materials and not only human safety. The environmental problems derived from nutrient and biocide dispersal, particularly in agricultural practices, are a residual from the past and need special action only in developing countries. In the more advanced nations there is a need for better coordinated registration procedures for new chemicals and for a periodical re-examination of products already on the market to take account of new knowledge. New research efforts for water recycling should be encouraged, to reduce the consumption of essential and strategic reserves. Chemicals long established for use in agriculture should be rapidly re-evaluated to verify whether they satisfy present quality standards.

3. CONCRETE ACTIONS TO REDUCE HUMAN PRESSURE

Although there are some signs of moves in the right but difficult direction of respecting nature, as in the case of EC Directive 78/659 on the conservation of freshwater quality, the current approach to setting environmental standards has two severe limitations. First, it is based on anthropocentric criteria, tending to protect humans, without consideration for other forms of life, under the illusion that we can survive in a greatly modified environment. Second, standards are often expressed as limits for concentrations at the point-source, without considering the mass flow-rate and the capacity of the receiving system.

Short-term actions should be directed at introducing more ecocentric criteria aimed at preserving environmental quality, and not just human health or some characteristics of a resource. It is well known that environmental degradation implies resource degradation and poor quality of life for humans.

The first strategic direction should be towards a gradual change of energy production and use. Uses of energy for air and water warming and cooling could be greatly reduced by means of heat pumps, based on the circulation of low-temperature geothermal waters, and in adopting special construction solutions. The use of bicycles for transport in small cities should be encouraged, by means of cycle tracks and publicity campaigns. The use of catalytic converters and low-fuel consumption engines may be a short-term solution, along with the improvement of public transport (using less energy per passenger per km). New communication technologies should be encouraged when they reduce the need for transport. In city planning, excessive concentration of human activities should be avoided by sustainable land-use policies. Considering agricultural practice, particular attention should be paid to preserving the quality of groundwater reserves. Leaching chemicals such as nitrates or some herbicides (for example atrazine, 1,2-dibromo-3-chloropropane) and those producing acid metabolites which contaminate groundwater (such as DCPA, 2,3,5,6-tetrachloroterephthalate) should not be applied in the recharging areas of important aquifers.

Long-term action should be directed at driving forward the changes which are already initiated. In the next 50 years traditional energy resources will be largely replaced by new technologies operating in a global market. Solar, hydroelectric or geothermal energy power plants will be small and near the user, to reduce the cost and distribution of long-range power lines. Cars and other vehicles will be powered by solar energy or fuel cells, greatly reducing (and practically eliminating) the problems of air pollution in the cities. The progressive reduction in the availability of fossil fuels and the consequent increase in the price will produce devastating effects on traditional economies and an international crisis which can only be avoided if effective alternatives are available. To drive these changes, governmental actions to change energy policy are necessary at international level, in order to achieve a restoration of environmental quality. The same is needed for urban planning, where 'small is better' and where more attention should be paid to balancing input and output, avoiding loss of water and nutrients, and increasing recycling of materials. This implies changes in production style, reducing package mass and materials, changing commercial distribution strategies and reducing the effect of the domestic chemical arsenal.

4. EXPECTED BENEFITS

The final aim of long-term actions should be the reintroduction of man into the natural system by adopting the same functioning principle: energy from perpetual or renewable sources, and materials recycling. This will produce a drastic reduction in environmental pressure and a recovery in quality of life. The idea of a Total Environmental Pressure Index as a basis for new environmental quality criteria is very attractive and could be applied in identifying major problems for a selected space and time scale. The general public is very interested in these issues, especially regarding the possibility of combining a high standard of living with lower environmental pressures. The objective of recovering environmental quality on both a local and global basis is exciting, especially when technological alternatives are offered at an accessible price. In the twenty-first century sustainable technologies are expected to compete in the global market and the governments of developed countries should accurately evaluate present development criteria, to avoid the risk of marginalization. These changes will probably modify present equilibria and create the possibility of a more balanced resource distribution. European countries should make an effort to improve links between know-how and technological applications in order to maintain a leader position in the world, and to create new and qualified job opportunities.

A. Renzoni221

REFERENCES

Alzieu, C., P. Michel, I. Tolosa, E. Bacci, L.D. Mee, J.W. Readman (1991), 'Organotin compounds in the Mediterranean: a continuing cause for concern', *Marine Environmental Research*, **32**: 261–70.

Arrhenius, S. (1896), 'On the influence of carbonic acid in the air upon the temperature of the ground', *The London, Edinburgh and Dublin Philosophical Magazine and Journal of Science*, **41**: 237–76.

Bacci, E. (1994), *Ecotoxicology of Organic Contaminants* (Boca Raton, FL: Lewis Publishers).

Beyer, E.M., Jr, M.J. Duffy, J.V. Hay and D.D. Schlueter (1988), 'Sulfonylureas', in P.C. Kearny and D.D. Kaufmann (eds) *Herbicides. Chemistry, Degradation and Mode of Action*, Vol. 3 (New York: Marcel Dekker); pp. 117–89.

Fleischer, S., G. Andersson, Y. Brodin, W. Dickson, J. Herrmann and I. Muniz (1993), 'Acid water research in Sweden – Knowledge for tomorrow', *Ambio*, **22**: 258–63.

Gibbs, P.E. and G.W. Brian (1986), 'Reproductive failure in populations of the dogwhelk, *Nucella lapillus*, caused by imposex induced by tributyltin from antifouling paints', *Journal of the Marine Biological Association of the United Kingdom*, **66**: 767–77.

Helmann, M. (1997), 'A review of the contemporary global carbon cycle and as seen a century ago by Arrhenius and Högbom', *Ambio*, **26**: 17–24.

Miller, G.T., Jr (1994), *Living in the Environment* (Belmont, CA: Wadsworth Publishing Company).

Odum, E.P. (1989), *Ecology and our endangered life-support systems* (Sunderland, MA: Sinauer Associated, Inc.).

Rodhe, H., R. Charlson and E. Crawford (1997), 'Svante Arrhenius and the greenhouse effect', *Ambio*, **26**: 2–5.

Ross, L., S. Nicosia, M.M. McChesney, K.L. Hefner, D.A. Gonzalez and J.N. Seiber (1990), 'Volatilization, off-site deposition, and dissipation of DCPA in the field', *Journal of Environmental Quality*, **19**: 715–22.

Scorer, R.S. (1994), 'Long distance transport', in J. Rose (ed.), *Acid Rain* (Yverdon, Switzerland: Gordon and Breach Science Publishers), pp. 1–33.

Thayer, A.M. (1993), 'Soaps & detergents', *Chemicals & Engineering News*, 25 January, pp. 26–47.

Zhang, J. (1994), 'Atmospheric wet deposition of nutrient elements: correlation with harmful biological blooms in the Northwest Pacific coastal zone', *Ambio*, **23**: 464–8.

25. Dissipation of toxics

H. Fiedler and O. Hutzinger

---

1. INTRODUCTION

As a result of our civilization, there exists a multitude of anthropogenic activities with severe impacts on the environment, ecosystems and humans. The environment also receives inputs from naturally occurring processes which may or may not release toxic compounds or severely damage the environment. Such processes include volcanic eruptions, forest fires, earthquakes, floods and hurricanes. Moreover, large amounts of organic compounds, including organochlorines, such as chloromethane (CH_3Cl), are formed via enzymatic processes, found in foodstuffs (aflatoxins, botulinus toxin, indole-3-carbazole) or formed during preparation of food (for example formation of nitrosamines, polycyclic aromatic hydrocarbons) or in consumer goods (for example nicotine and ethanol).

Before establishing concepts, some definitions should be clarified, such as toxin, risk, adverse effect (damage), and the environment to be protected.

2. DEFINITION OF RISK

Dose and Toxicity

The old Paracelsus statement of 500 years ago is still valid. It is the dose that makes a chemical a toxin. Thus any chemical compound *per se* can be toxic to an organism above a critical concentration.

As established by OECD, risk is defined as a function of dose and toxicity; or mathematically as:

$$\text{Risk} = f \text{ (Dose, Toxicity)}$$

Although the toxic potency of a chemical is constant, the dose or the potential of exposure to man or the environment can be reduced, for example by legislation. Moreover, to control exposure of the general population or environment, limit values, guidelines and recommendations can be issued. Thus risk assessment has to include a detailed description of the exposure pathway(s) and the target organism/environment.

Before establishing pressure indicators and assigning harmful activities, it should be clarified, first, which potentially toxic compounds have to be considered, and second, which environments should be protected, since a chemical may be harmful to one environment and harmless to another.

In general, four categories of chemicals can be considered to be toxic: radioactive compounds, heavy metals (see below), persistent organic compounds (when accumulation occurs resulting in chronic exposure with often unknown effects), and very reactive substances (radicals, epoxides; in many cases intermediates).

A special problem is associated with heavy metals, as many of these compounds are toxic to organisms at low concentrations (for example lead, cadmium and thallium) whereas others (for example selenium, copper and zinc) are 'biometals' essential to maintain the functioning of organisms. However, at higher organ concentrations the same compounds can be toxic and even carcinogenic (Forth *et al.* 1987). Examples are given in Table 25.1.

The dose of a chemical is dependent on the behaviour of the respective chemical. Thus a reactive compound can be as toxic as the parent compound. However, in most cases, it is the metabolite which is more toxic than the original chemical. Generally, reactive compounds exhibit acute toxicity, which can be determined more easily, and in most cases appropriate measures have been taken to minimize release of such compounds into the environment.

Chronic exposure may occur through two scenarios, either through permanent release of a chemical, or single or permanent release of persistent chemicals. The latter is more difficult to assess as the uncertainty is much higher. Besides the heavy metals which do not degrade and thus cannot disappear, many organic chemicals belong to the latter group.

As it is not known when and at what concentrations a chemical or an activity might cause irreversible damage to the environment, there are generally three possible precautionary alternatives (Meerkamp van Embden, 1990). First, zero emission, which means the stopping of any gaseous, liquid or solid emissions. This amounts, practically, to a complete cessation of industrial production. For some chemicals this was realized in the past (for example the end of PCB production). Second, emissions in the order of naturally occurring background concentration. Such an aim has not yet been achieved and, to date, background concentrations have only been used as orientation values. Third, emissions in the range of the tolerance capacity or degradation capacity of natural sinks, for which detailed information on the environmental behaviour of chemicals and ecosystems is necessary.

Table 25.1   Classification of heavy metals

Heavy metal	Essential for plants	Essential for animals	Toxic in plants	Toxic in animals
Lead			•	•
Cadmium			•	•
Chromium		•		
Cobalt		•		
Iron	•	•		
Gold				
Copper	•	•	•	•
Manganese	•	•	•	
Molybdenum	•	•		•
Nickel		•	•	
Platinum metals			•	
Mercury			•	•
Selenium		•		•
Silver			•	
Vanadium	•	•		
Zinc	•	•	•	
Tin		•		

Source: (Merian, 1984)

Exposure

There are three requirements for performing exposure analysis. First, activities and processes have to be identified which may release potentially toxic compounds into the environment. Second, environmental sinks have to be determined, in other words, in which environmental media (air, water, soil, sediment, biota) a given compound will be ultimately found and at what levels. Third, the transport and fate (distribution, accumulation, degradation) of a chemical have to be determined.

Possibility of Occurrence

Finally, an estimation of the possibility that a hazard may occur has to be made. For example, there may be a 100 per cent possibility that PCBs are found in cows' milk, or the possibility of a volcanic eruption may be low. Statistics can help to evaluate the frequency of accidents.

Acceptability

In this project, analytically sound environmental pressure indicators should be defined. However, it should be mentioned that, in general, humans accept risks much more easily when, first, a risk is self-inflicted (for example smoking, application of pesticides in own house or garden), second, the damage is reversible, and third, they have a financial benefit. Thus objective and measurable parameters must be identified.

3. CLASSIFICATION OF PROCESSES AND ACTIVITIES

In the development of pressure indicators, the pressures can be categorized in different ways (see section 5). One approach to assessing the environmental impact caused by a chemical is to determine the emission from a given source per year by multiplying the concentration of a compound of the respective emission (measured in g, mg, and so on) per unit of feed processed or produced (tonne or litre) by the amount of feed material processed or produced (tonne per year):

$$\text{Emission of source} = \text{Emission factor} \times \text{'production' term}$$

In order to make a source emission estimate, there are two information requirements: first, representative measurements for the compound of interest from a given source. In many cases, these estimates are very uncertain as emissions are deduced from anything from a few test results to a nationwide survey. If measurements do not exist at all, either numbers have to be taken from the literature or emissions are derived from similar processes. Second, the total amount of feed material processed or produced is needed. Very often, there is a high degree of certainty about such information.

Processes and Activities

Processes and activities can be divided into industrial and private (household) activities.

Industrial activities
Most countries use production figures of chemicals (or goods) for priority setting when evaluating risks to the environment or for establishing test criteria. Such an approach was taken by the German Chemical Society for the evaluation of existing chemicals which were produced and marketed before extensive chemical testing was established (Chemikaliengesetz). Within this

evaluation, first, chemicals which had production rates greater than 1000 tons per year were post-evaluated for impact on the environment (ecosystem). Although such a procedure is a practicable way to assess impact on the environment, the pure production numbers have to be corrected for amounts being exported and imported into a country (or region). Thus the actual (effect) amount (concentration) is more important than just the overall amount of production. Moreover, the amount of a product that is used as an interim product in the production of a final product has to be taken into account. Some industrial countries have such inventories within their declaration of emissions (mandated by national Clean Air Acts).

Most.importantly, the use pattern of a chemical has to be known and evaluated qualitatively and quantitatively. For example, pesticides applied in southern Europe may be shifted atmospherically and to a lesser extent via waterways to the more northern parts of Europe. In general, it does not seem too difficult to obtain production figures for given chemicals and goods from the respective manufacturers as today's legislation requires the recording of such information. Along with the pure production amounts, data on various emissions have to be given (such as amounts of waste generated, emissions to the air, and emissions to receiving waters or water treatment plants).

Private activities

Lifestyle and private activities mobilize and release many compounds and/or produce large amounts of by-products. In general, much less is known about the chemical identity of the compounds formed and released, and their amounts. However, applying the methods used in life-cycle assessment, such estimated information can be generated. This was done, for example, by Brunner and co-workers who undertook a mass balance of copper for the cities of Stockholm and Vienna.

As an example, in a mass balance for dioxins, it was found that within the city of Hamburg (1.65 million inhabitants) the impact from industrial activities on environmental categories such as air, waste, sewage sludge and valuable goods was approximately twice as much as the impact from private activities (FHH, 1995). Thus the amount of toxins generated by 'private' activities has to be taken into account.

4. APPROACHES: SUBSTANCE-BASED

Harm to the Aquatic Environment

Fiedler and Hutzinger (1990) have developed a simple scheme to assess chlorinated organic compounds for the United Nations Environmental Programme (UNEP, International Register of Potentially Toxic Chemicals). A chemical was considered to be hazardous to the aquatic environment when a substance met at least two of the following criteria:

- Octanol water partition coefficient (log KOW) >3
- Toxicity LC50 <10 mg/L
- Persistence >1 week
- As a minor criterion production >1000 tons/yr or generated in manufacturing processes (use pattern).

A list of relevant compounds can be found in Fiedler and Hutzinger (1990) or Fiedler and Lau (1997).

When no experimental data were available, log KOW was chosen as the basic criterion: a compound was considered to be harmful for the aquatic environment when log KOW was >3.

Environmental Risk Assessment for Chlorinated Pesticides

Pesticides, including insecticides, herbicides, fungicides and rodenticides, are widely used in many industrialized and developing countries. Generally, pesticides are end-products, commercially marketed and directly applied without further purification. It is well known that, depending on their mode of application, they generally enter the environment directly either as a solid (fumigation, dust) or as a solution (diluted in water, spray). Exposure may also occur during manufacture and formulation. Since pesticides are ubiquitous and those containing chlorine are still being used, they may enter surface waters. Therefore, it is necessary to perform a risk assessment by ranking pesticides according to their potential to damage the marine environment. Fiedler and Schramm (1990) have used the class of chlorinated pesticides as examples. Due to limited data, quantitative structure activity relationships (QSARs) were used to make predictions about the potential threat of chlorinated pesticides towards aquatic organisms and subsequently to rank these substances.

On the basis of physico-chemical data, such as water solubility and vapour pressure, as well as acute toxicity (LC50), an ecotoxicological model was developed for preliminary hazard assessment. By use of the reciprocal product from the decadic logarithm of Henry's law constant (log H) and the lethal concentration (LC50), a suitable ranking system was developed that allows prediction of potential damage to aquatic organisms via application of pesticides.

For a preliminary hazard assessment the values for Henry's Law constant H and the LC50 values for fish will give information if a pesticide should be considered as potentially toxic to aquatic organisms. In addition, the LC50 value is a direct measure of the toxicity of a substance. Compounds with a high Henry's law constant will not be found in water and vice versa. The Henry's law constant can be calculated as follows:

$$H = \frac{V_p}{S} \frac{(atm)}{(mol/m^3)}$$

To get a suitable equation we formed the reciprocal product of H (atm·m³·mol–1) and LC50 (mg·L–1):

$$F = \frac{1}{H \cdot LC_{50}}$$

Thus a high factor of F indicates a high toxicity potential of this compound in a water environment, whereas a small value of F indicates little toxicity potential. The ranking of the chlorinated organics is summarized in Table 25.2.

For persistent substances, heavy metals and lipophilic organic compounds, reservoirs such as contaminated sediments, sludge and other deposits, contaminated (production) sites and landfills might become more important the more actively emitting sources (production and manufacture of certain chemicals, better flue gas and effluent cleaning devices) are controlled or stopped. This may be relevant, for example, to PCBs and polychlorinated dibenzo-para-dioxins (PCDDs) and polychlorinated dibenzofurans (PCDFs). Release from such reservoirs can occur via leaching or erosion.

5. CLASSIFICATION – ACTIVITY-BASED

Besides a substance-based approach, human activities and naturally occurring processes can be compiled and correlated with environmental categories and the compounds involved. As can be seen from Table 25.3, most activities listed in the first column are of anthropogenic origin and are related to industrial processes including agriculture, or originate from such processes (for example release of contaminants from reservoirs). Finally, column 3 of Table 25.3 gives some indicator compounds (chemical substances) which may be involved or should be controlled for each category of activity, or unwanted effects caused by a given activity.

Table 25.2   Toxicity ranking system based on log H and LC50

Compound	Toxicity ranking factor (F)	Compound	Toxicity ranking factor (F)
Endrin	2 200 000 000 000	2,4,6-Trichlorophenol	646 000
Captafol	262 000 000 000	Methoxychlor	530 000
Carbophenothion	49 900 000 000	Dicofol	453 000
Lindane	19 400 000 000	Propachlor	212 000
Dieldrin	16 500 000 000	Flamprop-isopropyl	69 500
Chloroxuron	12 200 000 000	Aldrin	41 800
Fenvalerate	7 610 000 000	Hexachlorobenzene	38 700
Permethrin	2 870 000 000	2, 4-DB	37 100
DDT	1 505 000 000	Atrazine	35 400
Chlorfenvinphos	905 000 000	Diallate	31 300
Iodofenphos	172 000 000	Flampropmethyl	28 000
Fenarimol	166 000 000	Thiobencarb	27 800
Chlordane	107 000 000	Neburon	25 800
Chlorpyrifos	97 000 000	Quinonamid	19 100
Chloropropylate	81 400 000	Trichlorophenol 2,4,5	16 200
Chlorothalonil	77 400 000	Clorfenethol	12 700
Captan	22 300 000	Dichlorvos	11 700
Metolachlor	18 600 000	Trietazine	5 260
Iprodione	16 700 000	Chloropicrin	3 090
Pentachlorophenol	8 950 000	2, 3-Dichloro-N-(4-	
Diuron	7 730 000	fluorophenyl) maleimide	1.790
Propanil	2 170 000	2, 4-Dichlorophenol	1 230
Bromophos	2 000 000	2, 4-D	708
MCPB	1 010 000	Methazole	139
Chlordimeform	829 000	MCPA	133
Chlorobenzilate	749 000	Terbutylazine	91
Fenoprop	718 000	2, 3, 4, 6-Tetrachlorophenol	59
Heptenophos	682 000	Allyl chloride	3

Notes:
H = Henry's law constant = ratio of a chemical's concentration in air to its concentration in water.
LC50: Lethal concentration = concentration of a chemical that causes the death of 50% of the test population at 96 h exposure time.

No data were available for chloralose, chlormephos, chlorthiophos, coumachlor, crimidine, 2,4-DES-sodium, dialifos, endosulfan, heptachlor, leptophos, profenfos, triallat, trichloronate (lack of either Henry's law constant or log KOW).

Source: Fiedler and Schramm (1990).

Table 25.3 Activities causing potential harm

Activity	Target compartment	Compounds
Industrial Production: • Chemical prim./second. • Others, e.g. metal, textiles, etc.	Main emissions are the products; secondary emissions are the solid residues and aqueous effluents	
	Air, esp. from large stationary thermal source, e.g. waste (municipal, hazardous, clinical), combustion of fossil fuels, production and recycling of ferrous and non-ferrous materials, recycling processes involving high-temp. processes	All major combustion products, such as SO_2, NO_x, dust, CO, CO_2, but also by-products such as heavy metals (esp. particle-bound), PCDD/PCDF, polycyclic aromatic hydrocarbons (PAH), PCB
	Waste or valuable goods from combustion processes, e.g. fly-ash (highly toxic) and slag (less toxic)	Heavy metals, salts (leachability→ groundwater pollution); by-products, e.g. PCDD/PCDF
	Water, sediments or sewage sludge effluents from production or cleaning systems and devices	Heavy metals, organics.
	Final products, such as detergents, pesticides with direct application	Persistent organics, N and P ($\to$ eutrophication)
Energy production: • Combustion of fossil fuels (point-source) • Nuclear (point-source) • Traffic: cars, airplanes (diffuse)	Heat and energy production, traffic	Climate change
Use of CFCs and halons	Air greenhouse effect, ozone depletion	($\to$ phytotoxicity)

Resource recovery	e.g. non-renewable resources	Soil depletion, land use
Agriculture		Loss of biodiversity, impact via application of pesticides, nutrients, sewage sludge, liquid manure, compost (heavy metals, persistent contaminants)
Reservoirs	Remobilization of contaminants once concentrated	
Diffuse sources	Traffic (cars, aircrafts)	NO$_x$, SO$_2$, diesel exhaust, lead
Erosion and run-off from surfaces (streets, roofs)	Water, sewer plants	Particle-bound contaminants, heavy metals and lipophilic organics
Industrial and private activities		Nuisances (noise, smell) Heat, radiation
Long-range transport	Air, water translocation of contaminants	NO$_x$, SO$_2$, persistent organic chemicals (PCB, PCDD/PCDF, pesticides, e.g. toxaphene)
Waste: • Incineration • Landfill • Composting, etc.		Concentration of heavy metals and organics in solid emissions (fly-ash, bottom-ash), release of combustion by-products into the atmosphere. Leaching of pollutants from landfills. Heavy metals and persistent organic chemicals will re-enter the environment through application of compost

6. REDUCTION OF THE PROBLEM PRESSURE

Most of the 'problems' mentioned in this chapter relate to persistent compounds. As a consequence, recent actions taken to stop the release of unwanted chemicals (by-products) cannot solve the problem. In such cases, actions can only stop further damage and attempt to improve environmental quality. In many cases, definite actions are not possible, for example, the excavating of landfills to remove contaminants, or the dredging of whole rivers to improve the sediment quality. The target category very often determines the rapidity of improvement; for example, the quality of the atmosphere and of vegetation will rapidly change for the better if the actual release of contaminants is stopped. However, soil and sediment, as well as human body processes (for example the production of breast milk) have slower recovery times once they have received an input of persistent compounds, due to long half-life times in the respective matrix.

It is important to note that industrialized and advanced nations have a responsibility not to export 'bad' technologies or products to developing countries, thus causing the same problems elsewhere. In terms of active sources releasing contaminants into water and air, international and harmonized actions have to be agreed upon as the transport of pollutants does not stop at national borders. The same applies to international trade in foodstuffs and products.

REFERENCES

FHH (Freie und Hansestadt Hamburg): O. Hutzinger, H. Fiedler, C. Lau, G. Rippen, U. Blotenberg, H. Wesp, S. Sievers, P. Friesel, B. Gras, T. Reich, U. Schacht and R. Schwörer (1995), 'Dioxin-Bilanz für Hamburg'. *Hamburger Umweltberichte* **51/95**. Freie und Hansestadt Hamburg, Umweltbehörde (eds), Hamburg, September.

Fiedler, H. and C. Lau (1997), 'Environmental Fate of Chlorinated Organics', in G. Schüürmann and B. Markert (eds), *Ecotoxicology* (New York: John Wiley).

Fiedler, H. and O. Hutzinger (1990), 'Organochlorine Compounds in the Marine Environment', prepared for UNEP/IRPTC, Contract no. G/CON/89-01.

Fiedler, H. and K.-W. Schramm (1990), 'QSAR Generated Ranking System for Organochlorine Compounds in the Marine Environment', *Organohalogen Compound.* **4**: 391–4 (Bayreuth: ECO-INFORMA Press).

Forth, W., D. Henschler and W. Rummel (eds) (1987), *Allgemeine und spezielle Pharmakologie und Toxikologie* (Mannheim: Wissenschaftsverlag).

Meerkamp van Embden, I.C. (1990), 'Toxikologie/Ökologie: Verknüpfung toxikologischer und ökologischer Erkenntnisse', *Nachrichten aus Chemie, Technik und Laboratorium.* **1**(90): 85–114.

Merian, E. (1984), *Metalle in der Umwelt* (Weinheim: Verlag Chemie).

Merian, E. and T.W. Clarkson (eds) (1991), *Metals and Their Compounds in the Environment: Occurrence, Analysis and Biological Relevance* (Weinheim: Verlag Chemie).

PART VIII

Urban Environmental Problems

26. Introduction

A. Markandya and N. Dale

1. THE URBAN ENVIRONMENTAL PROBLEMS POLICY FIELD

The urban environment is both the source of a wide array of interrelated environmental pressures and the principal location of many environmental impacts. There are also great differences in environmental conditions and economic activities between urban areas across regions and countries. For these reasons the Urban Environmental Problems policy field is perhaps the most difficult to define. Furthermore, it is difficult to achieve a balanced set of indicators that adequately represent the many dimensions of the problems of this policy area.

In the first-round questionnaire the complexity of pressures on the urban environment was illustrated by the range of suggestions for pressure indicators that were received. These suggestions were screened for specific relevance and the number of experts who proposed them, to arrive at a list of 30 indicators for the second-round questionnaire.[1] These were arranged in 15 categories including indicators for land use (total built-up area, derelict area), urban air emissions (SO_2, NO_x, VOC, PM_{10}), water (water consumption per capita), waste (municipal waste by type), energy (energy consumption by uses and sources), mobility (registered motor vehicles), noise (people exposed to noise) and health (incidence of asthma).

2. RESULTS OF THE SECOND-ROUND QUESTIONNAIRE

Figure 26.1 shows the results of the second-round questionnaire for Urban Environmental Problems for the three quality questions and the core-ranking question (given as a percentage of experts including the indicator in their top five core ranking).

The top five rankings for these four questions were as follows:

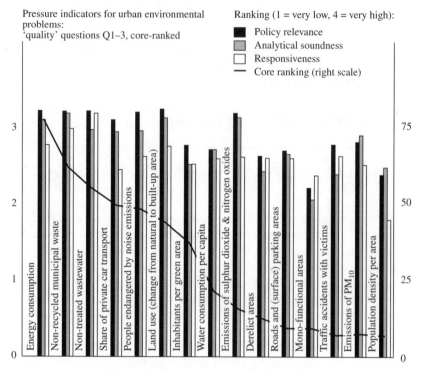

*Figure 26.1   Results of second-round questionnaire for the Urban
Environmental Problems policy field*

- Core-ranked indicators: energy consumption, non-recycled municipal
  waste, non-treated wastewater, share of private car transport, people
  endangered by noise emissions.
- Policy relevance indicators: land use (change from natural to built-up
  area), energy consumption, non-treated wastewater, people endangered
  by noise emissions, non-recycled municipal waste.
- Analytical soundness indicators: non-recycled municipal waste, land
  use (change from natural to built-up area), emissions of SO_2 and NO_x,
  energy consumption, non-treated wastewater.
- Response elasticity indicators: non-treated wastewater, non-recycled
  municipal waste, energy consumption, land use (change from natural
  to built-up area), traffic accidents with victims.

Despite the diverse nature of the lists of proposed indicators presented to
respondents, there is general agreement between the top five rankings for the

four questions with indicators for energy consumption, non-treated wastewater, and non-recycled municipal waste featuring in all four of the top five rankings. The land-use indicator features in three of the top five rankings. Further down the rankings there is less agreement between the four questions. Further details and discussion of these results can be found in the TEPI publication on *Indicator Definition.*[2]

3.   RELATIONS TO OTHER POLICY FIELDS

The Urban Environmental Problems policy field has complex links to most of the other policy fields since it is defined by the physical environment, while most are defined by environmental media, such as air and water, or specific issues, such as climate change and ozone depletion. This has resulted in a set of proposed indicators that cut across related policy fields, principally Waste, Air Pollution and Water, but are also central to the Urban Environmental Problems policy field.

The indicator for non-recycled municipal waste features highly in the questionnaire rankings, thus illustrating the clear linkage to the Waste policy field. However, in the Waste policy field the pressures are measured on a national basis.

Links to the Water policy field are evidenced by the high ranking of non-treated wastewater and water consumption per capita as Urban Environmental Problem indicators.

Air Pollution is closely associated with Urban Environmental Problems, in particular in relation to a variety of adverse health effects. The 'conventional' air pollutants, sulphur dioxide, black smoke and lead, were largely connected with urban combustion of fossil fuel. In recent years a new class of air pollutants, which includes nitrogen dioxide and ozone, has appeared. These are related to road transport and are especially evident in many urban atmospheres. Therefore, indicators such as share of private car transport and emissions of SO_2 and NO_x are strongly related to Air Pollution. The effects of acidification also fall within the Urban Environmental Problems policy field since severe damage has been caused to historical buildings and monuments that constitute part of the cultural heritage in European cities.

4.   APPROACH USED IN THE CONTRIBUTION

The chapter by Professor Fudge takes a broad interdisciplinary approach to the task of analysing urban problems and recommending actions to reduce environmental pressures. While examining the issues at European Union level, he recognizes that wider European and global environmental, economic and social processes should also inform the discussion.

The problems faced by European cities are set in the context of rapid global and European urbanization, with recent statistics indicating that the EU is around 79 per cent urbanized. The major urban problems in Europe are grouped under the nine themes of: social exclusion, lifestyle and equity; degradation of the urban environment; transportation and accessibility; the need for new forms of institutional capacity and governance; technological management: waste, water, air and resource use; urban dereliction and redundant buildings; urban economic uncertainty and unemployment; crime and personal safety; and leisure and tourism impacts.

In his recommendations for action to reduce the problem of environmental pressures Professor Fudge refers to the detailed recommendations of the *European Sustainable Cities Report* (CEC, 1996), drawn up by the European Commission's Expert Group on the Urban Environment. This report presents an integrated set of policies which 'draw on the inter-relationship of the substance of problems and the processes that create them', recommending a wide agenda of actions for the sustainable management of natural resources, covering air quality, soil, flora and fauna, water, energy conservation and waste management. The problem areas related to air, water, energy and waste correspond to the area covered by most of the highly ranked pressure indicators. The report also identifies actions for sustainability in the socio-economic context, at the levels of Member State governments and regional and local authorities, and for social sustainability.

The chapter also stresses the need for action to achieve sustainable urban accessibility as a vital step in the improvement of the urban environment. Professor Fudge draws on *The Future Development of the Common Transport Policy* (CEC, 1992) as a useful policy framework for issues of mobility and access. In conclusion, the importance of spatial planning systems as a basis for sustainable urban development is outlined. Recommendations are made for the development of land-use policy and practice based on those produced by the Expert Group on the Urban Environment (see above paragraph).

5.   INTERNATIONAL FRAMEWORK

The complex and broad-based definition of urban environmental problems means that it is difficult to reach simple and clearly defined goals for international agreement as was the case with, for example, ozone depletion. However, there have been several international initiatives for sustainable cities, which are outlined below:

- As a result of the need to implement the Local Agenda 21 (chapter 28) of the 1992 United Nations Conference on Environment and Development, the Local Agenda 21 Initiative was established by the International Council of Local Environmental Initiative (ICLEI) and the International Union of Local Authorities (IULA). It aims to develop a planning framework for local sustainable development focusing on actions such as consultation, audits, target setting and monitoring.
- The Sustainable Cities Project was set up by the European Commission's Expert Group on the Urban Environment in 1993. Their report, referred to in Professor Fudge's chapter, sets out recommendations for integrating urban environmental issues into EU, national and local policies. The project has also launched a Sustainable City Network for the exchange of information and experience.
- The OECD Environmental Group on Urban Affairs established the Ecological City Project in 1993 to identify integrated national strategies for urban environmental problems. This project has concentrated on issues such as urban renewal and redevelopment, transport infrastructures and energy consumption.
- The Healthy Cities Project is a global initiative set up by the World Health Organization (WHO) in 1991 working for the introduction of programmes for improving the urban environment and health. Under this project health-related environmental indicators are being developed.
- A further international significant initiative is the European Charter for Sustainable Cities and Towns, launched at the European Conference on Sustainable Cities in Aalborg in 1994.

NOTES

1. First questionnaire: December 1995; second questionnaire: October 1996. See Editors' introduction.
2. See Foreword.

REFERENCES

CEC (1992), *The Future Development of the Common Transport Policy: a global approach to the construction of a Community framework for sustainable mobility* (Luxembourg: CEC).
CEC (1996), *European Sustainable Cities Report*, Expert Group on the Urban Environment (Luxembourg: CEC).

27. Urban problems in Europe at the start of the twenty-first century[1]

C. Fudge

1. ANALYSING URBAN PROBLEMS

Urban problems can be understood from many different disciplinary perspectives, as part of a historical process or from different geo-political levels of analysis. In attempting to manage the discussion in this chapter, an interdisciplinary approach is attempted which recognizes the importance of history and the ways in which cities everywhere contribute, shape and are shaped by national and global development and change. In terms of geo-political analysis there are perhaps three levels of significance for Europe.

First, one could identify and address the problem of the urban system in Europe against the wider urban challenge facing the world through rapid urbanization. This level of analysis raises the question of the role Europe and its cities will play in the world economic, social and environmental order when coping with the potentially enormous problems associated with rapid urbanization, and the development of megacities in developing countries such as parts of Asia.

Second, urban problems may be addressed within the boundaries of a broader definition of Europe including the current Member States, other countries in 'Western Europe', Central and Eastern Europe, the Newly Independent States, Russia and the countries that border the Mediterranean on its eastern and southern coasts.

Third, one could become more insular and analyse the problems in the existing European Union (EU) towns and cities as some studies and policy reports have already done.

My own preference is to attempt to hold all three levels in play at the same time in a way that interconnects urban problems and issues at different levels of analysis, gives them some sense of relativity in terms of impact locally and globally, and allows the emergence of new thinking that could underpin urban policy for European towns and cities in relation to global economic, social and environmental change.

However, the analysis in this chapter focuses on the third level – the existing EU, examining issues experienced by towns and cities of the 15 Member States. Unfortunately, economic and environmental processes, and increasingly social change, are not contained by political boundaries and therefore the analysis at levels one and two will and must continuously inform our discussions.

In writing about urban problems, it is difficult to avoid a cataloguing process that at best shows some of the linkages between problems via matrices. This is understandable, given the complexity of the terrain, but is inadequate for a number of reasons. First, it does not provide a deep understanding of the often cyclical processes that interrelate problems (for example the private–public transport debate). Second, it tends to lead naturally to problem-solving of a sectoral or partial kind, often reinforced by professional perspectives on the problems of cities, that again is incapable of addressing the complexity of the causes and processes. Third, it does not lead automatically to the consideration of the holistic interrelationship of social processes, public policy and action, and the processes of governance. Finally, it tends to work against systemic analysis, which seems a useful descriptive (particularly ecosystems thinking) and possibly operational approach to the management of cities.

2. GLOBAL URBAN CHANGE

The EU is one of the most urbanized regions of the world. Statistics from 1992 show the EU to be 79 per cent urbanized, with corresponding figures for Japan 77 per cent, the USA 76 per cent, Central and Eastern Europe 67 per cent, and the developing world 35 per cent. Within the EU, urbanization was faster in the north than in the south. This is now reversing. The urbanized figures for Greece (64 per cent), Italy (69 per cent), and Spain (79 per cent), are all now close to or at the European average. Ireland and Portugal are still well below, at 58 per cent and 36 per cent respectively.

The world's urban population is now put at 2.6 billion out of a total population of 5.8 billion. Growth rates have fallen but another 86 million people are being added to the world total each year. The gradual drift to urban areas has become an avalanche. In 1950 there were 83 cities with a population of more than one million, 34 of them in developing countries. Today there are 280, with the number arguably expected to double by the year 2015. All of the new cities with a population of over one million are in developing countries, including 11 of the largest 15. Also in 1950 there were two so-called megacities, with 8 million population or more, New York and London. By 1970 there were 11 megacities and by 2015 it is predicted by the UN that there will be 33, 21 of which will be in Asia, with many having a population of close to 20 million. Many of these megacities, it is argued, will produce 70–90 per cent of their nation's GDP (*Guardian*, 1996).

Coupled with this predicted rapid urbanization are four other issues that potentially compound its significance – changes to climate, uneven availability of water, uneven patterns of food production and access, and uneven patterns of population growth/decline. Taken together, these major global concerns demonstrate the importance of how we manage our towns and cities locally, and the contribution that may well be required at a local or European level to these wider international issues. This not only affects urban policy and management in Europe, but more crucially must relate to global economic arrangements and world trade agreements.

The urban problems being faced in European cities include the following nine themes: social exclusion, lifestyle and equity; degradation of the urban environment; transportation and accessibility; the need for new forms of institutional capacity and governance; technological management: waste, water, air and resource use; urban dereliction and redundant buildings; urban economic uncertainty and unemployment; crime and personal safety; and leisure and tourism impacts.

In terms of recommendations to reduce the 'problem pressure' and the expected benefits of communicating the success or failure of such recommendations to the general public and to policy-makers via the proposed Pressure Index,[2] I refer to the detailed recommendations of the *European Sustainable Cities Report* (CEC, 1996). These recommendations are selectively reproduced here as suggestions for reducing the 'problem pressure'. They are holistic, integrated and draw on the interrelationship of the substance of problems and the processes that create them, presenting substantive policies, and management and governance processes that need to be developed.

2.   RECOMMENDATIONS FROM THE *EUROPEAN SUSTAINABLE CITIES REPORT*

Sustainable Management of Natural Resources

The issues of natural resources, energy and waste are closely interconnected. Cities are places of high energy intensity, and energy plays an increasingly important role in the operation of urban systems. The more energy that is consumed, the higher the need for natural resources to support energy production. Similarly, the higher the consumption of natural resources and energy, the more waste is accumulated. Because of this interrelationship, it is logical that several of the relevant policy options have multiplier effects. So by addressing one particular problem, the policy options may simultaneously solve one or more other problems.

Air

In relation to air the report states that the key goal of sustainable management is to ensure quality and supply. To achieve this the EU should continue to define and adopt stringent emission standards in relation to air quality. The EU, Member States and regional and local governments should adopt regulatory instruments and technical measures to reduce pollution sources and quantities. They should also develop policies and mechanisms to promote air generation and filtering, for example through the provision of more green elements in cities. It is further recommended that the measures designed to improve air quality and supply are developed within an overall framework of an action plan for air quality. This will, in effect, be a requirement once the EU's Directive on Ambient Air Quality Assessment and Management becomes operational.

Soil, flora and fauna

The general aim in relation to soil, flora and fauna is to increase the proportion of natural and human-made ecosystems within cities. Regional and local governments should facilitate the development of green corridors linking countryside to the various green elements within cities. This provides the best ecological framework for habitats, thus combining an increase in biodiversity with recreational value. A move from monoculture towards increased biodiversity is important in the sustainable management of cities. It is also recommended that green elements be used for education and awareness-raising in relation to the way ecosystems function and how urban functions can be integrated into the natural system.

Water

The principles of sustainable water management are related to water conservation and minimizing the impact of all water-related functions on the natural system. Regional and local governments should utilize measures to green cities by improving the water system. Maximizing the use of permeable surfaces facilitates the infiltration and cleansing of storm water, while creating ponds, ditches and wetlands facilitates the retention of storm water, purifies the water and enriches the flora and fauna.

It is also recommended that water-use efficiency be included as part of sustainable water management. Taking into account the end use of the water in determining the required quality, with measures such as collecting storm water for secondary uses and recycling grey water, is one way to achieve water conservation.

The EU, Member States and regional and local authorities are also urged to promote the implementation of more environmentally friendly sewerage solutions. Biological treatment plants and passive water treatment methods based on ecological functions should be more widely utilized.

Energy conservation
The basic aim of sustainable energy management is energy conservation. The key to energy conservation lies in behaviour of individuals and organizations, but also in energy production and distribution.

The EU should continue to support the setting up of urban energy agencies to tackle energy management and thus contribute to the environmental protection and sustainable development of cities. The EU should also consider the extension of other initiatives within the field of energy conservation, especially those targeted towards local authorities. National governments should provide the necessary frameworks for facilitating the implementation of energy conservation policies. Such frameworks may include fiscal measures, regulatory changes, new powers for municipalities and so on.

The EU and Member States should facilitate decentralization of energy management and production wherever appropriate, in order to increase the possibility of coordinating actors, of working actively towards reducing energy demand and increasing efficiency of production and distribution. The EU, Member States and regional and local governments should create the right conditions to replace non-renewable energy sources with renewable ones wherever possible.

Regional and local governments should apply sustainable design principles which facilitate energy conservation. Densities, siting, layout, bio-climatic architectural design, materials, insulation, orientation of buildings, micro-climate, green elements and the like should be considered in land-use planning and development control to minimize energy consumption. Regional and local governments should also undertake an energy audit of both internal and external activities, and of the city's own building stock, in order to move towards adopting suitable energy efficiency measures, thus contributing to energy conservation while reducing running costs. Greening the city's activities in such a way also provides a valuable example for other organizations and individuals to follow. It adds credibility to any awareness-raising initiatives undertaken by cities.

Waste management
Various solutions that utilize waste for energy production serve the dual purpose of conserving natural resources and making efficient use of waste products. The ultimate aim of sustainable waste management is, however, to minimize production of waste.

The report recommends, first, that the EU should take steps to provide policy guidance for an integrated system of waste management that allows for context-specific implementation in all Member States. Second, that the EU, Member States and regional and local governments should promote the reduction of packaging, and the increased use of reusable and recyclable packaging. And third, that regional and local governments should promote maximum separation at source and composting. The last measure will minimize waste production, reduce the level of contamination of waste, and turn some of the waste into useful forms, such as topsoil or biogas.

Other recommendations for waste management coincide with those for water management, especially those for liquid waste management.

Finally, the EU, Member States and regional and local governments should bear in mind that influencing behaviour through education, information and practical evidence is a key factor in achieving more sustainable urban systems. The relationship between influencing behaviour and sustainable management of natural resources is particularly evident. It is an area where people's behaviour affects the level of sustainability directly, and where they can see the results of changed behaviour in a transparent way.

Socio-economic Aspects of Sustainability

Population shifts and economic restructuring within the European urban system have affected cities differentially. Greater economic integration through the Single European Market, developments in Central and Eastern Europe and the expansion of the EU as new Member States join are having far-reaching effects upon the economies, social structures and environments of cities.

Economic management actions for governments

The EU and Member States need to create the conditions in which businesses can profit by operating in more environmentally sound ways, since the extent to which cities can encourage local businesses to be greener is very much constrained by the operation of market economics.

The EU and Member States should consider active economic management to promote sustainable behaviour of businesses. Examples of how this can be achieved include the following:

1. Promotion of the environmental business sector, for example by creating markets for environmental products and services through the use of regulations, taxation, incentives and investment.
2. The development of environmental standards for products and processes.
3. Regulatory frameworks for utilities which encourage demand management and tariff structures which reward lower use.

4. Management of the relationships between fixed and variable costs to make sustainable behaviour more attractive at the point of decision (for example, shifting car taxation from ownership to use).
5. Promotion of longer-term investment institutions.

Governments should further consider shifting taxation away from socially desirable activities such as employment towards environmentally undesirable activities such as energy use, resource depletion and the production of waste.

All policies need to encourage energy efficiency, since improved energy efficiency is now recognized as a key means of achieving both economic development and environmental quality objectives.

Member State initiatives involving the private sector should be encouraged. However, wherever services significant for sustainability are privatized, the regulatory framework must be designed to ensure that sustainability-enhancing policy choices are more profitable, and that unsustainable policy choices are prevented.

The use of pilot projects should be increased, but these should be more systematic in their approach so that a coordinated set of objectives for employment and the environment can be pursued and results measured.

Economic management actions for regional and local authorities
It is recommended that regional and local authorities take the following actions:

1. Explore ways of creating employment through environmental measures.
2. Encourage better environmental performance in existing businesses in their areas.
3. Target inward investment strategy towards types of economic activity which are more favourable in terms of sustainability.
4. Seek to build competitive advantage in relation to inwards investment by developing and promoting the environmental and quality of life attributes of their areas.

The scope for more radical action depends upon cities having powers to manage their local economies in more sustainable ways, subject to local democratic mandate. For example, cities should be enabled explicitly to consider local environmental, social and economic consequences in decisions about purchasing, tendering and company support; and to invest their resources according to social and environmental as well as economic criteria.

Action for social sustainability

In the field of social sustainability there is a need for the EU and Member States to strengthen their commitment and actions in striving towards the achievement of just societies that provide the necessary conditions for the well-being of all citizens. This includes the elimination of poverty and social exclusion, access for all to basic services, education, health care, housing and employment, and the facilitation of active involvement in decision-making by all groups of society.

The Expert Group recognizes the EU's initiatives in the establishment of the fundamental social rights of citizens as a constitutional element of the European Union, and the extension of the Social Charter to cover a wider range of individual rights and responsibilities, particularly if these may aid social sustainability.

In addition, the EU should continue to develop and implement initiatives that support the development of human resources through education and training, and especially the integration of young people into the labour market. At the national and local levels, Member States and regional and local authorities should take action in two ways. First, they should facilitate the adaptation of the workforce to changing needs and conditions of the labour market through the implementation of national and local training initiatives and programmes. Second, they should focus specifically on groups that are disadvantaged or segregated from society, and help them to help themselves through education and training as a key means of getting access to meaningful employment opportunities.

The EU and Member States should actively contribute to improving the health of their citizens through the integration of health protection measures in legislation and policy, and through taking actions together with regional and local authorities. These should include the provision of adequate health services, the development of education and training programmes, the collection of statistical data, the reduction of traffic and other polluting activities; and initiation of awareness-raising campaigns.

In the absence of a Community housing policy, the EU should promote the principle of adequate housing for all through pilot projects and initiatives focusing on promoting cooperation between agencies, exchanging information and experiences, and financial support to innovative experiments that further social aspects of housing and reduce homelessness. Member States should create the legal and financial frameworks for the implementation of innovative housing schemes building on public–private partnerships and aimed at providing good-quality housing well integrated within the existing urban structures to be available for rental at affordable prices.

Regional and local authorities should widen schemes aimed at enabling the allocation of social housing in accordance with urgency criteria, to take into account other aspects than mainly financial ones, for example racial prejudice and other reasons which might prevent people from gaining access to decent housing. They should also promote the conversion and use of derelict land and buildings for the development of social housing schemes or temporary shelters for the homeless through spatial planning, development control and creative use of housing finance.

In recognition of the social role that public places play, the EU and Member States should financially support public space and conservation strategies and projects. Regional and local authorities should facilitate the enhancement of the quality of public spaces, including the prevention of physical deterioration and the implementation of greening measures, the reclamation of those spaces for people rather than cars, and the creation of safe environments, for example by applying the 'public guardianship' concept.

4. SUSTAINABLE ACCESSIBILITY

Achieving sustainable urban accessibility is a vital step in the overall improvement of the urban environment and maintenance of the economic viability of cities.

A useful policy framework for mobility and access has been established with the publication of *The Future Development of the Common Transport Policy* (CEC, 1992) and the subsequent Green Papers 'Towards fair and efficient pricing policy in transport'and 'Citizens' Network – Fulfilling the potential of public transport in Europe'. The EU, Member States and regional and local governments should now develop transport policies which seek to minimize energy consumption, and the environmental and social impacts of motorized travel. The following paragraphs summarize the principal measures required.

When transport policies are drafted, targets should be set covering all aspects of the environment (for example, land take, noise and visual intrusion), and in the longer term all aspects of sustainability. These targets can be incorporated into evaluation and funding mechanisms. There should be an equitable system for evaluating different transport modes which takes effective account of all benefits and costs, including environmental impacts. It is essential to develop measures to reduce the need to travel rather than continuing to emphasize measures which seek to minimize travel time.

At city level there is a need for strategic planning in the management of urban transport systems, moving towards long-term time horizons and away from *ad hoc*, incremental responses to demand. Sustainability goals need to be developed for transport planning. Reducing demand for travel clearly requires close linkage between the management of urban transport systems and the strategic planning of future settlement patterns. As indicated above, transport and land-use plans are intrinsically interlinked. All transport plans should be assessed within a land-use framework.

Policies to ensure a transfer from private to mass transit are essential. The accessibility of mass transit should be improved to take into particular account the needs of people with reduced mobility. Existing tram and trolley systems should be maintained and optimized, and alternative means of transport developed, including walking and cycling. Attention should also be given to the role of restraint and pricing measures as essential elements of reducing private car travel through increased costs. Alongside this, new methods of communication, including telecommunications, should be fostered and promoted.

The use of the Structural and Cohesion Funds to assist transport which improves accessibility within urban areas while reducing the environmental impacts of motorized modes is recommended. All programmes for funding under the EU support framework should be assessed to ensure that they set out policies and actions which will reduce rather than increase the dependence on private motorized transport in cities. Support should be given to all projects which increase cycling and walking in cities, and more space should be given to these only truly environmentally friendly modes of transport.

The full social and environmental costs of urban transport need to be appreciated and absorbed by users, as agreed by European Transport Ministers. This requires the creation of new accounting mechanisms which would form the basis for improving both the price structure and the provision of transport infrastructure. The following are recommended for Member States:

1. The development of fiscal policy to reduce the relative price advantage currently enjoyed by those motorized modes causing the greatest environmental damage (for example, a carbon tax).
2. Adding taxation on usage to taxation on ownership, for instance, fuel taxes, road pricing and road licensing arrangements, in order that transport users acknowledge and pay for the urban environmental costs which they generate as a result of the frequency and extension of their transport habits, ultimately bringing about a change in behaviour.
3. 'Ring-fencing' or 'earmarking' of monies received from the taxation of environmentally damaging modes for the financing or subsidy of less harmful means of transport. However, such an arrangement is not at present acceptable to all Member State governments.

Member States should seek to design regulatory regimes which enable competition where desirable, while ensuring control over quality, access and the environmental impacts of transport.

Accomplishing these policy changes requires the establishment of appropriate administrative arrangements. Greater coordination is required between public and private transport (for example through creation of a separate joint administrative agency to manage urban transport in totality). City transport should be under the aegis of one authority only, preferably the same authority that has the remit for land use and development within the city.

Local governments should develop measures to facilitate the effective involvement of local communities in the formulation of transport policies. Similarly, they should encourage community-based solutions to urban mobility problems, for example, through intermediate modes between private and public transport, as happens in rural areas.

Incentives are needed to encourage employees of organizations in all sectors to use environmentally friendly alternatives to the car.

5. SPATIAL PLANNING

Spatial planning systems are essential for the implementation of city-wide policies for sustainable development. In developing policy and practice recommendations for land use in cities the Expert Group acknowledges the diversity of local problems and solutions, and seeks to strengthen existing spatial planning systems, especially by encouraging ecologically based approaches.

Land-use plans should advocate mixed uses rather than separation of uses through rigid zoning. Spatial planning systems which currently rely on zoning will need to become more flexible to accommodate this.

Sustainability requires a move to planning systems in which environmental carrying capacities at local, regional and global levels are accepted as guiding principles within which other considerations may be traded off. Capacity-based approaches are already being applied in certain Member States and should be encouraged.

Member States should seek to provide a coherent framework for spatial planning, such that plans prepared at municipal level fit within regional and national environmental policy frameworks. Where such overarching frameworks do not exist, Member States should allow municipalities increased scope to devise local solutions.

Planning should seek to be objectives-led. Objectives should determine strategic directions and specific levels of environmental quality, economic growth and social progress. Through them, plans should describe intended states of the environment. Plans should include both national and locally derived targets related to sustainability, and indicators should be developed to measure both the extent of problems and the degree of success in addressing them.

In order to reduce the need to travel, spatial planning should be complemented by fiscal and restraint measures such as road pricing and traffic calming, which are capable of producing results in the short term. Use of the planning system to influence urban form is a long-term mechanism since new development is a relatively small proportion of the total urban stock, but it is essential for the development of more radical measures in the future.

Urban regeneration should be used to meet goals of sustainable development in the following ways:

1. By strengthening social cohesion through involving residents of deprived residential areas in the regeneration process.
2. By ensuring the restoration of ecological links, and the strengthening and conservation of ecological values, as part of an integrated ecosystem.
3. By improving accessibility of existing areas. New infrastructure should be designed to complete the fabric of footpaths, cycle lanes and bus lanes, and public transport provision should be encouraged in order to provide opportunities for more sustainable transport patterns.
4. Urban regeneration sites near railway stations should be used for high-density developments which concentrate activities.

In relation to tourism, leisure and cultural heritage, the following are recommended:

1. Their planning should be integrated in national guidelines and regional policies dealing with economic, social, environmental and cultural aspects.
2. Tourism, leisure and cultural heritage issues should be an integral part of the spatial planning process.
3. Cultural and environmental policies require long-term planning. Planners and decision-makers should avoid the use of planning procedures that are inspired by short-term gains where they reduce opportunities for the achievement of long-term objectives.
4. A balanced urban structure should be created so that the historic centre and the new core support mixed uses which complement their roles, and protect and maintain existing elements with architectural or traditional values. The balance between human features and local environmental conditions should be kept.

Urban environmental problems

NOTES

1. It should be noted that this essay was originally drafted in 1997.Therefore the most recent developments in this policy field have not been included.
2. The condensation of the indicators into a set of indices has now moved further down the political agenda, although such a development is not excluded at a later stage. See Foreword.

REFERENCES

CEC (1996), *European Sustainable Cities Report*, Expert Group on the Urban Environment (Luxembourg: CEC).
CEC (1992), *The Future Development of the Common Transport Policy: a global approach to the construction of a Community framework for sustainable mobility* (Luxembourg: CEC).

PART IX

Waste

28. Introduction

B. Friis

1. POLICY RELEVANCE AND INTERNATIONAL FRAMEWORK

Waste represents a loss of resources, and the spread of emissions from treatment and disposal of waste to air, soil and water over a period. In addition, there is a risk of unintended emission of undesirable substances.

Waste is an environmental problem of growing concern. The principal question is 'how can we improve our welfare without continuously increasing the amounts of waste and the related environmental problems?'. Several policies have addressed this question, for example, the UN and the EU have adopted a well-known priority ranking for dealing with waste (waste minimization, recycling, treatment with energy recovery, sanitary landfilling).[1]

The Basel Convention on hazardous waste has been adopted by many countries, including the EU,[2] and more recently, Agenda 21[3] has highlighted waste as one of the topics to address.

At EU level, the Fifth Environmental Action Programme[4] has formulated a strategy to stabilize waste production at the 1985 level by the year 2000.

2. RESULTS OF SECOND-ROUND QUESTIONNAIRE

A second questionnaire submitted to waste experts asked them to rank the 30 indicators condensed from the first questionnaire[5] on the basis of three quality criteria defined as 'policy relevance', 'analytical soundness' and 'responsiveness'. Figure 28.1 shows the overall rankings for these three questions. The core ranking of the indicators is also presented, expressed as a percentage of experts who included the indicator in their top-five list of essential indicators.

It should be noted that there is some disagreement between the core rankings and the quality question rankings. The top two core-ranked indicators are 'waste landfilled' and 'waste incinerated', which relate to waste treatment, whereas the top two indicators for all three quality questions are 'hazardous waste' and 'municipal waste', which relate to waste types. There is also less

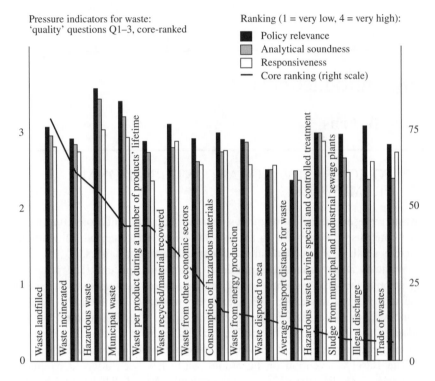

*Figure 28.1   Results of second-round questionnaire for the Waste policy
field*

agreement compared to some other policy fields between core rankings and
quality question ranking for indicators further down the rankings.

The highest core-ranked indicator representing a more broad life-cycle
approach is 'waste per product during a number of products' entire lifetime',
which is fifth, although it is ranked lower for the quality questions. Indicators
on various emissions from waste treatment are not represented.

3.   DELIMITATION OF THE WASTE POLICY FIELD

'Waste' is a word used in different ways in various countries. It is defined in
Directive 75/442/EEC as 'any substance or object in the categories set out in
Annex I which the holder discards, or intends or is required to discard'.

The policy field of Waste comprises hazardous and non-hazardous solid
waste from households, municipalities, industry, energy production, hospi-

tals, construction works and other societal activities. Exported waste should also be included since it might exert a pressure on the environment in the receiving country.

In some countries, certain wastes, such as nuclear waste, military waste, and manure, are covered by different legislation and are recorded separately from other types of waste.[6]

Links

For the Waste policy field the most important links with other policy fields are the following:

Dispersion of Toxic Substances
Waste is one way of dispersing toxins. The Dispersion of Toxic Substances policy field concentrates on the total production/consumption of various toxic substances, while the policy area of Waste includes the amounts of hazardous solid waste and their treatment. Contaminated soil from past activities is a state indicator and at present not included in the list of environmental pressure indicators. A pressure indicator measuring the annual increase in contaminated soil due to waste treatment is proposed for the Waste policy field.

Water Pollution and Water Resources
Waste can be a threat to water due to illegal discharge, leachate from landfills, and dumping into the sea. Sludge is in some Member States regarded as waste and counted together with other waste types. In other countries it is regarded as a potential problem for water resources. It can also be seen as a resource for agriculture. One of the proposed indicators for waste is sludge from sewage plants.

Resource Depletion
Waste can be regarded as a potential or lost resource. Energy consumption in production and waste treatment is included in the Resource Depletion policy field; however, recycling of waste is dealt with in the Waste policy field. Sludge and manure might be considered as a resource, a potential pollutant for water or even a waste. It is proposed that manure be dealt with under Resource Depletion.

Air Pollution
Treatment of waste (for example, incineration) can cause air pollution, depending on the waste type and the technology applied. However, treatment of waste is included in the Waste policy field; for example, one of the proposed

indicators is 'Dioxins emissions from waste incineration'. Air pollution indicators concentrate on the total emissions of various pollutants.

Ozone Depletion
Decomposition of waste at landfills generates methane, which contributes to
the depletion of the ozone layer. The methane can be converted to CO_2 if the
gas is incinerated, thereby reducing the effect on the ozone layer. An indication of such contributions to ozone depletion from the Waste policy field can
be given by registering which types of waste are landfilled at which kind of
landfill (for example, with/without incineration of landfill gas).

Urban Environmental Problems
Municipal waste is one of the topics dealt within the Urban Environmental
Problems policy field. The Waste policy field includes all types of waste
viewed on a national basis.

4. CONTRIBUTIONS IN THE WASTE POLICY FIELD

As a contribution to the development of indicators in the Waste policy field,
three experts were asked to write a chapter. Three different writers from three
different EU Member States were found. Dr Donald Huisingh is involved
with the new trends of cleaner production and sustainability, Peter Gössele
specializes in waste management, planning and statistics, and Professor Franco
Cecchi is concerned with research on waste treatment and monitoring.

The chapter by Jordan and Gössele (Chapter 30) describes the historical
Donald Huisingh's contribution (Chapter 29) poses questions about environmental pressure indicators and how they can be developed and used in
combination with other tools in order to facilitate progress of societies toward sustainability. Huisingh warns that the pressure indicators standing
alone are simplifications, focusing on end-of-pipe solutions and compartmentalization of environmental problems. He reminds us that environmental
problems are interconnected (one moment we have solid waste and the next
we have an emission to air or water) and encourages a further development of
pressure indicators within the new paradigm of waste prevention and cleaner
production. In addition, he suggests that closer links between environmental
pressure indicators, and governmental policies and instruments be established.

The chapter by Jordan and Gössele (Chapter 30) describes the historical
development of waste production. Efficient incentives are needed to reduce
quantities of waste and the levels of hazardous waste, and to ensure environmentally safe treatment. The solutions are not simple. For example, the
authors question the idea that recycling is always an environmental advan-

tage. Although – and because – the situation is complicated, Gössele and Jordan welcome the Eurostat development of a system of indicators to provide an overview for non-expert politicians, administrators and the public. The authors recommend that the problems of potential misinterpretation of data be avoided by professional use and regular reassessments·

The chapter by Professor Cecchi and Dr Pavan (Chapter 31) explains that waste must be considered as an integral part of production. The environmental problems related to waste can be expressed by the physical law on entropy, and the chapter sets out how this approach can guide industry and the public towards a better utilization of resources by using cleaner technology instead of 'downstream' technologies. Cecchi and Pavan discuss the present environmental problems related to waste and suggest that 'technical obstacles to economic exchange' be removed in order to improve the market for recyclables, to avoid 'over-production of waste' and in order to avoid decisions on waste management being taken on a short-term economic basis only.

The chapter lists a range of definite actions to be taken within waste management: for example, how to improve sanitary landfills and how to treat biological waste, together with sewage sludge.

Cecchi and Pavan expect that an environmental pressure index for waste will contribute to an improved communication with the public, and among administrators and politicians, and hope that this and other actions will result in an increased rationality in defining waste policy, in production decisions and in public opinion.

NOTES

1. Council Directive on Waste (91/156/EEC) (the 'Framework Directive').
2. Basel Convention on the Control of Transboundary Movements of Hazardous Waste and their Disposal, SBC No. 94/008.
3. Second UN Conference on Environment and Development in Rio de Janeiro (1992).
4. See terminology in Annex IV.
5. First questionnaire: December 1995; second questionnaire: October 1996. See Editors' introduction.
6. Directive 91/156/EEC on waste excludes from Article 2 radioactive waste, mining waste, some agricultural waste and explosives if they are already covered by other legislation.

29. How can environmental pressure indices be used to help societies monitor progress in achieving their Agenda 21 goals?

D. Huisingh

1. INTRODUCTION

The European Commission is to be lauded for its efforts to develop environmental pressure indicators/indices (EPIs).[1] Such initiatives are indicative of a growing awareness of the need for and the will to invest human efforts and financial resources in helping European societies monitor their progress towards the elusive goal of sustainability. During the process of development of these EPIs, extensive information was used and inputs from numerous people involved in waste management were solicited. Such broad-ranging consensus-building activities are very important and help us all to gain a deeper appreciation of the complexities facing us in contemporary society.

I am encouraged by this initiative but also seriously concerned that the proposed EPIs will do little to help our societies make the progress toward sustainable development that is so urgently needed. Because of this concern, much of the chapter is devoted to posing questions and making suggestions for developing and using other indices and other tools together with the proposed EPIs.

2. USE OF EPIs ALONGSIDE OTHER ENVIRONMENTAL QUALITY IMPROVEMENT TOOLS

Before the EPIs are implemented, we need to address the following questions to increase the opportunities for success.

- Overall, how will the EPIs be used to help EU countries make progress and monitor that progress in achieving their goals under Agenda 21?

- How will the effectiveness of these EPIs be measured? And who will monitor it?
- How will improvements in EPIs be implemented?
- What plans does the EU have to integrate these EPIs with other tools to foster and to monitor progress in making improvements in environmental quality and in human health?
- Assuming there is agreement that other tools must and will be used in combination with the EPIs, what other tools will be used? For example, what governmental policies will be used to foster the development, production and use of greener products designed to use fewer toxic substances and less energy, and to produce readily reusable resources at the end of the consumer-use phase?
- What regulatory, financial and peer group pressure 'sticks' and 'carrots' will be used to foster the reduction of hazardous and non-hazardous wastes at the product design and production sources, rather than continuing only to index tons of waste per capita and to resign ourselves to build more waste management capacity to treat the symptoms of our industrial and societal inefficiencies?
- If such integrative approaches are envisioned, how will the EU foster the implementation of such proactive and preventive approaches of cleaner production and cleaner products?
- How will the emerging, 'Branch-specific industrial benchmarks' be used to establish the toxic substance use reduction and waste reduction goals for members of each industrial sector?
- Equally important, how will work with the waste EPIs be integrated with results from biomonitoring and human health monitoring?
- How will education, training, technical assistance, financial instruments and other approaches be utilized to help ensure that the results of using the EPIs and other related indices will be used to foster continuous environmental quality improvements?

3. WILL THE SELECTED EPIs HELP OR HINDER SOCIETAL PROGRESS TOWARD SUSTAINABILITY?

I am seriously concerned that, while the selection process of these EPIs was a useful step, the EPIs' usage may slow down rather than accelerate waste reduction and toxic substance use reduction efforts if the proposed EPIs are not integrated with other initiatives. In this regard, will the use of these EPIs provide us with insights about cost-effective approaches for improving environmental quality? Are there better, more effective, approaches than the EPIs that can be implemented?

In seeking answers to these questions, EU policy-makers would do well to develop policies based upon more complete consideration of the Law of the Conservation of Matter stated by Miller as:

> Matter cannot be created or destroyed; it can only be changed from one form to another. Every waste material we believe we have managed, is still with us in one form or another; there is no away. (Miller, 1992)

From this and related basic laws of the operation of the ecosphere, what appears to be a solid body at one moment is constantly changing into or being mixed with the gaseous and liquid phases of the universe by biological and physical–chemical processes. Consequently, EPIs, if they are to be useful environmental management tools to help us monitor our progress in environmental quality improvements, should work with the realities of our interconnected and mutual dependence upon all facets of the atmosphere, geosphere and biosphere.

How can the proposed EPIs be adapted or combined with other tools to incorporate these realities? How can we link the proposed EPIs with initiatives such as sustainable product development and green chemistry that focus on developing products and processes that use less toxic substances and generate less waste?

Further, how can the EU combine the proposed EPIs with initiatives such as the US Environmental Protection Agency's highly effective, voluntary toxic substance use reduction initiative, the 33/50 Program? The first phase of that programme was so successful that it is now being expanded to encompass the phase-out or reduction of usage of many more toxic substances than were included in the first phase of the programme. Such initiatives, when coupled with the EPIs, could facilitate more rapid and focused progress in reducing the production, use and release of eco-toxic substances.

Also, how can the EPIs build upon initiatives such as the Dutch Environmental Covenants that are based on consensus agreements for waste and emission reductions among the stakeholders of different industrial sectors, the government, NGOs and consumers?

Moreover, how will the proposed EPIs address issues such as the phase-out of CFCs and other ozone-depleting substances (ODSs)? Such substances may be present in discarded consumer products such as refrigerators, air conditioners, fire-fighting equipment and so on, and if not properly managed, will be released as gaseous 'wastes' to the atmosphere as the 'solid waste', that once contained them, rusts in landfills. How will EPIs help us to be more responsible in managing ODSs so that our waste management practices do not continue to contribute to ozone layer depletion?

Finally, how will the proposed EPIs help society reduce the use and release of 'endocrine system disrupters'? Information about the diverse substances suspected of having endocrine system disruptive effects has been brought to our attention in several recent studies (for example, Colbourn and Clement, 1992). How will the proposed EPIs address such substances, which may include pesticides, surfactants, incinerator emissions such as dioxins and dibenzofurans, and products such as PCBs? How will the EU's activities be integrated with the numerous new research initiatives that are focused on the sources, nature and effects of such materials? This class of substances, perhaps more than many others, requires that our monitoring efforts be expanded to encompass many facets not currently assessed.

The longer-term objectives of the use of tools such as EPIs must be clearly enunciated before further decisions are made. We must be cautious not to develop and implement EPIs based solely upon data presently available. Instead, we must integrate the basic ecological concepts upon which our earth operates into the development of long-term strategies for the development and use of appropriate clusters of EPIs that reflect the interconnectedness referred to earlier in this chapter. Such longer-term issues must be addressed in research on the development and improvement of EPIs that can be useful for monitoring societal progress toward sustainable development.

In order to develop such sets of EPIs, research must be done to obtain answers to the following questions. First, which parameters should be monitored and how should they be monitored? Second, who should do the monitoring and how should the data be utilized to provide proper feedback to all societal stakeholders?

The process of developing more useful EPIs should respect and build upon the interconnectedness of all facets of the ecosystem. Previous EPIs have been inadequate because they did not build upon the cybernetic interconnections inherent in the ecosystem and the societies dependent upon them. Consequently, the result has been compartmentalization of environmental information and medium-specific regulations that are ineffective both environmentally and economically.

Unfortunately, the proposed EPIs continue to reinforce this division. They will continue to reinforce the old paradigms implicit in single-medium, end-of-pipe, curative approaches to environmental improvements. We now know that this paradigm is an inadequate guide for helping society 'solve' its sustainability challenges.

The new paradigm of 'waste prevention and cleaner production' encompasses a whole-process, preventive, continuous improvement approach. Using this approach, many companies are making progress in reducing toxic substance use and waste production, enhancing product durability and repairability, and in making other improvements that are ecologically and economically more effective than placing sole reliance upon waste treatment approaches.

4. CONCLUSION

In conclusion, what is my answer to the question posed as the title of this chapter?

Use of the proposed EPIs will provide useful information for governmental policy-makers, regulators, industrialists, scientists and citizens. If EU leaders realize the serious limitations of the proposed EPIs, and commit themselves to a process of continuous improvement of such EPIs and the integration of additional tools that will more adequately reflect the multi-media dimensions and the multi-year consequences of our activities upon the health of humans and the ecosystem, then more rapid progress will be made towards achieving the local and regional goals set under Agenda 21.

To achieve this there are four main requirements for the new EPIs. First, they should assess and report on the health of humans and the ecosystem, not only reflect upon single-medium aspects such as quantities of solid or hazardous waste produced per capita per year. Second, they should be clearly linked with governmental policies, programmes and fiscal instruments designed to foster continuous societal progress in the reduction of the volume and toxicity of wastes and emissions produced and released into the air, water and soil. Third, the EPIs should be linked with stimuli for corporations to utilize the concepts and approaches of 'cleaner production, sustainable products and industrial ecology'. Fourth, the new EPIs and associated educational and informational activities should be used to help all societal members understand how their purchasing and other lifestyle choices can contribute to societal progress towards achieving their Agenda 21 goals.

Future generations will judge us. What will be their judgement of our actions to foster a sustainable future for them? How will we use EPIs and other tools to help ensure that their judgement will be positive? I hope that the pressure indices, based on expert judgement, widely canvassed, will provide a basis for addressing these issues.

NOTE

1. The condensation of the indicators into a set of indices has now moved further down the political agenda, although such a development is not excluded at a later stage. See Foreword.

REFERENCES

Colbourn, T. and C. Clement (1992), 'Chemically-Induced Alterations in Sexual and Functional Development: The Wildlife/Human Connection', in *Advances in Mod-*

ern Environmental Toxicology, Vol. XXI (Princeton, NJ: Princeton Scientific Publishing Co., Inc.).

Miller, T.G. (1992), *Living in the Environment*, 7th edn (Belmont, CA: Wadsworth Publishing Company).

30. Proposals for the reduction of problems in connection with waste

K. Jordan and P. Gössele

1. WHY IS WASTE A PROBLEM?

Human activities throughout the ages have caused production of waste. We have learned about the skills and habits of our prehistoric ancestors from their rubbish heaps, where at most a few earthenware shards or some scraps of metal have lasted until today. Even the material from a 200-year-old dump is not much more diverse, with stones, ceramics, glass and metals still the main waste products, but the quantity is much greater, with a substantial increase in waste per capita.

Following industrialization, waste production accelerated proportionally with the production of goods. With the development of certain types of industry, such as chemistry and metallurgy, waste production not only increased but became increasingly hazardous. During the first two to three decades following the Second World War, industries were modernized, economies prospered and Western European societies developed a 'throw-away' mentality because resources seemed to be readily available.

Up to the early 1980s, the amount of household and industrial waste rose steadily. Since 1950, for example, the annual paper consumption in the Federal Republic of Germany has increased seven-fold and an annual increase of 1.5 per cent is anticipated to the year 2000.

In addition, the composition of waste has changed considerably. Due to changes in consumption patterns, a dramatic increase in packaging waste has been observed. Beverages such as beer, wine, mineral water and soft drinks, previously packaged in returnable bottles, are now increasingly bottled in one-way-glass, tin plate, aluminium, plastic or cardboard containers. From 1970 to 1988, the proportion of returnable packaging in Germany decreased from approximately 90 per cent to 74 per cent. This trend continues, though less sharply.

The amount of waste disposed of by public utility services has hardly increased since the beginning of the 1980s. This is, however, not the result of

Table 30.1   *Domestic waste from households, small enterprises and*
commercial services in the former West Germany (including
domestic-type commercial waste, bulky waste and garbage)

	1980	1982	1984	1987	1990
Amount of domestic waste					
in million tons	21.4	20.3	19.4	19.5	21.6
in kg per capita	347.4	329.3	317.6	318.8	339.2

Source: Statistisches Bundesamt (1994).

an avoidance of waste production, but relates to an increase in recycling activities and the separation of reusable waste products from household waste, as depicted in Table 30.1.

As a result of developments in treatment and processing technologies, it has been possible to increase the amount of collected paper and recycling considerably. Yet, during the same period, paper consumption and the usage of raw materials for paper products were also much higher.

In Germany, waste for disposal is generally deposited in landfills. In 1990, waste incineration plants, which primarily dispose of household waste, accounted for 8.4 per cent of the total amount of waste disposed of. In 1993, there were 263 landfill sites for municipal waste, of which a large number are to close in the near future. The chemical and biological processes taking place within the landfills are largely unknown and incalculable and have, in the past at least, frequently resulted in costly rehabilitation of affected sites.

The public has become aware of the consequences of thoughtless disposal of waste in recent years, caused by the quantitative growth in, for example, manufacturing, consumption, use of raw materials and use of land. The contamination of the groundwater by leaching from disposal sites, emissions of dioxins from incineration plants and the illegal transboundary export of hazardous waste have led to public and political discussion, not only concerning treatment and disposal practices, but also concerning consumer behaviour and the use of limited natural resources resulting from economic growth.

The hazardous potential that results from the volume and the composition of industrial as well as 'ordinary' household waste has meanwhile led to considerable increases in waste disposal costs. This cost factor leads to questions about whether future economic and social development can afford such trends. However, a characteristic of the ongoing waste disposal discussion is that the public continues to value the importance of environmental protection alongside economic issues such as the creation of jobs and the stability of the economy. Environmental and economic problems lead the field of political topics which are allocated the highest priority in sociological surveys.

2. WHY IS CENTRAL POLITICAL INTERVENTION NECESSARY?

In economic terms, Europe is already strongly interlinked and interactive. Waste is a traded good and is no longer a matter of merely local concern. Past experience shows that waste is regularly transported from 'expensive' and strictly regulated countries to countries with relatively cheap means of disposal or recycling opportunities. Because of less stringent regulations, the handling of waste generally implies higher risks of environmental hazards in such countries.

The so-called 'waste tourism' can only be avoided through international regulations and controls. The process of harmonizing national regulations within the European Union should take into account the differences of technological standards in Member States, but the harmonization needs to achieve the highest standards in waste management.

International interventions are also necessary in order to prevent market distortions in the field of secondary raw materials. For example, the separate collection of paper in Germany (regulated by a national packaging waste ordinance) has resulted in the collection of greater supplies than can be reused or recycled within the country and has therefore inhibited the development of national separate collection schemes in other Member States.

3. ACTIONS TO BE TAKEN

In most EU Member States, some kind of waste separation has been introduced recently, aiming at facilitating material cycles rather than dumping waste. This applies to municipal as well as to industrial waste.

There are many activities, including legislative measures, financial incentives, and development of new treatment technologies, which should promote the reuse and recycling of waste, reduce the potentially harmful effects of waste and prevent its storage.

Currently, most recycling technologies are so-called end-of-pipe technologies which, inherently, do not reduce the prevailing amount of waste, but slow down its rate of increase. A prerequisite for qualitative improvements is that the dispersion of toxic substances from different waste sources and to environmental media such as soil, groundwater and air is avoided. This can only be accomplished through strict source separation of waste. This separation also facilitates the development of tailored treatment and recycling processes.

In this context, the question arises whether the great variety of composite packaging material is really necessary. Furthermore, for various reasons it seems questionable whether an increase in recycling will, in the long term, reduce the amount of waste produced and have positive effects on the state of the environment in terms of the quality of groundwater and air, and the preservation of natural resources.

There are several reasons for these doubts about the waste-reducing potential of recycling. The environmental impact from recycling processes is not always known, and the recycling process itself produces waste. In many cases the resulting recycled products are of low quality and once they themselves become waste, this waste is either non-recyclable or only recyclable at a high cost. In this way, the waste problem is simply shifted into the future. The energy consumption (collection, transport, treatment and distribution) relating to the recycling process is in many cases not evaluated or simply neglected. Investments tend to favour technological developments which exploit natural resources rather than technologies which preserve them.

It is obvious that, in the long term, measures to prevent the effects of waste, once it exists, are not sufficient. For sustainable economic and social development of Western industrial societies, changes in public behaviour patterns (consumption patterns, nutrition, and recreational activities) are necessary as well as the consideration of environmental impacts, once development, production and distribution of goods are taking place. Possible actions are economic incentives: for example, the introduction of product liability, product labelling, restrictions for certain products, return obligations or concessions on returnables, and environmental tax systems.

Industrialists developing, manufacturing, processing, treating or selling products should take more responsibility. Products must be designed so as to lessen waste generation, and ensure ecological recycling and disposal. Furthermore, products should not be marketed at all if the environmental impact is likely to cause harm, for example by the release of noxious substances.

4.   ADVANTAGES OF A PRESSURE INDEX[1]

Today, most manufacturing processes and products are highly sophisticated. Neither politicians, administrators nor the general public are likely to be able to assess the environmentally hazardous potential of new technology or its products and the impact on waste management. It requires specialist knowledge and experience to forecast the 'response scenario' of a certain waste product. PVC, for example, does not in itself present a hazard, yet it becomes one following composite waste treatment.

The European Commission has tried to bring the available expertise together with the purpose of preparing a short, precise and comprehensive rating system for waste categories in relation to their environmental potentials and/or hazards. We can only congratulate them on this effort and wish them success.

The communication of anticipated problems and necessary actions for counter-measures in the field of waste management should enable non-expert politicians and administrators to avoid unqualified and expensive decisions. In this context, the environmental awareness of public opinion is an important regulator of administrative and political decisions. If a pressure index contributes to making waste policy more transparent, this should certainly strengthen public confidence and facilitate cooperation.

In the international context, a pressure index will support the harmonization of guidelines and policies, and guide Europe towards a single waste management approach.

Although pressure indicators are generally helpful for policy-makers, their limitations should be recognized. First, there is the danger that the indicators will be too rigid and will not respond to the changing relevance of pressures. Hence regular reassessments of indices are necessary in order to prevent misrepresentations of available data. A second problem arising from the use of such indicators is that they will be misinterpreted and people will draw doubtful conclusions, only to confirm their strong prior views. However, the usefulness of such an index, when viewed objectively and professionally, outweighs these objections.

NOTE

1. The condensation of the indicators into a set of indices has now moved further down the political agenda, although such a development is not excluded at a later stage. See Foreword.

31. Guidelines for an environmentally compatible management of waste

F. Cecchi and P. Pavan

1. INTRODUCTION

The problems of waste production and management can be understood with reference to the concept of entropy, which has been developed in recent years. According to the entropy law, all transformations in nature involve an entropy (disorder) increase, and waste must be considered as part of the production cycle. Therefore, entropy can be considered as a measurement of the required energy to restore a situation to the original state, before change. Applying this approach to waste production, we should look at entropy increase (disorder increase) in order to see how much energy is necessary to obtain the original situation. In fact, recycling or energy recovery from waste is a way of minimizing entropy (or disorder) increase. However, in applying this rule we should be aware that it is impossible to have 100 per cent process efficiency and that it is impossible to avoid dissipation of some amount of energy, however small, in any production process. Meanwhile, the optimal equilibrium depends on the market and political choices that are made worldwide. In fact, local modification of this equilibrium could create local negative repercussions on employment and production levels, and thus lead to negative social effects.

Although the quality of waste to be disposed of is an important aspect of the waste problem, the main problem related to waste is the trend for increased production, despite initiatives for separate collections, recycling and so on, which have been adopted in recent years. Difficulties are often caused by the continuing need to find markets for recovered products. These problems go beyond country boundaries, because the international trade in some of these recycled materials is sometimes underpriced, producing a negative impact on recycling activities in those countries where there is only a low level of recycling.

Another factor which makes waste a problem is the market distortion connected to the overproduction of waste and the availability of plants for correct final disposal. The latter often results in the need to deal with waste disposal on an emergency basis. Thus solutions to problems are often based on the short-term economic interests of waste managers, so that only limited technical approaches are considered which in general are those at lower cost, using inadequate technologies and causing a greater negative environmental impact.

The presence of toxic and noxious compounds in waste restricts the possibilities of recycling and reuse, and causes disposal problems for contaminated materials.

The increasing difficulties of construction of treatment plants due to public opinion worries (whether well founded or not) often results in inappropriate land planning, making waste disposal into a land problem.

The impacts of concern are those which cause permanent environmental modifications and those which affect human health. Those concerning the environment can be categorized as follows: local ecosystem modifications (micro-climate, groundwater, rivers, lakes), global ecosystem modifications (climate, groundwater, sea, atmosphere, forests), impoverishment of un-renewable resources, socio-economic gaps between different countries due to differences in environmental policies, and transfers of pollutants from one system to another (for example from air to water, from water to soil). Further to this, we should be concerned about the increase in the market for 'down-stream' technologies, encouraged by the policy approach of limiting and controlling pollutants, instead of the use of clean technologies. The necessity for such 'down-stream' treatment of wastes will affect production efficiency and consequently generate a variety of problems from country to country. Finally we should be concerned about the flow of natural or artificial compounds into the environment in amounts which are greater than those of natural streams.

Health impacts can be related to the life of waste: during production, transportation and final disposal. These negative impacts can be grouped as follows: exposure to pathogens, exposure to toxic/noxious materials, and physical injury.

These impacts are common for both municipal and industrial waste; however, industrial waste is sometimes related to higher risks. Disposal facilities are the most serious source of problems in terms of environmental pollution. This can be air pollution (particularly some pollutants generated by waste incineration), water pollution (due to waste landfilling), or soil contamination (inappropriate land disposal, landfilling).

These impacts can be related to controlled waste management and disposal, but the main impacts are the consequences of uncontrolled waste disposal and inappropriate choices in the management of disposal facilities. This contributes to reduced safety at landfill sites and treatment plants (reduced safety can result from a mixture of incompatible waste, insufficient biogas recovery, bad leachate collection and bad management).

2.   POLITICAL INTERVENTION AND SOCIAL DISCUSSION

As a consequence of the application of the thermodynamic entropy approach mentioned above to the economy, there can be significant repercussions on employment levels. It is possible, for instance, for productive plants to close due to loss of market competitiveness, and for market demand to move towards alternative products. Much depends on how the costs of waste management and disposal are shared. If the incidence is unequal, weak companies or countries may pay a disproportionate share of the costs. To avoid this it is necessary, among other measures, to remove some of the 'technical barriers' that presently impede the effective management of waste.

The removal of these technical obstacles requires, in most cases, the promotion of relevant interventions. First, significant financial support should be given from governments or the European Community for research and development of advanced technologies both in the field of minimizing waste producing processes and in the field of the treatment/disposal of the waste itself. This can also be achieved using demonstrative projects.

Second, international agreements must be developed to avoid unfair forms of competition among companies, and which take into account economic objectives and tax policies (for example, eco-labelling, environmental audit, depuration standards, transboundary transports, classification of waste, targets for recycling, extended producers' liability, quality of recovered materials: glass, plastics, paper, aluminium, access standard to final disposal facilities).

Furthermore, these interventions must be connected with the definition of appropriate social and economic indicators of the quality of life and thus require the involvement of the main social components (promotion of a wider dialogue between public administrations, universities, industries and so on).

The creation of international laws and control of their application is necessary in order to spread the correct approach and to educate future generations about the right approach to the waste problem.

3.   CONCRETE ACTION IN THE SHORT AND LONG TERM

It is necessary to take action to develop the awareness of both industrial producers of waste and the public of the present situation related to the production and final disposal of waste (that is, industrial and anthropic waste production, and the use of sanitary landfills and incinerators as the main disposal techniques). This must be done in order to improve the quality and reduce the quantity of waste produced at source, to reduce its environmental and health impact, to reduce the environmental impact of disposal technologies and to develop new, more appropriate technologies.

A first step is the development of an appropriate database system. This is necessary for several reasons:

1. For ecological management of anthropogenic and industrial waste production. This involves the control of energy consumption and raw materials in the production cycles, the analysis of the entire life-cycle of noxious and dangerous wastes, and separate collection and recycling of municipal solid waste, especially the three main types of waste: wet (biowaste), dry recyclable (plastics, aluminium, paper) and inert (stone, ceramics). In fact, biowaste treatment can be viewed as an element of a strategy which includes at least the following key elements: (a) reduction of the volume and toxicity of waste; (b) recovering energy both from biowaste itself by anaerobic digestion and the remaining dry waste by more appropriate burning technologies; (c) more appropriate utilization of landfills, mitigating their environmental impact (leachate formation, release of foul-smelling substances and gases involved in the greenhouse effect); (d) a further increase in the recycled proportion of waste; (e) containment, by composting uncontaminated materials and using the resulting conditioning soil material, of the progressive impoverishment of organic material of soils which at European level have often reached an organic matter content lower than 1 per cent.

2. To define unified, standardized methods and procedures of waste classification.

3. To create a qualitative–quantitative record of waste production which is updated continuously.

4. To create a territorial database of sanitary landfills, incinerators and other treatment plants, updated continuously.

5. To improve sanitary landfills from the construction and management point of view by adopting systems of a demonstrated efficiency (for example multi-barrier impermeabilization, appropriate leachate drainage systems, active biogas captation systems realized along the landfill filling, monitoring networks in the short and long term for detecting real-time contamination of groundwater and air, recovery of the area at the end of filling time) and promoting the disposal of inert wastes both from the chemical (slag, cinder) and biological (stabilized organic residues) point of view.

6. To create very reliable processes of thermo-destruction of waste, adopting energy recovery and promoting inertization processes of slag and cinder inside the incineration process itself (vitrification) to reduce the diffusion of pollutants in the environment and the volume of waste to be disposed of in sanitary landfill. The control of the management of the incinerators and the disposal of slag and cinder must be very effective with very strict protocols.

7. To create moving treatment plants for noxious and dangerous waste.

8. To improve the scrapping technique of bulky waste.

9. To overcome the sectionalism mainly due to the physical state of waste (solid, liquid, sludge), and consequently to realize the integration of solid waste management and wastewater treatment plants. For instance, the acidogenic fermentation of the organic fraction of municipal solid waste (MSW) and sewage sludge could be a source of easily biodegradable compounds for wastewater biological nutrient removal processes; the organic fraction of MSW can also be used as co-substrate with sewage sludge in the anaerobic digester for improving the energy balance of the wastewater treatment work; composting, landfilling, and incineration could improve their performances by adopting the co-disposal of sewage sludge and solid waste.

10. To define a general legislative reference for the utilization and the characterization of composts from waste to be utilized for agricultural purposes.

Other short-term actions to be considered are:

11. To develop appropriate, reliable environmental monitoring methodologies.

12. To develop appropriate, reliable environmental models for forecasting pollutant movements; in particular, this point is relevant to the noxious compounds which, in the short term, cannot be regarded as completely removed from waste, and are thus disposed of at landfills or burned in incinerators.

13. To decontaminate polluted soils caused by past inappropriate waste disposal, or by inappropriate management or localization of dangerous industrial activities.

14. To avoid the illegal international traffic of noxious and dangerous wastes.

15. To develop training programmes and/or modification of existing university teaching faculties on waste management as a response to the growing request of new professions connected with the new environmental targets to be reached.

16. To develop a European study on the effect on the European markets of separate collection of refuse. Goals of the study could be to assess the

possibility of marketing recovered materials at socially acceptable costs and the appropriate size of the market.

The long-term actions involve a completely different cultural approach to the problem. It is necessary to move from a culture of waste to a culture of secondary raw materials, and thereby to move from the present concept of landfill to one of final storage landfill for those materials that are unrecyclable and infinitely environmentally compatible. Consequently, this would lead from an increasing trend of waste production to a decreasing trend. This goal could be achieved in general by modifications of lifestyle.

Regarding industrial and commercial waste this goal would require five elements:

1. The adoption of eco-compatible products, that have minimum environmental impact and greater possibility of reuse.
2. The adoption of completely clean technologies, both concerning the type of raw materials used and transformation processes. This helps to eliminate noxious or other by-products harmful to the environment and health, and to produce an amount of waste compatible with thermodynamic principles.
3. The orientation of the market toward eco-compatible products.
4. The unification of agencies/organizations responsible for recovery/disposal of residues and a definition of the optimal size of authority area.
5. The unification of protocols of control.

Regarding municipal waste, a new approach is necessary to housing structure, collection and transportation. Thus for the dry portion of MSW we need to develop a system featuring a first sorting at residential level, a local unit plant and, subsequently, a district area plant. All these places can be connected using vacuum pipelines, thus avoiding/reducing transport by truck. The organic fraction of MSW could be directly disposed of into the sewerage system after sink-shredding and treatment at the wastewater treatment plant.

4.   EFFECTS OF A PRESSURE INDEX[1]

Due to growing public awareness of environmental problems, there is a need for further development towards a wider involvement of the general public and policy-makers. One aspect of this enlarged participation in environmental management is the communication of the results of the policy actions via a pressure index. The advantages of doing so can be summarized as follows.

It will increase awareness of the general public, especially concerning the possibilities offered by recycled materials and the correct ways to use them. It can provide a deeper understanding of existing technologies and their performance. This will help to allay irrational public worries about waste treatment plants and the optimization of waste separation. The index will define a priority list for a rational use of the available resources according to the weight within the specific pressure index, and will document the progress achieved and allow a faster feedback of the impact of actions. It will help to identify productive systems which cause lower environmental impact. It can reinforce the institutional structures of waste management with consequent increased rationality in defining the waste policy. Further, it will improve coordination of companies, consultant structures, the scientific community, and social and training/educational systems.

A survey of hazardous waste, in terms of types and amounts, could allow a better understanding of efficient resource use in terms of plant realization and the general management of these materials. The same applies to MSW, and would allow the reduction of landfilled waste and the promotion of a conservative use of organic compounds (compost, biogas, biofuels). A survey of the waste treatments, the products obtained and the materials recycling could provide essential data for the optimization of resource use and for the development of an effective market in recycled materials.

5. CONCLUSIONS

Considering the above points, it is possible to draw some conclusions about waste management and production.

Regarding industrial waste, this must be considered as part of the production cycle. The energy required to reduce the entropy produced is the energy needed for the treatment of the waste. Therefore, by minimizing waste, we minimize the energy loss. All factors that foster an environmentally compatible production cycle, from the choice of raw materials to the use of low environmental impact technologies, have to be considered as important to the efficiency of the process. Actions that evaluate environmental impact in the long-term should be adopted instead of short-term solutions, even if the apparent economic consequences may not immediately appear favourable.

Regarding municipal waste, the creation of well-defined streams of waste leads to the best use of resources. Channelling organic waste to biological treatments and dry waste to landfills will result in a higher level of safety and a lower environmental risk. The awareness of the public, and especially of political and administrative structures, about waste problems has to be improved, in order to promote financial support and to develop a more appropriate legislative framework worldwide. New processes, which consider green approaches, have to be studied and developed, and applied to the entire life of waste, from collection to final disposal.

NOTE

1. The condensation of the indicators into a set of indices has now moved further down the political agenda, although such a development is not excluded at a later stage. See Foreword.

PART X

Water Pollution and Water Resources

32. Introduction

A. Comolet and A. Garadi

---

1. THE RESULTS OF THE SECOND-ROUND QUESTIONNAIRE

The analysis of responses to the first questionnaire[1] produced a set of 31 indicators selected on the basis of the four criteria shown in Figure 32.1: pollution-emitting sectors, pressures in terms of quality and quantity, water quality parameters and types of water resources (surface/underground). The results of the second questionnaire were then used to classify these indicators

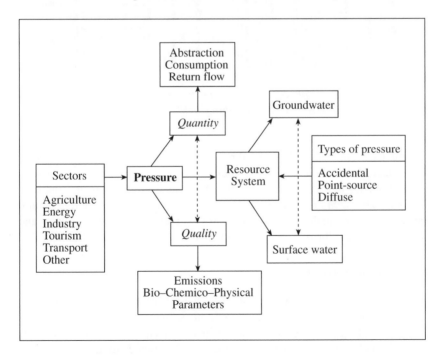

Figure 32.1   Criteria for selection of water pollution and resources indicators

Water pollution and water resources

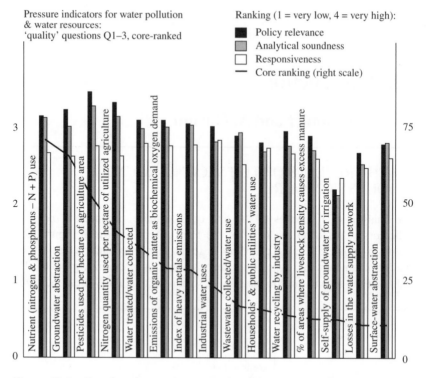

*Figure 32.2   Results of second-round questionnaire for the Water Pollution
and Water Resources policy field*

in order of rank on the basis of three qualitative criteria: policy relevance,
analytical soundness and responsiveness.

The overall top 15 rankings for the three quality questions and the core
rankings are given in Figure 32.2. These indicators cover the different natural
areas in Europe, qualitative and quantitative pressures on water resources and
their impact, and the different sectors which release polluting substances.

Pressure on Water Quality

Pressures on water quality are caused by the release of pollutants and toxic
substances produced by social and economic activity. Agriculture is the main
source of nitrogenous pesticide and fertilizer effluent. Agricultural pressures
are reflected by two highly ranked indicators: 'pesticides used per hectare of
utilized agricultural area' and 'Nitrogen quantity used per hectare of utilized
agricultural area'. Indicators associated with public use and urban areas

include 'emissions of organic matter measured as BOD'. Indicators related to industry are represented by 'Index of heavy metal emissions'. The final indicator in this category – 'Total nutrient (N + P) use (eutrophication equivalents)' – cuts across all sectors since the substances released are common to them all.

Quantitative Pressures

Quantitative pressures are those resulting either from excessive withdrawals and use, or from wastewater released into the environment with little or no treatment, which is measured in terms of effluent flows. In the case of pressures due to water abstraction, particular attention is given to underground water resources because of their sensitivity to over-abstraction. The indicator used is 'groundwater abstraction'. The impact of industry, as the major source of pressure related to water use, is reflected by the indicator on 'industrial water uses'. The main sources of effluent discharge are industrial and municipal, and pressures in this case are measured by indicators such as wastewater collected/water use.

Representativeness of the Selected Indicators

The indicators selected reflect problems associated with qualitative and quantitative pressures which occur during the different phases of the water cycle (resource systems, use and return flows) in the various natural areas in Europe, as well as the intensity of different social and economic uses of water in these regions (domestic, municipal, industrial and agricultural).

The polluting and toxic substances included in the indicators reflect the main impacts in terms of water quality: eutrophication, toxicity, organic pollution and – indirectly – acidification. In terms of quantity, the main emphasis is on groundwater resources because of their extreme sensitivity to excessive abstraction (resource renewal problems), and also on industrial water uses because of the toxicity problems liable to result from the discharge of industrial wastewater into aquatic ecosystems. Finally, this category also includes the indicators reflecting return flows, such as 'water treated/ water collected'. Discharges from these sources are largely responsible for the water quality problems mentioned above.

It should be borne in mind that several aspects are not taken into consideration: first, those aspects related to 'natural' pressures, with flooding and drought as the major impacts; second, salinization problems characterizing some southern European regions (for example, Spain) as a result of freshwater scarcity and inappropriate irrigation (for example, inadequate or non-existent drainage systems); and third, the problems due to changes in the water regime brought about by hydraulic installations, to changes in aquatic systems through development, or to changing land-use patterns.

2. DELIMITATION OF THE POLICY FIELD FROM OTHER POLICY FIELDS

Water is a non-substitutable resource that is vital both to ecological processes (*in situ* use) and to social and economic activity (*in situ* and *ex situ* uses), but it is the latter category that exerts the greatest pressures on the resource system.

Relevance to the Pressure System

Public utilities and the different economic sectors (agriculture, industry and so on) all use the natural environment to meet their water needs. The quantities of water abstracted therefore provide an indication as to the intensity of the pressures exerted by the different types of use. Once part of the water abstracted has been used and/or consumed, wastewater effluent is discharged into the same environment, which is therefore subject to two forms of pressure, both of which are primarily quantitative in the sense that both abstraction and discharge produce changes in the water regime.

The effluent discharged once the water has been utilized contains many different types of polluting – and sometimes toxic – substances, in concentrations which depend both on the type of activity and on whether or not the effluent is treated after use. Pressures are therefore also exerted on water quality, since the effluent alters the composition of the water resource. Interaction between the qualitative and quantitative aspects of water management also needs to be stressed, in the sense that pollutant emissions tend to limit the quantities of water available for certain uses, while over-abstraction may alter water quality in the environment.

Relevance to the Other PIP Policy Fields

Because water resources interact in so many different ways with social and economic activities in their various forms (through abstraction and wastewater discharges), as well as with other natural habitats and ecosystems (air, soil, vegetation, other natural resources and so on), water-related issues cut across many different policy fields. An analysis of the top ten 'overall ranking' indicators selected for each of the ten policy fields addressed under the PIP shows that the Water Pollution and Water Resources policy field is closely and directly linked to the Resource Depletion, Urban Environmental Problems and Dispersion of Toxic Substances policy fields. The linkages are described below.

- Water is a natural resource, so the Resource Depletion policy field is associated with three indicators which are directly related to quantitative aspects in the Water Resources and Water Pollution policy field. These are the indicators on groundwater abstraction by type of use (one for drinking water and one for agriculture/industry) and on overall water use per capita. The first two appear as aggregate indicators of total groundwater abstraction in the Water Resources and Water Pollution policy field, while, conversely, the 'total water use in industry' topic makes up part of the third indicator. In the current programme, water resources make up a policy field in their own right and, as a result, those indicators which are also associated with Resource Depletion need to be given top priority in the Water Pollution and Water Resources policy field. The Resource Depletion policy field could then focus more specifically on the analysis of pressures on natural resources other than water.
- In urban areas, net water consumption by public utilities and industries connected to public distribution networks is not very high since large quantities of wastewater are discharged through the sewage networks (from 60 per cent to over 90 per cent of all water used is subsequently discharged as wastewater). The Urban Environmental Problems policy field is associated with two indicators, respectively on untreated wastewater and on untreated wastewater which is directly discharged into urban surface water. These indicators contribute to both the overall wastewater treatment rate (with the relative proportion of untreated wastewater making up the remainder to the value 100) and the industrial wastewater treatment rate.
- Water carries pollution and therefore contributes to the dispersal of toxic substances. The Dispersion of Toxic Substances and Water Pollution and Water Resources policy fields are linked through three indicators. 'Consumption of pesticides by agriculture' in the former is linked to 'pesticides used per hectare of utilized agricultural area' in the latter. 'Emissions of persistent organic pollutants' in the former are reported as 'emissions of organic matter as BOD' in the latter. Finally, the former includes 'index of heavy metal emissions to water' while the latter includes 'index of heavy metal emissions'.

The last two topics are considered from the angle of wastewater discharges in the first case, and from the toxicity angle in the second. In so far as the aim is to describe pressures, it is suggested that the sectors in which the pressures originate should be given priority. In this case, if the indicator is also included in the Water Pollution and Water Resources policy field, it should be associated with the corresponding state indicator (concentration).

The Water Pollution and Water Resources policy field is also linked to the Marine Environment and Coastal Zones policy field, in so far as these two ecosystems are in continuity with each other. The two are considered separately under the PIP, since the first covers continental aquatic ecosystems, and the second marine aquatic ecosystems. Finally, there are indirect relationships with other policy areas such as Climate Change, which is likely to have a substantial impact on water resources through sea-level rise, increased or reduced rainfall and so on.

3. THE APPROACHES ADOPTED IN THE CONTRIBUTIONS

The first chapter for this policy field is by Joan Davis and Klaus Lanz and the second is by Josephina Maestu, Jose Maria Gasco, Jose Manuel Naredo and Federico Aguilera. The two contributions were analysed by means of a grid based on four criteria: the conceptual framework of each chapter, how types of pressure and their impacts were studied, what measures are suggested to reduce pressures, and how the PIP indicators were evaluated.

Conceptual Framework

Davis and Lanz analyse the topic on two levels: driving factors, which generate pressures on water resources (release of polluting substances), and symptoms, most of which are associated with pressure indicators. The authors distinguish between long-standing or 'traditional' problems associated with the renewal of resource systems in terms of both quantity and quality, and new problems which may be invisible (for example chemical pollution), complex and unpredictable (for example those associated in part with climate change, with the physical limits of water resources, and with wastewater collection and treatment). In considering the newer problems, Davis and Lanz stress the fact that there has been little or no reduction in underlying pressures, and, furthermore, that they are not considered as pressures at all in many cases, and therefore continue to harm the environment (for example pesticides and nitrates released by intensive agriculture).

Maestu et al. lay stress on the fact that qualitative and quantitative water resource problems are important for social, ecological and economic reasons. However, pressures on water resources vary from one European region to another, due to their edaphoclimatic diversity in particular. Pressures associated with water abstraction are critical in arid regions, while pollutants released by agricultural and urban activities reduce water availability throughout the European Union, as well as affecting human health and the integrity of ecosystems.

Types of Pressures and Impacts

Davis and Lanz identify three main causes of pressure. Increased water resource use by industry, agriculture and the population as a whole is the prime factor, followed by pollution. Visible pollution is highly apparent and often due to intensive agriculture (pesticides contaminating groundwater, nitrates and phosphorus causing eutrophication in lakes). 'Non-visible pollution' essentially results from the use of synthetic chemicals by industry. The third main cause identified by the authors is the deterioration of aquatic ecosystems, particularly as a result of wetland drainage to increase agricultural land surfaces.

Maestu et al. distinguish between pressures on water availability and pressures on water quality. The authors suggest that availability should be assessed on the basis of evapotranspiration demand after determining the water balance. Seasonal and geographical variations in distribution and demand should also be included to reflect cases where demand is not met or where conflicts arise between different uses. 'Natural pressures' are also taken into account, such as drought and flood risks, which may have considerable ecological, economic and social repercussions. Concerning water quality problems, salinization in the Mediterranean region is given as the main cause of soil deterioration, and also of reduced freshwater availability because of the need for additional freshwater input to dilute saltwater. Eutrophication is given as a consequence of excessive nutrient discharges, particularly in northern Europe. Organic pollution by substances released from urban centres and livestock farms is substantially reduced by wastewater purification and water treatment, but remains a major problem, particularly in southern European regions in summer, when high temperatures cause bacteria and micro-organisms to proliferate. Toxic pollution (by organic micropollutants, heavy metals and radioactivity) is a major problem in all European countries.

Proposed Pressure-reducing Measures

Davis and Lanz point out that reducing resource consumption, and therefore environmental pollution, requires both 'top-down' government measures (legislation, financial incentives) and 'bottom-up' measures (adequate information and incentives at community level, choice of appropriate indicators). The driving factors which determine change in pressures have to be addressed through long-term measures, while symptoms need to be dealt with in the short term. In the long term, major change requires not only measures which deal specifically with water, since water resources and water pollution are also affected by policy measures which address the social system and resource consumption patterns as a whole. In the short term, the most appropriate measures would be technical (introduction of water-saving processes, physical elimination of detergents, reduction in pesticide use through a shift away from crops such as maize, reduction in pesticide contamination) and economic (elimination of regressive tariff structures where these still apply).

Maestu et al. suggest a number of physical measures to reduce pressures on the available quantities of water. These would aim at improving both the water supply itself (inter-basin transfers, development of non-conventional resources including desalinized seawater) and water-use systems (improved management of trade-offs between conflicting uses, introducing water-saving processes, promoting change in social behaviour and customs). To reflect water quality, the authors suggest using an index, to be developed in line with the 'relative risk' concept, which would measure the absorption capacity of a given area. The index is defined as the capacity of an environment to receive, dilute and assimilate impacts. More concrete measures would include reducing the use of nitrates and pesticides in agriculture and controlling salinization by implementing reforestation policies and water sampling controls.

The Contributions and the PIP

Davis and Lanz stress that local water quality indicators are appropriate where the aim is to promote changes of attitude and action among the public, whereas aggregate indicators are more appropriate if the aim is to compare pressure indicators at international level. The PIP is designed to meet the latter objective.

Maestu et al. stress that pressure indicators can only be meaningful if they reflect situations in the different regions of Europe. Short-term and long-term measures as well as international comparisons should take account of this diversity.

4.   SOME COMMENTS ON THE APPROACHES AND EVALUATION BY THE AUTHORS

Both chapters underline the major quantitative and qualitative problems resulting from the pressure of social and economic activity on water resources, but each of them also raises some specific points.

Davis and Lanz's approach stresses the need to develop activities which meet the conditions required to guarantee the renewal of environmental resources, and which increase public awareness in order to promote sustainable resource use among citizens. To achieve these aims, the indicators selected should include not only official aggregate data, but also other data which may be more readily interpreted and assessed by the public at large in the communities or regions where problems arise. Experience has shown that motivation and environmental commitment among the public go hand in hand with participation and cooperation.

Maestu et al. stress the diversity of pressure-related problems in the different natural areas in Europe, and place particular emphasis on those which are specific to the Mediterranean regions, such as high evapotranspiration and salinization.

5.   A BRIEF DESCRIPTION OF THE INTERNATIONAL POLICY CONTEXT

The international policy context of the PIP is framed by the contribution of the United Nations Commission for Sustainable Development (UN CSD), by European water resource policy and by international agreements on transboundary water resource management.

Sustainable Development Indicators used by the UN CSD

Chapter 18 of Agenda 21 focuses specifically on the protection of freshwater quality and availability. A list prepared under the UN CSD's work programme on sustainable development indicators has been published in a 'Blue Paper'[2] and covers the major quantitative pressure-related problems addressed in Chapter 18: ground- and surface-water abstraction, household water consumption and wastewater treatment. Qualitative problems are addressed in the chapter through the topic of state indicators reflecting freshwater BOD and concentrations of faecal matter.

Indicators of pressures on water quality are described in the different chapters on activities considered as driving forces, particularly Chapter 14 (promoting sustainable agriculture and rural development), which deals with the indicators on pesticide and fertilizer use in agriculture. Emissions of some toxic substances, including heavy metals, are not addressed.

A Brief Description of European Water Policy

European water policy is essentially based on a corpus of regulations which establish either water quality standards for specific uses or emission standards for particular substances. The field of application of these regulations

Table 32.1   Main European water directives

Directives establishing quality standards for each type of use	• Directive 75/440/EEC on the quality of surface water used for drinking water • Directive 76/160/EEC on bathing waters • Directive 78/659/EEC on water used in aquaculture • Directive 79/923/EEC on water used in shellfish farming • Directive 80/778/EEC on drinking water
Directives establishing emission standards	• Directive 76/464/EEC on the discharge of toxic substances (+ sub-directives) • Directive 80/68/EEC on the protection of groundwater from pollution by toxic substances • Directive 91/271/EEC on urban residual water • Directive 91/676/EEC on agricultural nitrates • Directive 96/61/96 IPPC

has become quite substantial and is largely covered by the PIP indicators, which could therefore be used to monitor enforcement by EU Member States of the provisions set out in the directives, in particular through rates of compliance with quality and emission standards (see Table 32.1). These standards would then act as reference standards against which policy results could be evaluated or classified in order of importance.

European Union policy towards improved water management goes beyond the content of the 'water' directives, however. A number of other regulations, particularly those aimed at the sources of pressure on water resources, also target overall water resource management, for example, Directive 93/793/ EEC on environmental hazards, which applies to the use of chemicals, or agro-environmental Regulation 2078/92. All these instruments are included under the European Union's fifth Environmental Action Programme.[3] Table 32.1 lists the main EC directives in the 'water' area.

The Main International Agreements

Water management is also the subject of numerous international agreements focusing on international waters (seas and oceans, international rivers). These include the North Sea Conference, the Oslo and Paris Conventions, the Bonn Agreement (1983), the Hague Convention (1990), the Action Plan for the

Rhine (1987), the Convention on the Protection of the North-East Atlantic (Paris, 1992), PARCOM and others.

Some of these international agreements have established targets for the reduction of pollutant loadings. These agreements include the Convention on the Protection of the North-East Atlantic (reduction of pollution by agricultural nutrients in the North-East Atlantic), the Action Plan for the Rhine (reduction of phosphorus and nitrate effluent in rivers and seas to 50 per cent of 1985 levels by 1995), or the North Sea Declaration (withdrawal or strictly limited use of 18 active substances, 50 per cent reduction of pesticide effluent to marine waters).

NOTES

1. First questionnaire: December 1995; second questionnaire: October 1996. See Editors' introduction.
2. Indicators of Sustainable Development, Framework and Methodologies', United Nations, New York, 08/1996.
3. See 5EAP in Terminology (Annex IV).

33. Water pollution and water resources

J.S. Davis and K. Lanz

1. INTRODUCTION

Indicators are finding increasing use as an aid in evaluating our impacts upon nature. They can be particularly helpful when dealing with those impacts, the complexity of which hinders an overview as to cause and effect. In these cases, representative parameters can not only point out critical issues, but also help us determine the direction of change with respect to these issues.

Good indicators, however, go beyond raising awareness and showing direction. By promoting cooperation among individuals, institutes, businesses and officials, they can also contribute to steps in the appropriate direction. To further this cooperation of citizens, whether in their personal or professional lives, a selection of indicators should include, in addition to 'official' indicators, those which are readily understood and easily measurable by members of the communities or regions faced with the problems.

This point is of essential relevance for the growing discussion on sustainable resource use. Most of the changes necessary for the reduction of resource consumption and of environmental pollution demand immediate attention from us all. They cannot be postponed until governments have taken 'top-down' measures such as legal steps, or created financial incentives to encourage appropriate behaviour. Indicators can play a key role in speeding up changes through 'bottom-up' processes, by informing and motivating people at many levels to cooperate on measuring issues of concern, and by furthering activities which help their selected indicators to move in the right direction. This type of cooperative commitment and the resulting progress has itself become an indicator of success in projects[1] supporting sustainability.

With these thoughts in mind, the following discussion looks both at the factors behind our water problems and at the symptoms resulting from these problems. A number of these symptoms we have erroneously come to consider as the real problems themselves. This misinterpretation can mislead the search for solutions. However, being aware of both levels can help to set priorities as to where our efforts can be effectively invested. Both levels require attention and action, but measures are needed in different time scales.

The 'symptom level' (with which most of the widely used pressure indicators are associated) deals with shorter-term measures, while the underlying level involves longer-term changes and needs different criteria for representative indicators.

2. WATER POLLUTION AND WATER RESOURCES: IMPACTS OF CONCERN

The issues around water can be dealt with on various levels: the actual problems (past, present, future), how we are dealing with current problems, and how we need to deal with the problems to come.

Old and New Problems

Current practices in relation to water reveal scant understanding of the fact that, when it comes to life support, there is no substitute for this element. True, man's activities have always affected water, both quantitatively and qualitatively, but throughout most of history withdrawals and pollution did not exceed the capacity of nature to replenish the amount and to renew the quality of water. Only in recent decades have we gone beyond its recovery capacity quantitatively and qualitatively. While most of these problems are well known and well documented, we are currently creating new impacts, which differ significantly from the old ones. These new impacts often do not have the same 'advantages' of most of the past problems: they are less likely to be evident within a relatively short period of time and in many cases are difficult to measure. The new problems are characterized to a large extent by both non-visibility (chemical pollution), and a degree of complexity and unpredictability (partially associated with climate change factors) far exceeding that of past impacts. In both cases, once a problem can be confirmed, we are already so far along the path in the wrong direction that even immediate and drastic measures cannot significantly alter the impact within a functional period of time. This aspect has long been emphasized in the case of water, regarding the expected consequences of the increasing greenhouse effect.

A rise in atmospheric temperatures will, according to most models, lead to less frequent, but heavier, rains in virtually every region of the world. Semi-arid regions in particular will suffer because their already highly irregular rain patterns will become even more sporadic. More droughts and severe difficulties for agricultural production are predicted, notably for large parts of Brazil, south-western Africa, and western and northern Australia (WBGU: Jahresgutachten, 1997). Apart from quantitative and temporal variation in rainfall, rivers fed by glaciers (such as the Rhone and the Rhine) will experience much lower flows during the dry summer months due to a steady shrinking of glaciers.

Another example of unpredicted difficulties is the collection and treatment of domestic wastewater. For one hundred years, it was considered appropriate that water used in kitchens, bathrooms and toilets should be collected in a single sewer system and discharged to rivers or the sea. For the most part, the wastewaters are treated before disposal, but this varies considerably among countries and regions. Hundreds of billions of ECUs have been spent on sewers and wastewater treatment plants. Today, in times of financial restraint, it is gradually being realized that this system is neither affordable nor does it meet environmental needs. Via sewage systems a high percentage of nutrients is lost to agriculture, while at the same time causing nutrient overload in lakes, rivers and coastal waters. Further, persistent chemicals and pathogens are only partially removed by the wastewater treatment, the rest being discharged into rivers, raising the issue of their appropriateness as a source of drinking water, or even for bathing. However, the immense financial investment already made in wastewater infrastructure makes it extremely difficult to change the existing system. Attempts to retain and recycle the nutrients by transporting and treating toilet waste separately from the almost nutrient-free grey water are only just being started. Short-sighted decisions made long ago continue to exert their long-term effects, and modern society is having difficulty in making constructive changes.

Dealing with the Present Problems

One of the reasons why water problems have to be seen as significant issues is that the pressures creating these growing problems have not been reduced, and in many cases have not even been recognized as pressures. They thus continue to serve as sources of new problems.

Where we have dealt with water problems, we have aimed largely at the symptoms, and not at the underlying problems and pressures. This is particularly clear in the case of the intensive water use and pollution associated with our current system of agriculture. Intensive agriculture is often the main polluter of a region's water due to pesticides and nitrates contaminating the groundwater, and phosphates leading to eutrophication of lakes, rivers and coastal waters. Until now we have resorted to suppressing the symptoms technically, for example by removal of contaminants from drinking water or aeration of lakes. This symptom-oriented instead of problem/pressure-oriented approach in the agricultural field has a number of unwanted consequences. Among them are the extensive costs associated with technical measures, as well as the health threat associated with traces of chemicals not removed in the course of preparing drinking water from contaminated sources. Such consequences reveal the need for a transition to forms of agriculture which do not endanger water, and thus life itself. A change to an ecologically compatible agriculture will also benefit other water and environmental issues, for example by reducing soil erosion, increasing infiltration (raising groundwater levels, and decreasing run-off and flooding), lowering energy consumption (reducing CO_2 emissions), and increasing biodiversity.

Being aware of such chain reactions of effects is essential for planning the use of indicators, and evaluating their success. Effective indicators are reflected at the systems level, revealing changes in parameters in key places.

Looking at three long-standing causes of pressure for water, connections become apparent, revealing various points of intervention to reduce the pressure.

Water use
Water use in industry and households is still increasing in most areas, despite available technologies for improving the efficient use of water and widely held knowledge about ways to reduce wasteful use. However, the low price of water, coupled with the lack of understanding and appreciation of its real value to life systems, hinders us from making necessary changes.

The use of water in agricultural systems is drastically increasing worldwide, while pollution is also rising due to the intensive use of chemicals and the salinization of soils. This has been influenced by the increase in meat consumption which has placed tremendous pressure on the production of grains. The increased use of high-technology and high-breed grain types has altered soil characteristics, and as a result has vastly increased the need for irrigation.

Pollution
Pollution is still at a very high level in industrial countries/areas, and is markedly growing in those countries/areas undergoing development. While visible pollution has often been reduced in industrialized countries, there has been a simultaneous shift to non-visible pollution, caused mainly by long-lasting synthetic chemicals.

Deterioration of aquatic ecosystems
Drainage of wetlands has been extended due to the increased need for food, and the resulting demand for more farming area. In many coastal regions, wetlands and mangrove forests have recently been sacrificed to the development of aquaculture. Increased pressure on water systems for the production of hydropower has arisen from the growing demand for electricity.

Old and New Impacts of Special Concern

The impacts that *should* be of special concern to us are, for the most part, those that we are not currently dealing with as critically and intensively as needed. These impacts include influences both on the quality of water and on the quantity available.

First, there is widespread contamination by xenobiotic substances.[2] Some of the substances can act as eco-toxins, influencing entire aquatic ecosystems, even when present only in minute concentrations, for example, tributyltin compounds (Fent, 1996).

Second, contamination is not only a problem related to individual substances, but can also result from additive reactions, or more significantly synergistic reactions, of the many thousands of substances present in trace amounts in the rivers, lakes and drinking water of industrial areas.

Third, sinking groundwater levels can cause problems in urban areas for man-made structures (stability of building complexes), and in agricultural areas by restricting the availability of water for crops. In urban areas the drop in levels has two main causes, namely excessive withdrawals and a marked decrease in the recharging of groundwater caused by the increase in sealed surfaces such as buildings, streets and parking areas. In rural areas, the drop in levels is influenced both by the channelization of streams in agricultural areas and by changes in the soil structure resulting from the use of heavy farm equipment, synthetic fertilizers and chemicals. These factors reduce the moisture retention of soil, thus increasing run-off and erosion. This situation has become critical in many areas of intensive agriculture.

3. THE NEED FOR CENTRAL POLITICAL INTERVENTION AND SOCIETAL DISCUSSION

The changes required to benefit the environment need to be advanced by both top-down and bottom-up approaches. Central measures and decentralized activities are complementary in that they reach different people at different levels, they move people in different ways and they have their effects in different time scales.

The main role of central political intervention lies less in creating changes quickly (there are inherent delays in the political process) but in creating changes that are widespread and thorough. This includes changes which are legally founded, and can thus serve as a basis for further political measures. An example of effective top-down measures is building regulations with an impact on water, such as by-laws requiring on-site infiltration of rainwater at all new and renovated buildings, which would be the quickest way to raise urban groundwater levels. But in order to be truly effective, political measures also require cooperation at societal level. Discussions at this level can further cooperation by facilitating the spread of information. A key factor for the success of discussions at societal level lies in making the issues understandable in terms of what needs to be done, how it can be done and where, and what the options are at local, decentralized and individual level. Societal discussions can then initiate action in the short term, well before central political intervention can be implemented. In any case, when the discussions contribute to acceptance of the measures in advance of their implementation, the effect of central political intervention can progress more rapidly.

For the public to be able to assess the effect of everyday behaviour on aquatic ecosystems, information and education are crucial. For example, when people recognize that the chemicals used in conventional agriculture can affect not only the quality of groundwater, rivers and even drinking water, but also their own health (Colburn et al., 1997), they are more likely to choose organic products. Another example of the effects of recognizing significant connections has occurred in Switzerland, where awareness about the link between the excessive exploitation of alpine rivers for hydropower and the wasteful use of electricity has led to critical discussions on future water and energy policies.

4. CONCRETE ACTIONS FOR THE REDUCTION OF THE PROBLEM PRESSURE

Which measures are appropriate here will depend in part on the main sectors (industrial, household, agricultural) of water use as well as the source/type of pollution. While most of the points listed below involve some financial investment, there are also significant possibilities for water-use and pollution reduction by alteration of behavioural patterns and consumer criteria. Depending on the area considered, the decision/implemention can be very short-term (individual/private sphere) or may require decisions and actions extending over a longer period of time, though still within five years. The following categories are considered: industry, public buildings, households and agriculture.

Short Term

Actions for industry should include:

- use of closed-cycle water systems in process systems

- recycling of cooling water
- increased removal/recovery of chemicals from water before final discharge[3]
- reduction in use of chemicals
- alteration of types of chemicals used
  - use of biodegradable substances
  - use of easily removable (in process system) substances
- use of grey water and/or low-water-use appliances (for example, for sanitary purposes)
- physical water treatment[4] to lower detergent requirement in commercial laundries, increases efficiency of chemical reactions (thus lowering chemicals needed and reducing the amount of unwanted by-products)
- change in pricing structure of water and wastewater costs to industry (in particular, elimination of regressive tariff structures, where these are still in use).

Actions for public buildings, hotels and large building complexes should include:

- use of grey water and/or low-water-use appliances (for example, for sanitary purposes)
- physical water treatment to lower detergent requirement in hotel laundries
- reducing water/detergent use by reducing frequency of replacement of towels/linens during guest stay in hotels.

Actions for households should include:

- water-saving fixtures on taps and shower-heads,
- reduced water use for WC-flushing (low-flow toilets, urine-separating toilets, vacuum toilets)
- physical water treatment to lower detergent requirement in washing machines
- use of biodegradable detergents
- use of natural fibre clothing, which require less frequent washing, particularly for clothes worn next to the skin; also a decrease in the high turnover of clothing (clothing made of synthetic fibres tends to be discarded sooner than that made of natural fibres)
- re-design of property use: fewer lawns, which require frequent watering; garden design using plants which have lower water needs.

Actions for agriculture should include:

- conversion to organic farming, leading to:
  - reduction of loading of surface waters and groundwaters with fertilizers
  - elimination of contamination with pesticides
  - improvement of soil structure and water retention.
- reduction of meat production, leading to:
  - reduction of water use and pollution in fodder production (maize is a chemically intensive monoculture)
  - reduction in environmental loading due to slurry excess.
- restriction to appropriate crops, leading to:
  - reduction of water use, for example, the case of cotton shows clearly that planting a crop under inappropriate conditions can lead to drastic water consumption: up to 30m^3 water is required for 1 kg of raw cotton.

Long Term

For long-term considerations the major changes in water consumption and pollution will result not only from technical and structural changes, but also from significant societal changes.

Outlook

Estimates of savings via technical innovations vary. The same holds for the estimates of their costs, and thus of their widespread use. Even when a good two-fold saving is considered easily possible, this can hardly suffice in areas where increasing population and industrial growth place further demands on a dwindling water supply. Further, experience has shown that chemical pollution increases along with industrial development, thus adding quality problems to water consumption problems.

Although households need to remain a target for reduction of water use, more emphasis needs to be placed on industry as the major source of water use and pollution in industrialized regions. In Germany, for example, industrial use is about twice as high as household use. The reduction required can only partially be obtained from technological improvements, so a major contribution needs to come from changes within society. In this respect, the recently published study 'Sustainable Germany' (BUND, Misereor, 1996) gives an estimate of what is necessary. The study estimates an 80–90 per cent decrease in the use of energy and other resources as being necessary for sustainable resource use. Such major reductions in resource use in general will lead to a marked decrease in use and pollution of water.

Leverage points for changes

What are the main leverage points in bringing about such a major reduction of consumer goods, and thus of resource use? Looking at the main factors involved in high production and consumption indicates where we need to make changes in order to reduce both. Two main 'pushes' towards mass-production and consumption are found in the economic structure of our society, and in the societal and psychological factors which 'drive' us to purchase goods, well beyond the amount we can use. It is beyond the scope of this chapter to deal with these factors. It is, however, of obvious relevance to note that for the long term, major changes in total water use will come about less as a result of measures aimed specifically at water, but more as a result of basic changes in our society as a whole, as we attempt to move towards sustainability.

Transition factors

Several factors will be of particular significance in this transition. These are the transitions to longer-lasting goods, to quality goods where 'repairability' is a desired characteristic, and from consumer products as status symbols to goods serving product-associated purposes (some examples are clothes for comfort, warmth and good appearance, but not to meet continuous demands for fashion, and cars as means of transport, and less as status symbols). Also important is a shift in food preferences to fresh (non-processed) seasonal products, local production, organic products and less meat production.

While at a first glance these changes may not reveal their extensive consequences for water, it is clear that the sectors affected by these transitions are those which are strongly involved in current water use and pollution. The changes are therefore most relevant for long-term water savings and protection. Especially significant among the necessary longer-term changes is the need for more stringent control and product banning of a wide range of persistent synthetic chemicals. This long-term contamination endangers not only aquatic and terrestrial ecosystems, but also humans.

Change in attitude

Changes in consumer behaviour are essential, but not sufficient to reach and maintain the reductions required in water use and pollution. A change in our personal and cultural attitude to water is also required. This is an essential background for creating appropriate measures at the central political level. It is equally important at the private level in order to prevent excessive, conspicuous use of water, or other natural resources, in the private sector from becoming a new type of status symbol. This phenomenon can be seen already today, for example, intensively watered lawns in arid areas.

Criterion – value instead of price

Changing our attitude towards water involves being more aware of what water means for our life, and for the life of all on this planet. An understanding of the inestimably high value of water must replace our current view and actions regarding water, which are consistently influenced by its extremely low price. Low prices are often involved in water over-use and pollution. Again, agriculture is a clear example, with intensive use of chemicals lowering the cost of food production while increasing the costs of water protection and water treatment.

Even though more realistic pricing is necessary, incentives for reducing consumption should not only come from price structures, since price rises cannot be fully effective without increasing value appreciation. Further, we cannot overlook the danger that rising income will negate to a large extent the price effect. Water, as a 'free good', cannot be subjected purely to market mechanisms to control its use. Changes in value judgements also lie behind the willingness to invest in water-relevant developments such as ecological agriculture and new technologies for water protection.

5. THE EXPECTED BENEFITS OF COMMUNICATING SUCCESS OR FAILURE OF ACTIONS TO THE GENERAL PUBLIC AND TO POLICY-MAKERS VIA PRESSURE INDICATORS

The cooperation within a society towards making changes is to a large extent dependent upon the possibility of the individual understanding what is going on, and of feeling part of the change. This means providing understandable information both on the issues and on the way the everyday behaviour and decisions of the individual affect the problems or solutions. Participation is furthered by providing an indication of progress. Such are the theoretical and practical considerations behind the use of indicators in informing people of the progress that their changes in behaviour have helped to make. Experience has shown that a good indicator can be a good motivator. For example, after the link between algal blooms and phosphate had been established and recognized by the public in Germany and Switzerland, the use of phosphate in detergents virtually ended before the legal bans took effect.

The closer the tie between the indicator and the individual, politicians or the community, the stronger its effect upon the commitment of the citizens in helping to make changes. This has been one of the clear signals arising from local and regional sustainable indicator projects. The significant role of visible, understandable connections and indicators should not be underestimated here. For these reasons, the question of the type of indicator is critical. A highly condensed, composite indicator, containing the weighted evaluation of a number of parameters, will have a very different significance and role from those indicators that have a direct relationship to the everyday events and local surroundings of the people addressed. Both will have their place and are complementary.

The local, regional and national characteristics will influence the applicability of the indicator or indicators so that, for example, where water is plentiful, the issues will be different from those where it is scarce. And almost independent of scarcity, the type of water source also plays a role, so that water use in rainfed regions should be evaluated differently to regions where 'central' sources (dams) are dominant. Regional user characteristics add an extra dimension; for example, industrial regions will have systemically different problems and solutions from agricultural regions, with the result that different indicators will be applicable.

If the goal is to motivate citizens to take action and to make changes, then local indicators of water quality and use are appropriate. If the goal is to provide international comparison of pressure indicators, then the composite type may be more suitable. However, the inherent problem of choosing an appropriate weighting remains. Different factors have different significance in individual countries or regions, often depending on resource availability and financial capabilities.

6.   CONCLUSION

When looking for and creating composite indicators which can be used for 'single indicator'[5] and comparative purposes, the function of many individual indicators will need to be evaluated. This provides an excellent opportunity to identify relevant local and regional indicators. These could be used to promote cooperation in local areas and to motivate the people to take part in the improvement of the condition of local waters, as well as of the environment in general. An example of this is the setting up of a programme for local people to 'adopt' parts of streams or forests which can be effective in motivating participation. Active vigilance, documentation of changes and comparison among participants significantly contributes to progress.

Helping people to become involved in the process at local level could well help to improve those very factors associated with indicators at composite level. But the effect goes beyond this, as experience has shown that involvement, cooperation and feedback lead to further motivation and commitment to the environment, and to indicators of its health. This is a positive effect indeed, when a good indicator turns out to be a good motivator.

Looking at indicators in this light, it is clear that they can make significant contributions to pressure reduction. However, there is one characteristic of indicators which should not be left out when designing and evaluating them. Indicators reflect problems that already exist, and are recognized as such, but they do not have a precautionary role; that is they are not part of problem prevention. It is this aspect of precaution, of reacting to that which we know is a threat to humans and environment, even when we cannot yet measure exactly how much of a threat, that needs to be integrated into our daily decisions, be these at individual, community or governmental level. And this means that we need significant changes in the way science, politics and society react to what is known.

NOTES

1. One of the projects dedicated to sustainability and showing considerable/measurable progress by the use of indicators is that of 'Sustainable Seattle'. Information available from: Sustainable Seattle, Metrocenter, 909 Fourth Ave., Seattle, WA 98104, USA (or email: sustsea@halcyon.com).
2. The increasing reports on the endocrine disruptor effects of commonly used chemicals found in aquatic systems and associated with a marked loss of male fertility (in aquatic organisms as well as in man) is one example of the type of problem arising. See Colburn et al. (1997).
3. Reports on monetary savings in industry arising from such changes have been very positive: depending on the measure taken, pay-back times can lie in the range of only a few days or a few weeks. Many lie in the range of several months to a year. Relatively few required more than a few years.
4. Physical water treatment is understood here mainly as the application of magnetic or electromagnetic fields.
5. The condensation of the indicators into a set of indices has now moved further down the political agenda, although such a development is not excluded at a later stage. See Foreword.

REFERENCES

BUND, Misereor (eds) (1996), *Zukunftsfähiges Deutschland* (Sustainable Germany), (Basel: Birkhäuser Verlag).
Colburn, T., D. Dumanoski and J.P. Myers (1997), *Our Stolen Future*, 2nd edn, (New York: Plume/Penguin).
Fent, K. (1996), 'Ecotoxicology of Organotin Compounds', *Critical Reviews in Toxicology*, **26** (1): 117 (Florida: CRC Press).
WBGU (eds) (1998), *Welt im Wandel: Wege zu einem nachhaltigen Umgang mit Süßwasser* (*World in Change: Pathways to Sustainable Freshwater Management*), Wissenschaftlicher Beirat der Bundesregierung für Globale Umweltveränderungen (Berlin, Heidelberg, New York: German Government Advisory Panel on Global Change).

34. Water resources and water pollution

J. Maestu, J.M. Gasco, J.M. Naredo and F. Aguilera

1. INTRODUCTION

Water is important for economic, ecological and social reasons, and both quality and quantity are affected by human activities. This chapter stresses the pressures exerted on water resources from water abstraction, which is the critical issue in arid regions in Europe. In addition it is important to explain how pollutants from agriculture and urban uses limit the availability of water, and affect human health and the integrity of ecosystems.

Water resources, water problems and pressures on the water environment vary across the different regions of Europe. This reflects the edaphoclimatic diversity of Europe. In this chapter we attempt to develop an argument about the differences between southern, central and northern Europe, and how pressures might need to be understood differently in each region. It is argued that water policy and the development of policy instruments in different countries reflect these differences already and that European water policy should be based on data and indicators that also reflect these differences. Good examples of the type of analysis that needs to be considered in building indicators can be found in the *Dobříš Assessment* (European Environment Agency, 1995a), which introduces this diversity using complex risk models and spatial analysis.

This chapter reviews the current pressures on the water environment from different human activities and gives examples of how the diversity of edaphoclimatic conditions is important in understanding pressures on the aquatic environment. It focuses more on issues of water quantity but argues that the interrelationships between water quality and quantity need to be understood. It is not possible to have a water quality policy that leaves aside the quantitative element.

2. PRESSURES ON WATER RESOURCES: WHY IS THIS A CONCERN?

Pressures on Water Availability

The relative importance of evapotranspiration demands
Human activities exert pressure on the availability of water resources. Pressure on water resources is greater in 'xeric'[1] (in Mediterranean regions) and 'aridic' (in southern regions) edaphoclimatic zones than in 'udic'[2] (most central and northern European regions) edaphoclimatic zones (see Gasco, 1992).[3] This is not only due to human activities and limited supply but also to natural evapotranspiration demands, before and during water use.

There are few regions in southern Europe where there is no water stress during the warmer and potentially more productive summer months. Evapotranspiration demands tend to use up most of the rainfall throughout the year in arid climates and during the summer months in semi-arid climates, with little net contribution to available underground- or surface-water resources.

An analysis of the pressures on water resources needs to consider not only total abstraction by different uses in relation to water availability (as in the *Dobříš Assessment* and other international publications) but also needs to take into account losses due to evapotranspiration demands. Table 34.1 shows how, by adding evapotranspiration demand, the relative pressure on water resources in Spain and France better reflects what we commonly perceive to be the relative scarcity and water availability in both countries. The table shows that, taking into consideration evapotranspiration, only 23 per cent of total water resources are unused in Spain, as opposed to 86 per cent with the previous indicator.

Table 34.1   Water use in France and Spain (as % of availability)

	France	Spain
% use of renewable underground water	25	100
% use of water in lakes and dams	–	92
% use of water in rivers	10	7
% water use (urban, industrial and agriculture) in relation to pluviometry	6	14
Corrected % of water use including effective real evapotranspiration demands in relation to pluviometry	53	77

Source: Naredo and Gasco (1996).

Seasonality of rainfall and water demand

Another differential characteristic in xeric in contrast to udic climates is the seasonal deficit of water. During summer months water in reservoirs is fundamentally important not only as a source of urban water supply but also for the survival of aquatic ecosystems in rivers, reservoirs and wetlands. This is because water in dams can be used to keep a minimum water flow in rivers and supply water to wetlands as required (the so-called ecological flow). Therefore, the use of dammed water and also the underground water supply helps to deal with seasonal irregularity.

The seasonality of water demand (greater needs for irrigation and tourism) at the time of higher temperatures and evapotranspiration, when rainfall is at its lowest, has meant a need to keep seven times as much water in dams in countries such as Spain compared to France. These dams in turn modify both the natural flow of water and the natural landscapes, and hence affect natural ecosystems.

The main consumers of available water in xeric and aridic climates are evapotranspiration and irrigation, while in udic climates they are population and industry.

Local competition for water and over-exploitation of aquifers

In addition to the seasonality of the demand, we have to consider the coastalization of demand, particularly in the warmest months of the year, when urban and agricultural uses compete in the flat plains near the sea, producing local shortages. In the summer period water bodies dry up (naturally or due to human abstraction), making it difficult for aquatic life to survive and making the protection of wetlands more problematic.

This complexity of pressures on water quantity in aridic and xeric climates leads to regional competition for the resource. Complex systems of water infrastructure (water dams and transfers) and planning, integrated water management and dispute resolution systems are required that rarely exist in udic climates.

Groundwater resources have been over-exploited during the summer months and particularly during droughts. This over-exploitation of groundwater, as the last remaining water source at local level, is a concern because it has led to saltwater intrusion in coastal areas, the reduction of supply to rivers, and the drying up of dependent wetlands. The use of the highly saline water for emergency watering also leads to deterioration of soil conditions and vegetation cover.

Water stress and floods

Floods can lead to irreversible deterioration of the aquatic environment. They are a special concern in arid climates because of their contribution to erosion by washing top soil to the lower part of valleys (particularly when vegetation cover has been lost after a long drought). The impact of this phenomenon is related to the changes in land use (urbanization, reforestation and deforestation) and is being affected by climate change.

The canalization of rivers to prevent human casualties and the loss of production as a result of floods affect natural ecosystems and reduce the self-purification capacity of rivers.

European water shortages versus local shortages – national versus local data

Pressures on water availability need to be understood at a local level. Although at European level there could be said to be no water shortage, this does not mean that some localities are not suffering from serious shortages, even in northern Europe. Shortages are local or regional in character and have important consequences for natural ecosystems and economic sustainability.

Pressures on Water Quality

Natural composition of water

The natural composition of water varies according to climate and geochemical conditions. In udic climates soils have less salts and more organic components, and there are areas with high content of reduced iron (for example Denmark), fluoride (for example Germany), arsenic and strontium (in some mountainous countries) (see EEA, 1995b). These elements can be found naturally in water. By contrast, in Spain, for example, 42 per cent of water bodies have a salt content above the potability level (0.75 ds/m) resulting from the arid soils. In addition different species of flora and fauna may be adapted to the different conditions, including sudden changes of temperature.

Water pressures need to be understood against this background of natural characteristics, since the impact of the same human activities might vary between different ecoregions and for different ecotypes within these regions.

Different concerns according to differential risk

The main sources of pollution and concern for water bodies in less heavily industrialized and populated countries in the south are animal and human excreta, and other sources of organic pollution. Warmer temperatures exacerbate this pollution problem and its effects on human health. In central and northern European countries this problem has been largely resolved and acid pollution has become a main concern, reflecting the higher risk of acid deposition in some of these countries (EEA, 1995b).

Salinization: why is this a concern?
In the Mediterranean basin salinization remains a major concern. During droughts, as good-quality water becomes scarce, irrigation farmers are forced to consider poor-quality supplies from surface or underground sources, increasing the risk of salinization of soil. This leads to reduced crop yields and excessive accumulation of salts in soils. The vicious cycle is such that soil degradation leads to the loss of vegetation and contributes to desertification. Additional water would be required to reverse this process and wash salts away in order to re-establish the salt balance of soils.

Eutrophication and nutrients
Nitrates in run-off water and leached through the soil pollute both underground and surface water in intensive farming systems. After harvest the residual biomes in the soil and crop residues are broken down by microbes, and nitrates are produced by mineralization of organic materials. A proportion of nitrates is also directly leached from fertilizers. Leaching of nitrates is more likely in shallow and well-drained soils (sandy soils), and during wet periods or in udic climates (O'Hare, 1988). The nitrogen cycle, by which nitrates are produced, varies according to the type of soil. Nitrification is inhibited by high acidity, poor soil aeration, low temperatures and lack of moisture.

The differential impact of nitrates is related to rainfall patterns (less risk in countries with lower run-off), slope, soil composition and temperature. According to the *Dobříš Assessment* (EEA, 1995a) there is higher leachate and higher risk of nitrate pollution in north-west European countries.

Phosphates from fertilizers and detergents in urban wastewater systems are a major nutrient for plants and a major cause of eutrophication. They are problematic when associated with nitrates. The effect of phosphates on eutrophication is greater than that of nitrates because it is the limiting nutrient for phytoplankton production in water bodies.

Eutrophication caused by excessive nutrients (nitrates and phosphates) has ecological and health consequences. Excessive phytoplankton growth, as a consequence of nutrient loads, leads to increased turbidity and to the disappearance of submerged plants. Also the production of toxins by blue-green algae can poison fish, cattle and humans. When algae decay, the oxygen in the water is depleted by the respiration of decomposing organisms, leading to anaerobic conditions that do not support fish or benthic invertebrates. Eutrophication leads to taste and odour problems in drinking-water supplies which then need pre-treatment, treatment and filtration. Treatment by chlorinating to eliminate bacteria can in turn have consequences for human health.

Organic pollution: why is this a concern?

Organic pollution originates from the discharge of sewage either from urban centres or from livestock farms. Organisms that break down organic matter, such as bacteria, use up in the process the dissolved oxygen in water. If the oxygen falls below certain thresholds, many organisms may suffer, and fish and invertebrates will die. The decomposition can release ammonium that under high temperatures and pH conditions can be converted into ammonia that is poisonous to fish. Self-purification is limited and heavy discharge loads can kill aquatic life. High temperatures, in the summer in southern Europe, accelerate the process of reproduction of bacteria and microbial organisms, increasing oxygen depletion and the risk to human health. Treatment of wastewater and purification of drinking water have reduced this problem substantially. However, widespread purification with chlorine can cause cancer in combination with other substances.

Dilution of discharges into rivers is limited in water-scarce countries, in contrast to udic climates, making the effects of organic pollution in the aquatic environment and on drinking-water supplies more severe and increasing the needs for purification of these supplies.

Toxic pollution: a main priority?

Toxic pollution (organic micropollutants, heavy metals, radioactivity) caused by industrial activities is a major concern throughout Europe. Toxic pollution is probably the single most important threat to life and the stability of the biosphere.

Toxic pollution from industrial and domestic effluents is harmful not only to the aquatic ecosystems but also to human health. Heavy metals concentrations that may not be harmful to humans may affect the aquatic biota, although metals such as copper and lead can have their impact diminished in harder water with high alkalinity.

Organic micropollutants originating from widespread industrial sources are of particular concern. They are poisonous, and tend to persist and bioaccumulate in living organisms by entering the food chain and accumulating in selective organs (brain, liver, kidneys). Even in small quantities they can be lethal. Many new synthetic organic compounds are being released into the environment even though the consequences of many of them are still unknown.

3. PHYSICAL ACTIONS TO REDUCE THE PRESSURES ON WATER

The problem pressures need to be reduced fundamentally at source, but there is room for some fine-tuning to reduce pressures on water availability in the different seasons of the year. This means fundamentally working on the demand side to make better use of existing resources, and on the supply side to improve water availability through regulation and using non-conventional sources of supply. Often the choices depend on the cost-effectiveness of the alternatives.

Reducing Pressures on Water Quantity

Reducing pressure on water availability has traditionally been achieved by improving supply: new regulation (to deal with interseasonal imbalances), transporting water from water-rich to water-poor areas (water transfers) or, more recently, using unconventional sources of supply (desalinization plants) where pluviometry is low, as in aridic climates.

Programmes to reduce pressure on water availability need to consider issues of 'linking compatible uses'. In xeric climates 80 per cent of run-off water is used in irrigation and most of it evapotranspirates and does not return directly to the water bodies; 20 per cent of the water is used for domestic and industrial uses, where most of the water returns to water bodies after treatment. Ordering the uses of water, by using it first in the least consuming system (urban users) and later in the systems that are more consuming (like irrigation with the adequate precautions) can increase water availability. It can also help avoid regional and local competition between types of uses.

Farmers in xeric and aridic climates already manage water scarcity efficiently. They operate to maximize the yield of pluviometry to promote the infiltration of water in the soil. Conversely, in udic climates farming practices attempt to improve drainage. In xeric and aridic climates the way the land is worked for non-irrigated crops has the objective of achieving transpiration and not evaporation. Water is directed only to the crops, and farmers prevent the growth of surrounding vegetation (this is especially important in countries where potential evapotranspiration is higher than pluviometry).

Pressure on water availability can also be reduced by water saving, both through reducing losses in the distribution system and through reduction of water consumed per hectare, per capita or per unit of production, thus increasing the efficiency of water use.

Increasing water availability is expensive, and existing water resources can be used more efficiently. A more careful use of existing resources and reallocation of water among different types of users can be a partial substitute for new water infrastructure being built. This also means avoiding environmental side effects of the new infrastructures. Often the problem is that there are not enough incentives to save water and use it wisely.

In irrigation farming there is room for improvements that will reduce pressures on water availability. The average quantity of water necessary to correct the deficit in the soil is about 4500 m³/ha/year. About 20 per cent should be added to this to establish the salt balance of the soils. Existing average provision of 7000 m³/ha/year (when there is water) in Spain leaves room for improvement. This includes the improvement of channels and infra-structures to reduce leakage and losses during transport, and further improvements in irrigation technology (moving towards drip irrigation, using sprinklers and irrigation on demand). Changes in technology have given impressive results in Almeria, with production under plastic and using sandy soils resulting in a water consumption per hectare well below the average. Increased efficiency may lead to extending the cultivated area or augmenting the crops cultivated in the year without increasing the pressure on available water.

An important part of programmes to reduce water pressures involves con-sidering the behaviour of evapotranspiration in relation to the uses of land. Transpiration rates vary with vegetation type, age and standard crop cover. Interception losses can vary, especially where there are trees. Vegetation reduces run-off and soil erosion, improving water infiltration into the ground. The water yield, that is the water that remains after transpiration and inter-ception loss and that is available for river flow and groundwater recharge, is the effective rainfall that is available for abstraction. Reducing pressures on water quantity might mean changing vegetation type and crop cover or even reducing vegetation, especially where potential evapotranspiration is greater than pluviometry.

Finally, in conditions of competition, especially in coastal areas, reducing the pressure might mean making hard choices between different land uses (tourism versus high-yielding agriculture). Land-use planning and changes in agricultural practices become important issues in such circumstances.

The choice of alternatives needs to be informed by (a) the differential cost of providing water for each of them, (b) the saving potential, and (c) the social and environmental cost of the alternatives such as water transfers, groundwater abstraction, wastewater reuse, conventional and eolic de-salinization, reducing leakages in urban and farming distribution networks, and improved efficiency in irrigation (Aguilera, 1996).

Reducing Pressures on Water Quality

Pressures on water quality need to take account of the dilution and insulating capacity of rivers. This is related to the quantity of water in water bodies and the concentration of pollutants in the discharges. In xeric and aridic climates, especially during the summer months, the dilution capacity of rivers and water bodies is substantially reduced while the quantity of pollutants remains the same.

The physical actions that will help reduce pressures on the water environment of both point and non-point pollution during summer months will require the introduction of systems for accumulating discharges or diverting them away (to slurry ponds) to ensure that quality objectives, as designed in water quality and health legislation, are met. An increase in treatment requirements during the summer months to reduce the concentration of pollutants being discharged may also be required. The key point is that it is important in terms of pressure on the water environment to consider the discontinuity of water flows in xeric and aridic climates.

One response might be to have an index of absorption capacity (index of 'industriability') of a specific territory. This should be defined in relation to the ability of that environment to take/dilute/absorb impacts (Gasco, 1992). This index entails the idea of 'relative risk' of different areas, as presented in the *Dobříš Assessment* in reference to relative risk of acid rain, leachate of nitrates, the impact of phosphorous, and pesticides.

Improved use of chemical fertilizers and pesticides in agriculture can lead to significant reduction of pollution. The use of fertilizers and pesticides, often without technical control, needs to be corrected. Reducing the amount of fertilizers used might be possible without affecting productivity. A recent study in Almeria's Palmerillas Experimental Station (Spain) showed that similar productivity levels were maintained when the use of fertilizer was reduced by 75 per cent, together with reduced water doses. The improvement in the timing of application and appropriate usage according to type of soil can lead to reduced pressure from chemicals. In xeric and aridic climates reduction of the pollution effects from chemical fertilizers might be achieved by using organic fertilizers (especially stable dung from livestock farms or sludge from treatment plants in adequate sanitary condition). This would improve the organic component of land, which is not abundant in this climate.

The concept of 'relative risk' is important when programming reduction of pressures. It is not as important to limit or reduce water consumption per capita in udic climates as it is in xeric or aridic climates. In the same way, in the latter there is less concern with reducing acid deposition, which is a priority in countries with low-alkaline soils. The definition of the 'sustainability level' requires defining the sustainable total deposition of acid substances in each type of soil area (such as in Hammond et al., 1995), and also defining the right salt balance and organic discharge balance. It will mean establishing intermediate targets towards meeting the sustainability levels. Priority targets cannot be the same between different countries and different seasons. In aridic and xeric climates, eutrophication, salinization and organic discharges have different and, in some cases, more serious consequences than in udic climates.

Reducing the salt content of surface waters will require reforestation policies which will avoid washing away of salts in the soil. The problem of seawater intrusion due to over-exploitation of aquifers can be addressed by greater control of abstractions and changes in crops and watering systems, and might justify the installation of desalinization plants for agriculture (as is happening already in Murcia and the Canary Islands, Spain).

4. THE NEED FOR WATER POLICY AND PROGRAMMES, AND THE BENEFITS FROM COMMUNICATING SUCCESS OF ACTIONS VIA THE PRESSURE INDICATORS

The Need for a Water Policy

There is a long tradition in European countries of engineering-dominated programmes to manage water resource development and distribution. Water quality has now become a priority in all countries and the European institutions have an important role in developing common standards and policies, and in funding projects and programmes to achieve an overall level of environmental protection.

Southern countries have been traditionally concerned with dealing with the availability of water resources and coping with the devastating consequences of the water cycles (drought and recurrent floods). National governments have tried to prevent the worst consequences of these natural cycles by building dams, channels and flood defence infrastructures. Some Northern countries have focused on the prevention of floods and have been preoccupied with issues of water quality, reflecting the long-standing and dense industrialization in some regions. However, water availability is now becoming a concern in the north, in countries such as the United Kingdom, due to increased water consumption by the population.

It is important to have common standards and clear common policies towards global issues and common problems. At the same time it is important to deal with differences between regions when deciding about policy priorities in relation, for example, to the different types of pollutants.

Under conditions of scarce financial resources, different regions in Europe need to choose where to concentrate efforts, basing decisions on the relative risk of a programme failing. The setting of 'critical' and 'target loads', according to the capacity of the different basins and ecotypes within them to stand different levels of pollution, can in part be made by national or international institutions (as for those proposed for acid pollution).

The Usefulness of Indicators

Indicators developed at international level can help in comparisons between different countries and focus on the appropriate policies needed according to different problems. They seem especially useful if they measure the parameters agreed in international conventions and European directives.

The arguments and examples presented in this chapter lead to the conclusion that some problem pressures may need to be added to the policy agenda in order to reflect the conditions of xeric and aridic climates. To meet the criteria of policy relevance, indicators need to be able to reflect the differential risk in terms of the different sustainability levels for each problem pressure in the different regions of Europe.

This may mean that indicators and sustainability levels need to be defined at national or regional level first (according to an agreed set of criteria) and then used for comparisons and policy-making. Short-term and long-term actions will need to be defined based on this approach.

The question of whether the same indicators might be relevant for different countries in different ecoregions is an important one. As we have argued, the same indicator might have a different meaning in different climatic zones and ecoregions, hence preventing simplistic international comparisons. This means that a water pressure index might need to take this into consideration, perhaps by giving different 'weights' to the same indicator for different ecoregions.

Establishing policy priorities for water resources and water pollution might mean that once we have established the level of protection we want to achieve, we should then decide the least-cost alternative. To operationalize this, indicators need to describe physical phenomena, such as reductions in water resources and quality, in monetary terms. This might help to set priorities about where economic resources should be allocated and decide what opportunity costs are involved. Relevant indicators for policy-makers need to be expressed in such a way that they facilitate the best decisions on public and private expenditure, given that there are limited resources.

The importance of having indicators presented in monetary terms should not be overlooked because they allow policy-makers to make comparisons with other non-environmental decisions, discuss options and solve conflicts with other users of resources. This permits decision-making on an economically coherent basis.

5. CONCLUSIONS

It is important that the EU, in consultation with national and regional agencies, takes a lead in identifying key indicators that are relevant for European water policy. EU policies and indicators, however, need to be based on an understanding of the range of natural circumstances in which water policy must be defined and enforced, or it will create a much worse situation than the one that currently prevails. Now, at least we have practices tailored to the needs of each basin and region. It would not be desirable to have a situation in which some regions are forced to comply with standards which have been developed by using regions from other climatic zones as benchmarks.

This chapter defined for itself a simple task. It sought to explain the differences between the water quality problems and practices in central and northern Europe in comparison with arid regions in Europe, using the example of Spain. We have pointed out typical misunderstandings in the way statistics are developed in relation to evapotranspiration. We have also raised other themes which are relevant in the south, such as the importance of considering the discontinuity of water flows and the discontinuity of demand in coastal areas, the impact of this on ecosystems, the over-exploitation of coastal aquifers, and the need to consider different scenarios in water policy (droughts, floods and 'normal' scenarios). We have also pointed to the issues of the differences in natural background to water quality characteristics.

If we fail to recognize these differences, we might set up universal policies with the same indicator or target figures that are not appropriate and cannot be met in certain climates. One proposal would be to have a two-tier system. A higher-level policy would define the criteria to be used in defining policy and key indicators in each region. Then policy indicators and targets could be defined for each region and ecotype on the basis of the higher-level policy.

Some of the higher-level principles should, in our view, be founded on principles of 'best available techniques' in which programmes of action are based on practicability issues, including affordable costs. This might operate as an effective check against one set of regional interests dominating the policy process, and resulting in affordable costs for one region and massive costs for other regions which would be expected to adapt their practices and standards. As we have said, it would not only be unfairly expensive but doomed to failure in the long run because the regional conditions are so different.

NOTES

1. Xeric edaphoclimatic zones are characterized by a lack of moisture.
2. Udic edaphoclimatic zones are characterized by the presence of moisture.
3. Europe cannot be assumed to have a temperate humid climate (as in the *Dobříš Assessment*, p. 74).

REFERENCES

Aguilera, Federico (1996), 'Economia de los Trasvases de Agua: Una aproximación al caso Español', in *Economía del Agua*, Ministerio de Agricultura, Pesca y Alimentatión, serie estudios no. 69.
Armengol, J., J.L. Riera and J.A. Morgui (1991), 'Major Ionic Composition of Spanish Reservoirs', in *Verhandlungen International Vereinigung Limnology*, **24**: 1363–6.
European Environment Agency (1995a), *The Dobříš Assessment* (Copenhagen: EEA).
European Environment Agency (1995b), *Environment in the European Union – Report for the Review of the Fifth Environmental Action Programme* (Copenhagen: EEA).
Gasco, Jose Maria (1992), 'Economia y Ambiente: Caracteristicas diferenciales del caso Español', *Informacion Comercial Española*, no. 711, November, Secretaria de Estado de Comercio.
Hammond, A., A. Adriaanse, E. Rodenburg, D. Bryant and R. Woodward (1995), *Environmental Indicators* (Washington, DC: World Resources Institute).
Maestu, Josefina (1994), 'Is there a case for Southern Europe?: the case of Spain', paper presented at the 1994 Financial Times Conference on the Water Industry.
Naredo, Jose Manuel and Jose Maria Gasco (1996), *Manual de Cuentas del Agua en España*, Direccion General de Calidad de las Aguas, MOPTMA.
O'Hare, G. (1988), *Soils, Vegetation, Ecosystems* (London: Oliver and Boyd).
STOA (1995), *Assessment of EU Water Quality Policy* (Luxembourg: Scientific and Technological Options Assessment, EU).

PART XI

Annexes

Annex I Lists of ranked pressure indicators[1]

(A) HIGHEST CORE-RANKED PRESSURE INDICATORS FOR EACH POLICY FIELD

Ozone Layer Depletion (Top 10)

1. Emissions of chlorofluorocarbons (CFCs)
2. Emissions of bromofluorocarbons (halons)
3. Emissions of hydrochlorofluorocarbons (HCFCs)
4. Emissions of carbon dioxide (CO_2)
5. Emissions of nitrogen oxides (NO_x)
6 Emissions of methyl bromide (CH_3Br)
7. Emissions of chlorinated carbons
8. Emissions of methane (CH_4)
9. Emissions of nitrous oxide (N_2O)
10. Emissions of methyl chloroform (CH_3CCl_3)

Resource Depletion (Top 15)

1. Water consumption per capita (including groundwater abstraction)
2. Use of energy per capita
3. Increase in territory permanently occupied by urbanization; infrastructure; waste-tipping and quarrying
4. Nutrient balance of the soil (nutrient input/nutrient output)
5. Electricity production from fossil fuels (mineral oil, natural gas and coal)
6. Timber balance (new growth/harvest)
7. Use of mineral oil as a fuel
8. Surface-water abstraction (for drinking water/agriculture/industry)
9. Exceedance of fish catch quota
10. Groundwater abstraction for agricultural/industrial purposes

---

1. The development of the list of 60 indicators is explained further in the main 'TEPI' publication, version 1 (June 1999) and version 2 (to appear in 2000); see Foreword.

11. Extraction of mineral resources (sand, clay, gravel, marl, salt, sulphur, etc.)
12. Use of natural gas as a fuel
13. Use of artificial fertilizers
14. Electricity production from wind,water and solar power
15. Electricity production in nuclear power stations

Dispersion of Toxic Substances (Top 15)

1. Consumption of pesticides by agriculture
2. Emissions of persistent organic pollutants (POPs)
3. Consumption of toxic chemicals
4. Index of heavy metal emissions to water
5. Index of heavy metal emissions to air
6. Emission of radioactive materials
7. Emission of heavy metals by consumption
8. Production of chlorinated compounds
9. Consumption of household toxic chemicals
10. Vehicle distribution by technology type and fuel
11. Nuclear power plant distribution by type of technology
12. Toxic chemical processing plant distribution by type of technology
13. Emission of dioxins
14. Combustion plant distribution by type of cleaning technique
15. Storage of toxic chemicals in industrial plants

Climate Change (Top 12)

1. Emissions of carbon dioxide (CO_2)
2. Emissions of methane (CH_4)
3. Emissions of nitrous oxide (N_2O)
4. Emissions of chlorofluorocarbons (CFCs)
5. Emissions of nitrogen oxides (NO_x)
6. Emissions of sulphur oxides (SO_x)
7. Emissions of particles
8. Removals of carbon dioxide (CO_2)
9. Emissions of non-methane volatile organic compounds (NMVOCs)
10. Emissions of hydrochlorofluorocarbons (HCFCs)
11. Fluorocarbon emissions
12. CO emissions per year

Urban Environmental Problems (Top 15)

1. Energy consumption
2. Non-recycled municipal waste
3. Non-treated wastewater
4. Share of private car transport
5. People endangered by noise emissions
6. Land use (change from natural to built-up area)
7. Inhabitants per green area
8. Water consumption per capita
9. Emissions of sulphur dioxide (SO_2) and nitrogen oxides (NO_x)
10. Derelict areas
11. Roads and (surface) parking area
12. Monofunctional areas
13. Traffic accidents with victims (injured and/or dead)
14. Emissions of PM_{10}
15. Population density per area

Air Pollution (Top 15)

1. Emissions of nitrogen oxides (NO_x)
2. Emissions of non-methane volatile organic compounds (NMVOCs)
3. Emissions of sulphur dioxide (SO_2)
4. Emissions of particles
5. Consumption of gasoline and diesel oil by road vehicles
6. Primary energy consumption
7. Emissions of ammonia (NH_3)
8. Emissions of selected persistent organic pollutants (POPs)
9. Use of pesticides for agricultural purposes
10. Electricity consumption
11. Coal and oil products consumption
12. Total emissions of dioxins
13. Emissions of carbon monoxide (CO)
14. Total emissions of CFC and brominated compounds
15. Road vehicle distribution by type of fuel and technology used

Marine Environment and Coastal Zones (Top 15)

1. Eutrophication
2. Overfishing
3. Development along shore
4. Discharges of heavy metals

5. Oil pollution at coast and at sea
6. Discharges of halogenated organic compounds
7. Priority habitat loss
8. Wetland loss
9. Tourism intensity
10. Faecal pollution
11. Erosion
12. Physical intertidal and sub-littoral sediment distribution
13. Intensity of agriculture
14. Debris (litter/waste)
15. Aquaculture intensity

Waste (Top 15)

1. Waste landfilled
2. Waste incinerated
3. Hazardous waste
4. Municipal waste
5. Waste per product during a number of products' entire lifetime
6. Waste recycled/material recovered
7. Waste from other economic sectors
8. Consumption of hazardous materials
9. Waste from energy production
10. Waste disposed to sea
11. Average transport distance for waste
12. Hazardous waste having special and controlled treatment
13. Sludge from municipal and industrial sewage plants
14. Illegal discharge
15. Trade of wastes (export and import)

Loss of Biodiversity (Top 15)

1. Protected area loss, damage and fragmentation
2. Wetland loss through drainage
3. Agriculture intensity: area used for intensive arable agriculture
4. Fragmentation of forests and landscapes by roads/intersections
5. Clearance of natural and semi-natural forested areas
6. Change in traditional land-use practice
7. Loss of genetic resources: non-utilization of available crop species and varieties
8. Pesticide use on land
9. Loss of forest diversity: increase in exotic monoculture

10. Riverbank loss through artificialization
11. Fertilizer use on land
12. Air pollution: total SO_x and NO_x deposition
13. Loss of corridor elements or linear habitat features in rural areas
14. Loss of natural and semi-natural rangelands
15. Loss of genetic/habitat integrity: anthropogenic introduction of exotic species

Water Pollution and Water Resources (Top 15)

1. Nutrient (nitrogen and phosphorus – N + P) use (eutrophication equivalents)
2. Groundwater abstraction
3. Pesticides used per hectare of agricultural area
4. Nitrogen quantity used per hectare of utilized agricultural area
5. Water treated/water collected
6. Emissions of organic matter as biochemical oxygen demand (BOC)
7. Index of heavy metal emissions
8. Industrial water uses
9. Waste water collected/water use
10. Households and public utilities' water use
11. Water recycling by industry
12. Percentage of areas where livestock density causes exceedance of manure application standards of nitrates directive
13. Self-supply of groundwater for irrigation
14. Losses in the water supply network
15. Surface-water abstraction

(B) FULL LIST OF CORE-RANKED PRESSURE INDICATORS RESULTING FROM THE SECOND QUESTIONNAIRE

The first column (core ranking) corresponds to the ranking of the indicators by the expert groups consulted as a result of the second questionnaire in October 1996; the second column (original numbering) given in parentheses refers to the numbering of the indicators as submitted to the expert groups in October 1996, that is, before ranking. More than one set of parentheses means that the indicators have been clustered, thus resulting in a single pressure indicator: for example the core indicator 'Emissions of CO_2' includes the indicators: CO_2 emissions per capita, CO_2 emissions per GDP, CO_2 emissions per GJ energy consumption, CO_2 emissions per economic activity, CO_2 emissions from energy per capita, and CO_2 emissions from energy per GDP.

Core ranking	Original numbering	Indicator name/Policy field
		Air Pollution
AP-1	(AP-2)	Emissions of nitrogen oxides (NO_x)
AP-2	(AP-4)(AP-14)	Emissions of non-methane volatile organic compounds (NMVOCs)
AP-3	(AP-1)	Emissions of sulphur dioxide (SO_2)
AP-4	(AP-5)	Emissions of particles
AP-5	(AP-22)(AP-25)	Consumption of gasoline & diesel oil by road vehicles
AP-6	(AP-20)	Primary energy consumption
AP-7	(AP-3)	Emissions of ammonia (NH_3)
AP-8	(AP-10)	Emissions of selected persistent organic pollutants (POPs)
AP-9	(AP-18)	Use of pesticides for agricultural purposes
AP-10	(AP-19)	Electricity consumption
AP-11	(AP-21)	Coal and oil products consumption
AP-12	(AP-11)	Total emissions of dioxins
AP-13	(AP-6)	Emissions of carbon monoxide (CO)
AP-14	(AP-12)	Total emissions of CFC and brominated compounds
AP-15	(AP-24)	Road vehicle distribution by type of fuel and technology used
AP-16	(AP-7)	Emissions of heavy metals

Core ranking	Original numbering	Indicator name/Policy field
AP-17	(AP-23)	Production statistics for all industrial branches
AP-18	(AP-16)	Amount of animal waste
AP-19	(AP-26)	Mileage for the air transportation of persons and goods
AP-20	(AP-15)	Livestock population by type of animal
AP-21	(AP-17)	Total amount of nitrogen-containing fertilizer used
AP-22	(AP-9)	Emissions of methane (CH_4)
AP-23	(AP-8)	Emissions of nitrous oxide (N_2O)
AP-24	(AP-27)	Mileage for the sea transportation of persons and goods
AP-25	(AP-13)	Total amine (methylamines) emissions
		Climate Change
CC-1	(CC-1)(CC-2) (CC-3)(CC-4) (CC-5)(CC-6) (CC-7)	Emissions of carbon dioxide (CO_2)
CC-2	(CC-9)(CC-10)	Emissions of methane (CH_4)
CC-3	(CC-11)(CC-12)	Emissions of nitrous oxide (N_2O)
CC-4	(CC-21)	Emissions of chlorofluorocarbons (CFCs)
CC-5	(CC-17)(CC-18)	Emissions of nitrogen oxides (NO_x)
CC-6	(CC-19)	Emissions of sulphur oxides (SO_x)
CC-7	(CC-20)	Emissions of particles
CC-8	(CC-8)	Removals of carbon dioxide (CO_2)
CC-9	(CC-13)(CC-14)	Emissions of non-methane volatile organic compounds (NMVOCs)
CC-10	(CC-22)	Emissions of hydrochlorofluorocarbons (HCFCs)
CC-11	(CC-23)	Fluorocarbon emissions
CC-12	(CC-15)(CC-16)	CO emissions per year
		Loss of Biodiversity
LB-1	(LB-27)	Protected area loss, damage and fragmentation
LB-2	(LB-21)	Wetland loss through drainage
LB-3	(LB-1)	Agriculture intensity: area used for intensive arable agriculture

Core ranking	Original numbering	Indicator name/Policy field
LB-4	(LB-5)(LB-7)	Fragmentation of forests & landscapes by roads/intersections
LB-5	(LB-4)	Clearance of natural & semi-natural forested areas
LB-6	(LB-2)	Change in traditional land-use practice
LB-7	(LB-8)(LB-9)	Loss of genetic resources – non-utilization of available crop species & varieties
LB-8	(LB-12)	Pesticide use on land
LB-9	(LB-10)	Loss of forest diversity – increase in exotic monoculture
LB-10	(LB-22)	Riverbank loss through artificialization
LB-11	(LB-11)	Fertilizer use on land
LB-12	(LB-15)	Air pollution – total SO_x and NO_x deposition
LB-13	(LB-3)	Loss of corridor elements or linear habitat features in rural areas
LB-14	(LB-6)	Loss of natural and semi-natural rangelands
LB-15	(LB-25)(LB-26)	Loss of genetic/habitat integrity – anthropogenic introduction of exotic species
LB-16	(LB-16)(LB-17)	Evolution of built-up and related land, demand for housing
LB-17	(LB-18)(LB-19)	Hunting of wild fauna, collection of wild flora
LB-18	(LB-14)	Surface pollution incidents
LB-19	(LB-20)	Dryland habitat change through irrigation
LB-20	(LB-28)	Traffic intensity in protected areas
LB-21	(LB-24)	Accidental fires in protected and sensitive forests
LB-22	(LB-13)	Surface disposal of mineral workings deposits
LB-23	(LB-23)	Agricultural waste generation

Marine Environment & Coastal Zones

ME-1	(ME-2)	Eutrophication
ME-2	(ME-20)	Overfishing
ME-3	(ME-23)(ME-13)	Development along shore
ME-4	(ME-1)	Discharges of heavy metals
ME-5	(ME-5)(ME-6)	Oil pollution at coast & at sea
ME-6	(ME-8)	Discharges of halogenated organic compounds
ME-7	(ME-16)	Priority habitat loss
ME-8	(ME-10)	Wetland loss

Core ranking	Original numbering	Indicator name/Policy field
ME-9	(ME-22)	Tourism intensity
ME-10	(ME-4)	Faecal pollution
ME-11	(ME-14)	Erosion
ME-12	(ME-11)	Physical intertidal & sub-littoral sediment disturbance
ME-13	(ME-25)	Intensity of agriculture
ME-14	(ME-7)	Debris (litter/waste)
ME-15	(ME-21)	Aquaculture intensity
ME-16	(ME-9)	Loss of coastal green space
ME-17	(ME-15)	Flooding
ME-18	(ME-19)	Freshwater abstraction
ME-19	(ME-17)	Entry of invading species
ME-20	(ME-26)	Oil and gas abstraction
ME-21	(ME-3)	Increase in suspended solids from dredging and industry
ME-22	(ME-12)	Interference with freshwater flow to the coast
ME-23	(ME-18)	Accidents in coastal zone & at sea
ME-24	(ME-24)	Density of marine transport
ME-25	(ME-27)	Ore extraction

Ozone Layer Depletion

OD-1	(OD-1)(OD-2) (OD-3)(OD-4) (OD-5)(OD-6) (OD-7)(OD-8) (OD-9)(OD-10)	Emissions of chlorofluorocarbons (CFCs)
OD-2	(OD-11)(OD-12) (OD-13)(OD-14)	Emissions of bromofluorocarbons (halons)
OD-3	(OD-19)(OD-20) (OD-21)(OD-22)	Emissions of hydrochlorofluorocarbons (HCFCs)
OD-4	(OD-25)	Emissions of carbon dioxide (CO_2)
OD-5	(OD-23)	Emissions of nitrogen oxides (NO_x)
OD-6	(OD-18)	Emissions of methyl bromide (CH_3Br)
OD-7	(OD-15)(OD-2) (OD-3)(OD-4) (OD-5)(OD-6) (OD-7)(OD-8) (OD-9)(OD-10)	Emissions of chlorinated carbons

Core ranking	Original numbering	Indicator name/Policy field
OD-8	(OD-26)	Emissions of methane (CH_4)
OD-9	(OD-24)	Emissions of nitrous oxide (N_2O)
OD-10	(OD-17)	Emissions of methyl chloroform (CH_3CCl_3)

Resource Depletion

Core ranking	Original numbering	Indicator name/Policy field
RD-1	(RD-17)(RD-15)	Water consumption per capita (incl. groundwater abstraction)
RD-2	(RD-9)	Use of energy per capita
RD-3	(RD-22)	Increase in territory permanently occupied by urbanization; infrastructure; waste-tipping & quarrying
RD-4	(RD-20)	Nutrient balance of the soil (nutrient input/ nutrient output)
RD-5	(RD-10)	Electricity production from fossil fuels (mineral oil, natural gas & coal)
RD-6	(RD-26)(RD-27)	Timber balance (new growth/harvest)
RD-7	(RD-5)(RD-6)	Use of mineral oil as a fuel
RD-8	(RD-13)(RD-14)	Surface-water abstraction (for drinking water/ agriculture/ industry)
RD-9	(RD-23)(RD-24) (RD-25)	Exceedance of fish catch quota
RD-10	(RD-16)	Groundwater abstraction for agricultural/ industrial purposes
RD-11	(RD-3)	Extraction of mineral resources (sand, clay, gravel, marl, salt, sulphur, etc.)
RD-12	(RD-7)(RD-8)	Use of natural gas as a fuel
RD-13	(RD-19)	Use of artificial fertilizers
RD-14	(RD-11)	Electricity production from wind, water and solar power
RD-15	(RD-12)	Electricity production in nuclear power stations
RD-16	(RD-4)	Use of chlorine in chemical industry
RD-17	(RD-1)(RD-2)	Production of ferrous and non-ferrous metals from raw, non-recycled resources
RD-18	(RD-21)	Increase in territory used by agriculture
RD-19	(RD-18)	Use of animal feedstuffs

Core ranking	Original numbering	Indicator name/Policy field

Dispersion of Toxic Substances

TX-1	(TX-2)	Consumption of pesticides by agriculture
TX-2	(TX-15)	Emissions of persistent organic pollutants (POPs)
TX-3	(TX-1)	Consumption of toxic chemicals
TX-4	(TX-6)	Index of heavy metal emissions to water
TX-5	(TX-5)	Index of heavy metal emissions to air
TX-6	(TX-21)	Emissions of radioactive material
TX-7	(TX-14)	Emissions of heavy metals by consumption
TX-8	(TX-23)	Production of chlorinated compounds
TX-9	(TX-4)	Consumption of household toxic chemicals
TX-10	(TX-26)	Vehicle distribution by technology type & fuel
TX-11	(TX-31)	Nuclear power plant distribution by type of technology
TX-12	(TX-30)	Toxic chemical processing plant distribution by type of technology
TX-13	(TX-18)	Emission of dioxins
TX-14	(TX-24)	Combustion plant distribution by type of cleaning technique
TX-15	(TX-29)	Storage of toxic chemicals in industrial plants
TX-16	(TX-8)	Emission of cadmium
TX-17	(TX-20)	Emission of phthalates
TX-18	(TX-16)	Emission of PAH
TX-19	(TX-17)	Emission of PCB
TX-20	(TX-7)	Emission of mercury
TX-21	(TX-3)	Consumption of non-agricultural pesticides
TX-22	(TX-27)(TX-28)	Toxic chemicals transported on land and by boat
TX-23	(TX-9)	Emission of lead
TX-24	(TX-19)	Emission of persistent flame retardants
TX-25	(TX-12)	Emission of chromium
TX-26	(TX-25)	Small-scale combustion distribution by type of cleaning technique
TX-27	(TX-22)	Mining and metal processing
TX-28	(TX-11)	Emission of nickel
TX-29	(TX-10)	Emission of zinc
TX-30	(TX-13)	Emission of silver

Core ranking	Original numbering	Indicator name/Policy field
Urban Environmental Problems		
UP-1	(UP-21)(UP-8)	Energy consumption
UP-2	(UP-19)(UP-18)	Non-recycled municipal waste
UP-3	(UP-15)(UP-14) (UP-16)	Non-treated wastewater
UP-4	(UP-22)(UP-23) (UP-25)	Share of private car transport
UP-5	(UP-26)(UP-27) (UP-28)	People endangered by noise emissions
UP-6	(UP-2)	Land use (change from natural to built-up area)
UP-7	(UP-6)(UP-7)	Inhabitants per green area
UP-8	(UP-13)	Water consumption per capita
UP-9	(UP-9)	Emissions of sulphur dioxide (SO_2) & nitrogen oxides (NO_x)
UP-10	(UP-5)	Derelict areas
UP-11	(UP-3)	Roads and (surface) parking area
UP-12	(UP-4)	Mono-functional areas
UP-13	(UP-24)	Traffic accidents with victims (injured and/or dead)
UP-14	(UP-11)	Emissions of PM_{10}
UP-15	(UP-1)	Population density per area
UP-16	(UP-17)	Soil contamination
UP-17	(UP-10)	Emissions of VOC
UP-18	(UP-20)	Household hazardous waste
UP-19	(UP-12)	Emissions of lead (Pb)
Waste		
WA-1	(WA-19)(WA-18) (WA-24)(WA-25) (WA-26)(WA-28) (WA-29)(WA-30)	Waste landfilled
WA-2	(WA-17)(WA-14) (WA-15)(WA-16) (WA-27)	Waste incinerated
WA-3	(WA-8)(WA-4) (WA-11)	Hazardous waste
WA-4	(WA-7)	Municipal waste

Core ranking	Original numbering	Indicator name/Policy field
WA-5	(WA-34)(WA-31)	Waste per product during a number of products' entire lifetime
WA-6	(WA-13)	Waste recycled/material recovered
WA-7	(WA-6)(WA-1) (WA-2)(WA-5)	Waste from other economic sectors
WA-8	(WA-32)	Consumption of hazardous materials
WA-9	(WA-3)	Waste from energy production
WA-10	(WA-20)	Waste disposed to sea
WA-11	(WA-33)	Average transport distance for waste
WA-12	(WA-21)	Hazardous waste having special and controlled treatment
WA-13	(WA-10)	Sludge from municipal and industrial sewage plants
WA-14	(WA-22)	Illegal discharge
WA-15	(WA-23)	Trade of wastes (export and import)
WA-16	(WA-12)	Waste treated by biological treatment with utilization of compost/fertilizer products
WA-17	(WA-9)	Organic waste from separate collection

Water Pollution & Water Resources

WP-1	(WP-31)(WP-20)	Nutrient (nitrogen & phosphorus – N + P) use (eutrophication equivalents)
WP-2	(WP-2)(WP-1)	Groundwater abstraction
WP-3	(WP-19)	Pesticides used per hectare of agriculture area
WP-4	(WP-18)	Nitrogen quantity used per hectare of utilized agriculture area
WP-5	(WP-11)(WP-14)	Water treated/water collected
WP-6	(WP-25)	Emissions of organic matter as biochemical oxygen demand (BOD)
WP-7	(WP-23)(WP-1)	Index of heavy metals emissions
WP-8	(WP-7)(WP-8)	Industrial water uses
WP-9	(WP-16)	Wastewater collected/water use
WP-10	(WP-6)(WP-17)	Households & public utilities water use
WP-11	(WP-15)	Water recycling by industry
WP-12	(WP-26)	Percentage of areas where livestock density causes exceeding of manure application standards of nitrates directive
WP-13	(WP-5)(WP-4)	Self-supply of groundwater for irrigation

Core ranking	Original numbering	Indicator name/Policy field
WP-14	(WP-12)	Losses in the water supply network
WP-15	(WP-3)	Surface-water abstraction
WP-16	(WP-30)	Number of aquifers in coastal areas suffering from salinization
WP-17	(WP-27)	Net result of deforestation/reforestation as percentage of total forest area
WP-18	(WP-22)	Number of transport accidents involving toxic substances
WP-19	(WP-13)	Losses in the sewage collection network
WP-20	(WP-24)	Emission of suspended particulates
WP-21	(WP-29)	Percentage of drainage areas/utilized agriculture area
WP-22	(WP-28)	Percentage of irrigated areas/utilized agriculture area
WP-23	(WP-21)	Number of industrial accidents in plant covered by Seveso directive
WP-24	(WP-10)	Tourism water use
WP-25	(WP-9)	Water use in cooling during electricity production

Annex II Specialized institutes for each policy field

Air Pollution

Dimitris Lalas and Stelios Pesmajoglou
National Observatory of Athens
PO Box 200 48, GR-118 10 Athens

Climate Change

Jan Feenstra and Ella Lammers
The Institute for Environmental Studies (IVM)
Vrije Universiteit, Amsterdam, De Boelelaan 1115, 1081 HV Amsterdam
http://www.vu.nl/ivm

Loss of Biodiversity

Jonathan Mitchley and Karen Pack
Wye College
University of London, Environment Section, Ashford, Kent
TN25 5 AH, UK

Marine Environment and Coastal Zones

Karin Dubsky
Coastwatch Europe Network – E.S.U.
187 Pearse Street, Trinity College Dublin, IRL-Dublin 2

Ozone Layer Depletion

Ella Lammers
The Institute for Environmental Studies (IVM)
Vrije Universiteit, Amsterdam, De Boelelaan 1115, 1081 HV Amsterdam
http://www.vu.nl/ivm

Resource Depletion

André Viergever and Willem Sauer
INFOPLAN Environmental Consultants
Phoenixstraat 66, NL-2611 AM Delft
André Viergever is now director of E*M*A*I*L, P.O. Box 310, NL-2301 DA
    Leiden
http://www.e-m-a-i-l.nu

Dispersion of Toxic Substances

Ake Iverfeldt and Per Ostlund
IVL
PO Box 21060, S-100 31 Stockholm

Urban Environmental Problems

Marina Alberti and Alessandra Valentinelli
Ambiente Italia
Via Carlo Poerio 39, I-20129 Milano

Waste

Birgit Friis
Carl Bro a/s Energy & Environment
Consultant Engineers and Planners
Granskoven 8, DK-2600 Glostrup

Water Pollution and Water Resources

Arnaud Comolet and Ahmed Garadi
Planistat Europe
80, rue du Faubourg Saint-Denis, F-75010, Paris

Methodological Support (editors of the collection)

Anil Markandya and Nick Dale
University of Bath and Metroeconomica
Claverton Down, Bath, BA2 7AY, UK

Annex III   List of contributors

Air Pollution

Dave Guinnup and Christine Sansevero, United States Environmental Protection Agency
Professor Panos Papagiannakopoulos, University of Crete, Greece
Bjarne Sivertsen, Norwegian Institute for Air Research (NILU)

Climate Change

Hartmut Grassl, Director, World Climate Research Programme, Geneva
Sir John Houghton CBE FRS, Royal Commission on Environmental Pollution, London
John Sweeney, Department of Geography, National University of Ireland, Maynooth

Loss of Biodiversity

Pierre Devillers, Institut Royal des Sciences Naturelles de Belgique, Bruxelles
Marianne Lefort, Bureau des Ressources Génétiques, Paris, France

Marine Environment and Coastal Zones

Margarida Cardoso da Silva, National Laboratory for Civil Engineering, Lisbon, Portugal
Harry Coccossis, University of the Aegean, Greece

Ozone Layer Depletion

Marie-Lise Chanin, Directeur de Recherches, Service d'Aéronomie, CNRS, France
Ivar S.A. Isaksen, Department of Geophysics, University of Oslo, Norway.
Guido Visconti, Dipartimento di Fisica, Università degli Studi, L'Aquila, Italy

Resource Depletion

Øyvind Lone, Deputy General Director, Norwegian Ministry of the Environment

David Pearce, Associate Director, Centre for Social and Economic Research on the Global Environment, Norwich, UK

Jean-Louis Weber, Director of International Affairs, Institut Français de l'Environnement, France

Dispersion of Toxic Substances

Heidelore Fiedler and Professor Otto Hutzinger, University of Bayreuth, Germany

Aristo Renzoni, Department of Environmental Biology, University of Siena, Italy

Urban Environmental Problems

Colin Fudge, Dean of the Faculty of the Built Environment, UWE, Bristol, Chair of the EU Urban Environment Expert Group

Waste

Franco Cecchi, Dipartimento di Chimica Ingegneria Chimica e Material, Università Di L'Aquila and Paolo Pavan, Department of Environmental Sciences, University of Venice

Karin Jordan and Peter Gössele, ARGUS, The Technical University of Berlin, Germany

Donald Huisingh, Professor of Environmental Sciences, Cleaner Production and Sustainability, Erasmus University, Rotterdam, The Netherlands

Water Pollution and Water Resources

Joan S. Davis, Swiss Federal Institute of Environmental Science and Technology, Dübendorf, Switzerland and Dr Klaus Lanz, Aquatic Chemist, Consultant, Hamburg, Germany

Josefina Maestu, Jose Maria Gasco, Joe Manuel Naredo and Federico Aguilera, ECOTEC Research and Consulting, Madrid, Spain

Annex IV Project terminology: list of main acronyms, symbols and abbreviations used

5EAP	EC Fifth Environmental Action Programme (O.J. C 138 of 17.5.93): Resolution of the Council and the Representatives of the Governments of the Member States meeting within the Council of 1 February 1993 on a Community Programme of policy and action in relation to environmental and sustainable development – Towards Sustainability
AFEAS	Alternative Fluorocarbon Environmental Acceptability Study
BOD	Biochemical oxygen demand
Br	Bromine
BS	Black smoke
CAP	Common Agricultural Policy (EU)
CEC	Commission of the European Communities; Luxembourg/ Brussels (Belgium)
CFCs	Chlorofluorocarbons
CH_3Br	Methyl bromide
CH_4	Methane
Cl	Chlorine
CO	Carbon monoxide
CO_2	Carbon dioxide
COP	Conference of Parties of the Montreal Protocol
CORINAIR	CORe Inventories AIR (Corinair90-pan-European & Corinar 94-EU-15+3)
CORINE	CO-oRdination of INformation on the Environment
CSD	UN's Commission on Sustainable Development
DG XI	European Commission's Directorate-General XI (Environment, Nuclear Safety and Civil Protection)
DG XII	European Commission's Directorate-General XII (Science, Research & Development)
DNA	Deoxyribonucleic acid
Dobris+3	EEA's 1998 follow-up report to *Europe's Environment: The Dobříš Assessment* (EEA, 1995)

E*M*A*I*L	Environment Management And Information Liaison; Leiden, The Netherlands (TEPI publication)
EC	European Community (formerly EEC)
ECU	European currency unit (replaced by Euro)
EEA	European Environment Agency: Copenhagen, Denmark
EEC	European Economic Community (replaced by the European Community)
EIA	Environmental impact assessment
EMEP	Cooperative Programme for Monitoring and Evaluation of the Long Range Transmission of Air Pollution in Europe
EPA	Environmental Protection Agency
EPI	Environmental pressure index/indicator
EU	European Union, 15 Member States (Belgium, Denmark, Germany, Greece, Spain, France, Ireland, Italy, Luxembourg, The Netherlands, Austria, Portugal, Finland, Sweden, United Kingdom)
EUCC	European Coastal Conservation Conference, 1991
Euro	EU's currency unit
Eurostat	Statistical Office of the European Communities; Luxembourg/Brussels (Belgium)
FAO	UN Food and Agriculture Organization
FCCC	United Nations Framework Convention on Climate Change
GDP	Gross domestic product
GNP	Gross national product
GWP	Global warming potential
H_2O	Hydrogen
ha	Hectare
Halons	Bromofluorocarbons
HCFCs	Hydrochlorofluorocarbons
HFCs	Hydrofluorocarbons
HELCOM	Helsinki Convention on the Protection of the Marine Environment of the Baltic Sea Area (1974)
INSEE	Institut National de la Statistique et des Etudes Economiques, France
IPCC	Intergovernmental Panel on Climate Change
IPPC	International Pollution Prevention Control
IUCN	International Union for Conservation of Nature and Natural Resources
km	Kilometre
LB	Loss of Biodiversity policy field in the PIP
LRTAP	UNECE Convention on Long-Range Transboundary Air Pollution

m	Metre
m³	Cubic metre
MAP	Plan Bleu's Action Plan for the Mediterranean
mg	Milligramme
MSW	Municipal solid waste
N	Nitrogen
N₂O	Nitrous oxide
NATO	Northern Atlantic Treaty Organization
n.d.	data not available
NGO	Non-governmental organization
nm	Nanometres
NMHC	Non-methane hydrocarbon
NMVOCs	Non-methane volatile organic compounds
NOₓ	Nitrogen oxides
O₃	Ozone
ODP	Ozone depletion potential
ODS	Ozone-depleting substance
OECD	Organization for Economic Cooperation and Development
Oeko-Institute	Öko Institut, Darmstadt branch, Germany (TEPI publication)
OSPAR	Oslo Convention for the Prevention of Marine Pollution by Dumping from Ships and Aircraft (1974) and Paris Convention for the Prevention of Marine Pollution from Land-Based Sources (1978)
P	Phosphorus
PAP	Priority Actions Programme
PARCOM	Paris Commission (see OSPAR)
Pb	Lead
PCB	Polychlorinated biphenyls
pH	number used to express acidity/alkalinity of a solution
PIP	Eurostat's Environmental Pressure Indicators Project
PM	Particulate matter
ppb	Parts per billion
ppmv	Parts per trillion by volume
PSR	Pressure–state–response (framework for environmental indicators)
RAMSAR	RAMSAR convention on wetlands of international importance, 1971
RD	Resource Depletion policy field in the PIP
RIVM	National Institute of Public Health and the Environment; Netherlands

SAG	Scientific Advisory Group (of the Eurostat Pressure Indicators Project)
SEA	Strategic environmental assessment
SI	Specialized institutes dealing with the ten policy fields of the PIP
SIP	Sectoral Infrastructure Projects (Eurostat)
SO_2	Sulphur dioxide
SOE	State of the environment
SO_x	Sulphur oxides
TAU	TAU Consultora Ambiental; Madrid, Spain (TEPI publication)
TEN	Trans European Transport Network
TEPI	Towards Environmental Pressure Indicators for the EU (Eurostat's publication)
UN	United Nations
UNCED	United Nations Conference on Environment and Development
UNCSD	United Nations Commission on Sustainable Development
UNDP	United Nations Development Programme
UNECE	United Nations Economic Commission for Europe
UNEP	United Nations Environment Programme
UNFCCC	UN Framework Convention on Climate Change
UV	Ultraviolet
UV-A	Ultraviolet-A radiation
UV-B	Ultraviolet-B radiation
VKI	Institute for the Water Environment, Hørsholm, Denmark (TEPI publication)
VOC	Volatile organic compound
WCED	World Commission on Environment and Development
WCMC	World Conservation and Monitoring Centre
WHO	UN World Health Organization
WMO	World Meteorological Organization, Geneva, Switzerland
WRI	World Research Institute
WTP	Willingness to pay

Index